AF270525

MIND THE GAP

SCALING BUSINESSES ACROSS CULTURES

VINCENT LAURIA
STEFANO PELLEGRINO

WITH CONTRIBUTIONS BY:
PROF. SAVANID (NUI) VATANASAKDAKUL

WILEY

*To Edward Lauria, whose craftsmanship and work with his
own hands created the opportunities that shaped my life and who
always told me, "You can accomplish whatever you put
your mind to."*

CONTENTS

About the Authors   *vii*

Introduction: *Starting the Journey*   *xi*

1   ***It's an Adventure:*** *The Promise (and Perils) of Going Global*   *1*

2   ***Prepare to Be Unprepared:*** *In a Culture New to You, Expect the Unexpected*   *9*

3   ***Getting Ready to Expand:*** *Why, Where, and How Will You Go?*   *25*

4   ***You Have to Be There:*** *Build Trust and Knowledge on the Ground*   *39*

5   ***How to Get the Deal Done:*** *Different Systems, Different Finish Lines*   *57*

6   ***The Power of Transcreation:*** *Working Where Tech and Culture Intertwine*   *83*

7   ***Cultural Code-Switching:*** *The Way to Evolve and Thrive*   *95*

8 ***When "Yes" Means "No":*** *Some Fine Points of Code-Switching*   107

9 ***Deals Are Human:*** *Align the Human Factors, or You'll Fail*   127

10 ***Strategy in a Strange Land:*** *How to Launch and Build and How Not To*   147

11 ***Hiring Teams Across Countries:*** *Talent Eats Strategy for Breakfast*   173

12 ***Managing Teams Across Countries:*** *Talent Eats Strategy for Lunch*   197

13 ***The Convergence of Business and Society:*** *Explore and Work Where the Realms Meet*   229

14 ***Stories from the Frontlines:*** *How the Playbook Works in the Real World*   245

15 ***The Global Expansion Checklist:*** *A Summary of All Key Takeaways*   263

Notes   287

Acknowledgments   289

Index   293

ABOUT THE AUTHORS

Vincent "Vinnie" Lauria

Vinnie Lauria is a two-time Silicon Valley entrepreneur turned venture capitalist. He is the founding partner of Golden Gate Ventures, a global early-stage VC firm launched in 2011 with US$300M in AUM and investments in more than 100 companies across three continents. Over the past 15 years, Vinnie has served on more than a dozen start-up boards, including Asian unicorns like Carro and Carousell. He was an early investor in Stripe and AngelList and helped guide start-ups like Lomotif to a public listing on the NASDAQ.

Vinnie began his career on the technical side. He joined his first start-up as a web developer while still in high school and later worked in IBM Research, helping shape the company's early thinking around social software. After graduating from Boston University with a degree in computer engineering and a minor in business administration, he co-founded two start-ups in Palo Alto. Meetro, one of the earliest location-based social apps, gave him a firsthand education in the challenges of timing and product adoption. Lefora, a community-platform start-up, grew to more than 100,000 online communities before being acquired in 2010 by a public media company.

Along the way, he founded Silicon Valley NewTech, which became one of the Bay Area's largest monthly demo events, and later became a Fellow in the Kauffman Fellows Program, Class 17. He has guest-lectured at Stanford, Berkeley, Carnegie Mellon, and the National University of Singapore.

Beyond investing, Vinnie has been instrumental in building start-up ecosystems. Over the past two decades, he has helped shape start-up communities in Silicon Valley, Singapore, and Vietnam through mentoring, early investing, and creating ecosystem-building events. In Singapore, his firm has been widely credited as a catalyzing force in the ecosystem's early growth. Through organizations such as Endeavor, he continues to help globally minded founders scale across cultures and continents.

Stefano Pellegrino, PhD

Stefano Pellegrino is a three-time founder and zero-to-one business builder with deep operating experience across Southeast Asia. He is the co-founder and CEO of Aquila, a climate technology company backed by leading venture firms in Southeast Asia and Europe. His work sits at the intersection of fintech and green hard-tech.

Before launching Aquila, Stefano was the co-founder and country head for Vietnam at Aspire, one of Southeast Asia's fastest-growing fintech companies and a Y Combinator company. He built the business from incorporation and licensing through to a 75-person team and hit profitability within nine months. He later served as head of business development and international expansion, where he led strategic partnerships across five ASEAN countries and helped drive sustained multiyear revenue growth. Earlier, as the head of credit, he managed a 50-person team across four markets, scaling revenues while materially reducing credit risk.

Stefano began his career in Europe as New York qualified lawyer at a top international law firm. He later relocated to Asia where he advised major international companies on cross-border M&A, project finance, and renewable energy transactions. He structured and negotiated more than 750 MW of solar projects and participated in deals totaling more than US$3.2 billion. He also served as General Secretary of EuroCham Vietnam, helping strengthen one of the country's largest business associations, and lectured in international contract law at universities in both Vietnam and Italy.

Stefano is an attorney qualified in New York and Italy. He earned his PhD in Private Law from the University of Pavia with highest honors, completed an LLM at Berkeley Law, and conducted post-doctoral research at the Max Planck Institute in Hamburg. He remains active in climate-finance circles as the Ho Chi Minh City Ambassador of Investors for Climate.

Dr. Savanid (Nui) Vatanasakdakul

Professor Savanid "Nui" Vatanasakdakul of Carnegie Mellon University is a cross-cultural traveler. Born and raised in Thailand amid a rich mix of Asian cultural influences, she developed an early interest in how people, technologies, and social norms shape each other. Nui's career has taken her across four continents as both an academic and an entrepreneur. Today she teaches in Information Systems at Carnegie Mellon's campus in Qatar.

At CMU-Q, Dr. Vatanasakdakul leads the development of the Tech Entrepreneurship Minor, a pioneering multidisciplinary program that empowers students to ideate, build, and pitch technology-driven start-ups in the GCC region. Her Tech Start-Up Launchpad course and its culminating pitch events have become signature experiences, inspiring student entrepreneurship and fostering collaboration across Qatar's higher education ecosystem.

Her commitment to teaching excellence has been recognized with the Meritorious Teaching Award from Carnegie Mellon University— one of the institution's highest lifetime honors—and the Teaching Excellence Award from Macquarie University in Australia.

Her pedagogical approach integrates experiential learning, interdisciplinary collaboration, and global-local ("glocal") perspectives.

An active scholar, Dr. Vatanasakdakul conducts research in digital transformation, socio-cultural IT adoption, and technology entrepreneurship. Her work bridges theory and practice, offering insights particularly relevant to emerging markets.

A respected community leader, she has played a central role in advancing the Information Systems (IS) research communities, particularly supporting scholars in the Middle East and Asia. She serves as founding president of the Thailand Chapter of the Association for Information Systems (AIS), past president of the Qatar Chapter, and co-founder of SIGGreen, a global AIS initiative focused on sustainability. As the local chair of ICIS 2024, she led the first-ever hosting of this premier IS conference in Southeast Asia in its 45-year history, fostering meaningful collaborations between global scholars and regional innovators. In addition, she has been instrumental in building and strengthening the IS scholarly community across the GCC region, culminating in the establishment of the first GCC IS Symposium.

INTRODUCTION

Starting the Journey

We are writing to you from Ho Chi Minh City in Vietnam. We live here because this city is an exciting business hub, a place where international ambitions can meet local opportunities. Nearby in our neighborhood is an American coffee shop, operated Asian-style by a company based in Hong Kong. Walking down the street to get there, you see fleets of motorbike drivers weaving through traffic, each with a passenger on the back or a package to be delivered: the drivers who wear green jackets work for a Singapore company. And a lot of the talk at the coffee shop is about outbound trips or incoming visits to meet with people from Germany or Abu Dhabi or Australia. Everywhere there are deals to be done.

This book is meant to help. What inspired us to write it was seeing all the international deals that *didn't* get done: the opportunities lost or mishandled, lost revenues that could've been had, and the dead apps sitting on customers' phones from start-ups that died. The problem is global, not confined to Vietnam. There are icebergs waiting for Titanics in waters worldwide. We hope to show you how to navigate past them so your global journey stays on course.

Often the root of the problem is something that many businesspeople fail to grasp. When companies try to launch or scale from one country to another, they aren't just crossing a border. They are crossing a cultural gap. They are not just entering a new "market," which can be quantitatively analyzed and mapped out in a slide deck. They are entering a new realm of the human psyche, where people may think and act in mysterious ways—mysterious, that is, to market entrants who think their own ways will connect. Often the disconnects are what sink the ship.

The disconnects may happen in subtle ways that are hard to detect. We have seen whip-smart founders and operators enter new countries believing their biggest challenges were product or strategy. They walk into meetings with top local people, hoping to win them as partners or investors. But their carefully crafted pitches get undermined almost from the start. Their confidence comes across as arrogance, or frank statements as foolish blunders. They negotiate too fast and miss cues, not recognizing when a polite "yes" actually means "no." They think the same approaches that worked for them back home will work here, assuming the logic will carry over unchanged.

Worse yet, they pitch to the wrong prospects. Or they make the wrong hires. Or they don't fine-tune the product and strategy to resonate with the beats that people live and transact to.

We haven't just seen these kinds of mistakes; we have made them. It took us years to understand the nature of culture gaps. Longer to learn to navigate across them. And even longer to accept that there is no universally "correct" way to communicate or negotiate or sell. Every country, industry, and culture has its own norms, signals, decision rhythms, and expectations. The sooner you learn them, the faster you grow.

We hope our book will show you how to "mind the gaps." And we hope this, in turn, might save you some years of learning lessons the hard way. We want international leaders to avoid needless frustration, to stop assuming the other side is wrong, and to complete negotiations feeling positive, respected, and energized—not confused or defeated. Building mutual trust across cultures is the key foundational step. If you can do that, you're on your way to closing better deals and serving the market properly—so that people will find it worthwhile to buy what you serve.

By reading this book, you will learn how to navigate unfamiliar markets with more clarity, avoid avoidable mistakes, and build trust with people who think and operate differently than you do.

Who We Are

The two of us, Vinnie Lauria and Stefano Pellegrino, come from opposite sides of the world. When we first crossed paths in Ho Chi Minh City, we were more than 10,000 kilometers from our home countries, the United States and Italy, respectively. We had arrived in Southeast Asia through different journeys but were both drawn into the same challenge: how to build and scale businesses across cultures that were completely new to us.

Vinnie is a two-time Silicon Valley entrepreneur turned global venture capitalist. As the founding partner of Golden Gate Ventures, he has two decades of experience, including scaling his VC firm across three continents while backing more than 100 start-ups, including companies that grew into household names in their home markets. He has taught and mentored founders at Stanford, Berkeley, and NUS, and through programs like Endeavor, he has worked closely with teams expanding into markets that operate very differently from the United States.

Personally, Vinnie has evolved quite a bit since his early days. Back then he was following a typical all-American path to success. He'd been coding since high school and then sharpened up to next-level with an engineering degree at Boston University and early work experience at IBM. From there Vinnie headed west to Silicon Valley, where he earned his spurs as a start-up cowboy. His second start-up was acquired, which left him with a successful exit, a small pile of cash, and the question, *What next?*

Vinnie calls that period an inflection point. He had recently married someone with a real thirst for travel and for experiencing different cultures. So when the young couple sat down to plan their next steps, they decided to go out and explore. They set off on a one-year backpacking trip across Asia.

Their pan-Asia experiences opened up Vinnie's view of himself, and the world. With his wife, he hiked through the jungles of Borneo and wandered through hidden corners of Beijing. They raced a tuk tuk across India and had the opportunity to train with Shaolin monks at a Buddhist monastery. Every place challenged assumptions Vinnie didn't know he had—including the assumption of where "home" was. He and his wife settled in Singapore. In 2011 Vinnie launched Golden Gate Ventures. . .and we'll pick up more of the story later.

Stefano is a three-time founder and international business builder who began his career in Milan as a corporate lawyer at DLA Piper, back then the largest law firm worldwide. He broadened his horizons by moving to the United States to earn a Master of Laws degree at UC Berkeley, passed the New York bar exam, and then went back to Europe where he completed his PhD.

He moved to Asia in 2014 with his wife, as they both wanted to explore a new continent. There Stefano specialized in cross-border mergers and acquisitions for global companies and launched the renewable energy practice of his law firm—for which he closed $750 million worth of solar power deals. Those years were spent working on high-stakes, cross-border deals where cultural code-switching (a skill described in this book) mattered as much as legal structure.

Next, he took a country manager post at a fintech company expanding across Southeast Asia. In that role, he launched the company's Vietnam business and grew it into the firm's most profitable. He then managed their largest team across Singapore, Indonesia, Thailand, Vietnam, and Malaysia, and finally kick-started the international expansion of the company beyond Asia.

After the fintech company had completed a successful $100 million fundraising round, he decided to launch his own company. Today, as founder and CEO of Aquila, a climate technology company backed by global investors, he continues to scale businesses at the intersection of cultures.

Together we have more than 40 years of combined experience operating, investing, negotiating, teaching, and learning across markets as varied as Asia, the Middle East, Europe, and the United States.

And here is an intriguing aspect of the experience we've gained. While being "outsiders" in various cultures has presented challenges, we think it has given us an advantage. By coming into unfamiliar settings, we learned to keep our eyes and minds wide open constantly. And that has helped us see patterns that locals might overlook or take for granted—from how teams make decisions to how trust is built, and what people mean beneath what they say.

We never set out to become students of culture, but the life adventures that took us across continents made it unavoidable. Learning to build companies across cultures has been a long and often unpredictable adventure. The mistakes we've made, and the humblings and corrections we were subjected to, have been hard prices to pay but the ROI is beyond measuring. The rewards have been meaningful on both professional and personal levels. We wouldn't trade this life for any other.

How Southeast Asia Shaped Us

The Southeast Asia region, where we've built our companies, is one of the most culturally complex business environments in the world. It is a landscape of many nations, languages, and histories, with no single dominant cultural or regulatory anchor. Every market requires a different rhythm. Every conversation demands a different lens. Every partnership, deal, and team is a negotiation across expectations.

That is why Southeast Asia became our most important teacher. Working across multiple countries at once forced us to develop instincts we could not have learned in Silicon Valley or Milan. We had to learn how to "read the room" in rooms where people's silent signals and indirect communications conveyed encoded meanings, and the code differed from one room to the next.

Nor did the lessons come only in boardrooms and offices. Spending time *living* in other countries makes it clear that you cannot force your own norms onto a culture. You can't will the environment to behave the way you expect. You will go crazy trying. You have to accept people, rhythms, and practices as they are, not as you wish they were.

That mindset became the foundation for how we learned to operate anywhere in the world.

Our skills turned out to be transferable. The frameworks we developed in Southeast Asia helped us work with founders and partners in other corners of the globe like the Middle East and Latin America.

Once you have been trained in an environment as fragmented and fast-moving as ours, other global markets feel familiar. New York has the famous saying "If you can make it here, you can make it anywhere." Southeast Asia, with Singapore at its center, is the global business version of that. If you can build across cultures here, you can take those capabilities almost anywhere in the world.

A Third Lens

We invited Professor Savanid "Nui" Vatanasakdakul to contribute to this book because she brings a depth of expertise that complements our lived experience. Originally from Asia and now part of the global faculty of Carnegie Mellon University's Qatar campus, Nui bridges four continents in her work. She is a globally distinguished professor with more than 25 years of experience across Asia, Australia, the Middle East, and the United States. Her research connects technology, management, and cross-cultural collaboration, reflecting the same international ties we explore throughout this book.

Nui focuses her studies on how people communicate, interpret meaning, and build and use technologies across cultures. One of the most valuable ideas she contributed is the difference between translation and "transcreation." Translation gives you the right words; transcreation gives you the right meaning. In global business, two people can speak the same language yet understand entirely different things, because culture shapes how intent is expressed and how signals are received. Nui has helped us articulate things we had observed or intuitively sensed for years without having the vocabulary to express them.

Our lives and hers sometimes intersect in ways that feel almost surreal. Over Turkish food in Qatar, we found ourselves comparing the cultural norms we had each encountered, while Nui shared stories from her unexpected second career running Alaturca, a Turkish restaurant and Doha favorite. Stepping into that world pushed her into an entirely different cross-cultural environment. Many of the people around her had very limited formal education. She had to learn, once again, how to communicate and teach—this time with staff who came from different mindsets and backgrounds than in professional circles, and from various cultures as well. The back of the house was a place where street smarts mattered more than textbook smarts and where intuition, survival instincts, and lived experience guided daily decisions. Conflicts among staff sometimes escalated beyond words and even turned physical. Navigating these moments became a leadership challenge grounded not in academic theory, but in patience, empathy, conflict management, and real-world human complexity.

What makes Nui's experience unique is her learning to master two worlds at opposite ends of the spectrum: the high-achieving academic and digital innovation realm, and the gritty, unpredictable reality of running a small shawarma restaurant. Nui's stories reminded us that cultural differences show up everywhere, in every kind of workplace where people are shaped by their diverse upbringings, environments, and lived experiences. Her insights sharpened our understanding of what this book needed to be.

What the Book Offers and How You Can Use It

This isn't a textbook. It is a handbook built from lived experiences—not only ours and Nui's but also those of about three dozen international leaders we've interviewed. They live and have their HQs in places from China to Sweden to Nigeria to Mexico. They include a Parisian active throughout Europe and an Estonian who collaborates with a Japanese team to invest across borders. You will read their stories along with ours. You will get their perspectives, to complement ours. Throughout the book, we'll also take you inside the mindsets of the people on the other side of the table so you can understand not only what they do but why they do it.

The book is therefore a global compendium of collective knowledge. The reading experience we've aimed for is that when you dive into a subject area, you'll get a real-world 3-D view that brings out multiple facets of it.

Do common themes emerge? They do, and it would be hard to miss them. You've read a sampling already. In practical terms, the book offers some principles that apply universally, everywhere—starting with "mind the gap." But what you are unlikely to come away with is a one-size-fits-all master formula for doing business internationally. In fact, a theme the book hammers home is that "one-size-fits-all" doesn't work. You cannot use the same business model, marketing, or whatever in every country you want to enter. Entry will be denied.

Besides, we write this book as people who are still learning, not as people who have it all figured out. Culture is too deep and too alive for anyone to claim mastery over it.

So instead, think of the book as a toolkit. A collection of the best tools we have found for perception, decision, and action across borders. By the end of this book, we want you to see the world through a broader lens. You'll recognize your own assumptions faster, understand others more clearly, and make decisions with a sharper sense of how culture shapes trust, timing, and outcomes.

As you move through the chapters, you'll find a short set of key takeaways at the end of each one. They are there to help you step back for a moment, reassess your assumptions, and consider how your own instincts or biases might shape what you notice or miss in a new cultural setting. Think of them as prompts to see the same moment from different angles, the way a rainbow refracts one wavelength into many colors. You can flip back to these takeaways anytime—and we've collected the most concise versions again in Chapter 15 for quick reference when you need them most.

All told, this toolkit included a pretty comprehensive range of tools. Several chapters explore how to use them for tackling the big jobs that have to be done when taking a business international:

- Getting ready to expand (which includes choosing *where* to expand)

- Scouting the terrain

- Making good deals that last, with partners and allies

- Choosing strategies for entry and deployment

- Hiring cross-border teams, and managing them

- Working at the intersections of business and society

Cultural awareness is ingrained throughout these action-oriented chapters.

But a key "job" that supports them all is cultivating a cross-cultural mindset and key cross-cultural skills. These are what enable you to perceive clearly and act effectively. Chapters on mindset and skills include:

- The art of "preparing to be unprepared"
- Transcreation: what it is, why it's powerful
- Cultural code-switching (two chapters!)

You can read the book straight through or jump directly to the chapters that match your next expansion, negotiation, or cultural challenge. Use the stories to anticipate what might happen before you enter a new market or to make sense of what has already happened when you find yourself confused by a conversation, a decision, or a sudden shift in tone.

We'd also suggest this: carry the book with you as you move across borders, meet new teams, sit in unfamiliar rooms, and work with people who see the world differently than you do. Every market teaches you something. The book will help you recognize the lesson faster.

As for hopes and wishes, we hope most deeply that our book enables you to move through the world with more clarity, more confidence, and more curiosity. Writing it has been an adventure for us. We wish you to read it in the same spirit—as you take on the great adventure of doing business that makes the world better. Let's get started.

1 It's an Adventure

The Promise (and Perils) of Going Global

There was nothing left to do but sign the deal, a complex transaction between an Australian multinational company and a local Vietnamese group worth more than $5 million. Both teams had sent high-level executives to Hanoi to finalize the details. After several days of discussion, all parties came to an agreement. Stefano—who then worked for a global law firm and was representing the Australians—stayed up all night putting the terms into formal contracts.

The plan was for all parties to meet again in the morning over breakfast. Only one business item remained: the simple formality of collecting signatures on paper. Then, after a bit of mutual celebration, both sides could go home happy. Stefano's clients would be paying the Vietnamese those millions and getting much-needed services in return.

Except it didn't work out that way. As soon as everyone settled in together in the morning, the owner of the Vietnamese group spoke up. He said he'd been thinking about the deal. And he had decided he needed an additional $20,000.

Stefano could hardly believe what he was hearing. Twenty thousand was a mere fraction of a percent of the deal's total value. The amount seemed just enough to be annoying but not enough to cover any foreseeable cost or risk. Why, why, why?

That state of bafflement lasted only a moment. The lead executive for the Australians shot up out of his chair. He was furious, and he let the whole room know how he felt. He didn't care whether the owner wanted an extra $20,000 or 2¢. The ask, in itself, was a breach of trust. *We already agreed what the deal was,* he said. *We shook hands on it. And now you want to change the terms after less than 12 hours?* In his experience, the man said, a person who can't be trusted in small matters could not be trusted with important matters going forward, let alone for a long-term partnership. The deal was off.

With that, the Australians filed out of the room, drove straight to the airport, and didn't look back. Game over.

Fortunately, Stefano had learned a lesson about how to play the game. There came a time not long afterward when he served as counsel for a US company seeking entry to the Vietnam market. Different industry, different type of deal—and yet, the same scenario that he'd seen recently began to play out again. The Americans came to Vietnam and met with their prospective partners. After a couple of days negotiating, they had a handshake agreement. The Americans were jubilant that evening. They thought the deal was in the bag. Stefano laughed and told them, "Uh-uh, wait till tomorrow. There might be one more step; let me give you a heads-up . . . ."

Sure enough, before signing a contract the next day, the lead rep on the Vietnamese side asked for a small sweetener. Which the Americans gladly conceded, because they had been forewarned.

Stories like this are common when you step into a culture that isn't your own.

Crossing borders to do business in a new country, with a culture distinctly its own, is an adventure of high order. And the first rule of adventure is simple: there will be surprises.

The surprises you meet abroad are different from—and in addition to—the ones you face in your home market. You'll still deal with the usual business uncertainties, like unexpected moves by competitors. But layered on top of those are the surprises that come from culture gaps. These tend to knock you off course. They can feel confusing or even unpleasant in the moment, and sometimes the business consequences are painful. That's why learning to recognize and respond to them becomes so important.

In our international careers, we've sometimes been able to recover and course-correct quickly. But the persistent condition of living with uncertainty and perplexity can be reduced only gradually over time, not eliminated entirely. It's part of the adventure—and part of the work.

Stefano soon learned that what he had seen wasn't an isolated incident. In deal after deal, the same pattern emerged. At the last minute, after it seemed that all the terms were nailed down, negotiators on the Vietnam side said they needed an add-on. Maybe a slight increase in franchising rights or an added sliver of revenue share. Always, it amounted to no more than a cherry on top of the cake, or a few crumbs beside the cake. But always, the little extra was essential to closing the deal.

One could ask Vietnamese businesspeople why many of them do this. One could theorize on the deeper reasons behind the practice. Either way, you'd be likely to come up with a range of answers. Some would say that getting a little extra is a face-saving (or more accurately, a face-*building*) move for many people: it's a prize they can bring home to their spouses and tell their friends about, to show that they really know how to operate and come out on top. Some would say that in an emerging market like Vietnam—where widespread prosperity is a new thing and large segments of the population still live tenuously—negotiations are different than in post-scarcity economies like those of North America or Western Europe. Citizens of emerging countries are liable to see more value in every crumb and cherry.

All of the above may be true. Certainly it pays to dig for deeper understanding, whenever you encounter practices that seem strange to you. But meanwhile, there is the ongoing imperative to stay ahead of the game so you can ward off other mishaps.

Often, the seeds of failure are planted long before anyone recognizes a problem. Cultural misalignment begins with small assumptions and unspoken expectations. The earlier you learn to notice these signals, the easier it becomes to navigate new markets. It helps to reserve judgment whenever you encounter a culture gap, because people doing something differently from what you expect does not mean they are wrong. What matters is recognizing that your assumptions may not match the reality in front of you and learning to test those assumptions before they harden into conclusions.

When people begin to recognize culture gaps, something important shifts. They start to bridge them, not by changing who they are but by understanding the people around them more deeply and therefore knowing what to do. Over time, this becomes a reliable skill, one that turns confusion into clarity and turns unfamiliar environments into places where real connection is possible.

Another story from our experience helps bring the point into sharper focus.

Vinnie is one of many Silicon Valley veterans who made the switch from being an entrepreneur to a venture investor. The path is a logical one to follow: by launching start-ups, you learn what it takes to make them work. Which should then equip you to evaluate start-ups, invest in the most promising ones, and coach them up to their potential. It's a straightforward case of knowledge transfer. Many in the Valley have done it within the Valley.

The difference was that Vinnie chose to launch his VC firm in Singapore, a world away. That made him a pioneer. At the time, few VCs existed in or around Singapore, and there were plenty of tech start-ups that could use assistance with their ventures. It was smart of Vinnie to recognize unmet demand, and realize that by shifting from his previous role as a start-up founder, he could step in to give the market what it needed. There was just a slight catch.

A new VC firm is, itself, a start-up. You have to go around raising money for your first fund—pitching people with money to invest in you, so you can invest on their behalf.

Vinnie figured he knew how to fundraise. He'd done it in the Valley for his tech start-ups. But in Singapore, the slight catch turned into a major obstacle because the business environment and culture were not like those he'd known in the Valley.

Silicon Valley has an open culture, where trust is granted quickly. Once people decide that your credentials look good, you're qualified to pitch. If you pitch them a good enough idea, they'll jump on it. Vinnie remembers a fundraising meeting for his tech start-up at a coffee shop. It took only 20 minutes. He met the potential investor, presented his idea, waited while the man took a quiet moment to think, and when the investor looked up, he said "I'm in." Handshake agreement; both parties moved on; that was it.

Singapore culture didn't function that way. The speed of trust and the process of gaining trust were different. Credentials from Silicon Valley were enough to secure meetings with wealthy individuals and heads of business conglomerates, but Vinnie soon discovered that in Asia a single meeting rarely leads to a yes. And when he arrived for those meetings, the setting was often nothing like the casual coffee shops he'd known.

One potential investor granted Vinnie an audience at the VIP's table in a fancy restaurant, inside an upscale hotel *owned* by the investor. It was like being received at the court of a king, and elaborate rituals were required to win the man's ear. No quick-quick, get-it-done transactions were possible. Instead came a lengthy process of personal conversation and feeling out the personal timbre of the visitor and introducing Vinnie to family members and friends in attendance at the occasion (who likewise had *their* feelers working and would no doubt confer afterward to share their judgments). Just getting the pre-qualifications to pitch was a new kind of game here.

Furthermore, the ultimate responses were unlike those Vinnie had gotten in the Valley. Once, he'd had a chance to meet Reid Hoffman, the legendary PayPal veteran and cofounder of LinkedIn. The meeting wasn't to raise funds, just to connect over coffee. As the friendly visit wrapped up, Hoffman asked Vinnie: "How can I help you?" A generous offer, and one reflective of the Valley's culture. People see value in reaching out to extend and build their networks. A young stranger who appears to have a good disposition and innovative ideas is always worth welcoming into the loop, and that question stayed with Vinnie. It taught him the value of paying it forward, a habit he carries to this day.

But this wasn't the case with the Singapore investors Vinnie tried to court. They were people who had helped to build Singapore into the thriving place that it was—an achievement much to their credit. What counted in their loop was ability to contribute to their momentum, their way. Vinnie's pitch, when he was able to deliver it, did not meet that test. A venture capital fund? Responses ranged from "It won't work here" to "You're not the person to do it." Or, at best, "We'll think about it"—which turned out to be the code for "no."

Vinnie didn't raise a dollar, initially, from that tranche of investors. (They would come in later once they saw proof of concept.) To his credit, Vinnie eventually understood that the problem wasn't with his idea—nor was the problem that a lot of Singapore's top businesspeople were a bunch of clueless old reactionaries, an unmerited judgment. They weren't "wrong." They were part of a culture that had a pace and value system of its own. The problem was that Vinnie hadn't grasped the disconnects, the gaps. He'd been pitching the wrong idea to the wrong people at the wrong time.

So Vinnie adjusted. He raised the initial fund from investors outside Singapore and from Singapore's government—where people operating from a different perspective *within* the culture had actually created a financial incentive program to attract outsiders with new and valuable ideas. (Lesson: There are cultures within cultures. Target the ones that align with what you're doing.)

Fast-forward 10 years.

Vinnie's VC firm was now established in Singapore and investing across Southeast Asia, in multiple countries. One of them had been trending to top-of-mind.

Vietnam was looking more and more like a major growth market for early-stage tech investment. With a population topping 100 million and with a contract manufacturing base that was adding hands-on experience to an educated workforce, the country called for Golden Gate Ventures to have an increased presence. That meant an actual, physical presence. Although a flight from Singapore can reach Vietnam in just two hours and a few minutes, Vinnie knew that to properly *understand the culture* and nurture the contacts needed for intelligent, targeted investing, he would need to embed himself in life on the ground. (This is the focus of Chapter 4, "You Have to Be There.")

So Vinnie, his wife, and their children moved to Ho Chi Minh City. Before their furniture arrived, they found a bare, unfurnished apartment with enough room to harbor a growing family. And soon they met a neighbor who became a close friend. He was about Vinnie's age, invited Vinnie to join him for early-morning workouts, had children who quickly took to playing with his—and, at the very start of the friendship, when a money-transfer glitch left Vinnie's family with an empty apartment and no bed, he lent the American couple the money for a *mattress*. It was a small loan but a big gesture of trust.

You have been introduced to the kindly neighbor. His name is Stefano Pellegrino.

And that mattress was more than a gesture of friendship. It symbolized what this book is about: building trust across cultures in ways that textbooks don't cover. Closing deals isn't just pitch decks and spreadsheets. It's people, cultures, and connections.

Key Takeaways

- **Surprise is the starting point.** In a new culture, the first thing you'll encounter isn't opportunity, but unfamiliar behaviors that challenge your assumptions.

- **Growth accelerates outside your comfort zone.** When you step into unfamiliar cultures and environments, your assumptions get tested, and your learning curve sharpens fast.

- **Small gaps cause big consequences.** Most cross-cultural failures begin with tiny misunderstandings that snowball when assumptions go untested.

- **Reserve judgment when things feel "wrong."** What looks irrational or unprofessional through your lens often makes perfect sense within the local context.

- **Learn the pattern behind the behavior.** A surprise tactic is only surprising once; after that, you gain an advantage by understanding why it happens and preparing for it.

- **Trust moves at different speeds in different places.** A handshake in one culture seals a deal, while in another it's only the beginning of proving you're trustworthy.

- **Connection is the real work.** Closing deals across borders is ultimately about reading people, earning trust, and adapting to how relationships are built locally.

2 Prepare to Be Unprepared

In a Culture New to You, Expect the Unexpected

When Marco Polo first encountered paper money in the court of Kublai Khan, he could hardly believe what he was seeing. In Europe, value lived in metal: gold and silver coins you could hold in your hand. In China, value flowed on ink and paper, backed not by weight, but by the authority of the Khan. To Polo's eyes, it felt strange, almost like a magic trick. Yet it worked. People accepted the notes, trade moved, wealth accumulated.

That is what entering a new culture often feels like. You walk in with one mental model of how the world *should* work and then discover a completely different system that functions just as well, or even better, than your own.

As we've said, a basic fact about doing business across borders is that there will be surprises. Even if you study up on your target country in advance, the cultural traits you've read or heard about will pop up in surprising forms or in situations where you weren't expecting them. And the culture is liable to have traits you didn't expect at all.

The question then is how to prepare. Although "Expect the unexpected" may seem like an empty cliche, it's genuinely helpful just to know that something will be coming at you and that you won't know what the something is. Furthermore, there is a way to minimize the frequency of incoming surprises: spend time on the ground in a culture before starting a business there. Go there to get oriented. While books and reports can do a lot to prepare you, there is no substitute for learning a culture on the ground.

Vinnie's decision to move to Vietnam, before ramping up venture investments in the country, was motivated largely by the need to get a direct grasp of the business environment and breed contacts. Speaking more broadly, it helped ensure that he wouldn't walk into deals like a naive schoolboy. He schooled himself to a higher state.

We recommend at least a year on the ground in a new culture. This will prepare you for some (though not all) of the new twists you'll encounter when the stakes are high and will have a fundamental benefit as well. It will begin acclimating you to think in the ways that people in the culture think. Not with perfect mental/emotional fluency, but on the same wavelengths. That is a major leap in terms of capability to interact.

Before Stefano launched his Vietnam-based start-up company, he spent nine full years on the ground, working in a variety of roles in Vietnam and other parts of Southeast Asia. By the time he became a founder and CEO, he was ready in more than the sense of having business experience. His mind was set to a high level of thinking and acting interculturally.

But simply putting in time isn't enough, in itself, to acquire a proficient intercultural mindset. What you do while you're on the ground matters. There's an old joke about doing any kind of work: some people have 20 years of experience, and some just repeat the same year 20 times. We suggest doing all of the following on the ground.

Active Listening and Mindfulness

You will need to be keenly aware of what's going around you, while maintaining inner balance.

The state of mindfulness includes but is more than "being present." That is the part that keeps you attuned to what's going on around you. There is also an internal dimension—being aware of what's going on inside you.

Vinnie offers a simple example of the latter. His meditation studies had taught him to be inwardly aware of his breathing. One day, while crossing a street in a Southeast Asian city, he noticed that his breaths had grown tight and shallow, an instinctive threat response. Immediately he glanced around to see if a car was about to hit him. No danger there. He realized, through the change in his breath, that a stressful business thought was starting to form. By noticing it early, he was able to let it go before it took hold.

Few of us are inclined to pursue Vipassana meditation, as Vinnie has. However, many methods exist for developing mindfulness, and there will be value in learning one. Doing business across cultures can place unusual demands on a person; it's like living on high alert. The ability to dance through the swirl of external uncertainties while maintaining inner balance will increase your chances of success and reduce the risk of burnout.

Mindfulness becomes even more valuable when negotiations turn tense. In one deal with a Vietnamese company, Vinnie felt the conversation growing tense—not because of what was being said but because his breath had shifted, growing shorter and more pressured. That physical cue was the early warning. Instead of reacting from frustration or jumping in to argue, he paused, listened more closely, and repeated back what he heard. That small moment of self-awareness prevented an emotional spiral and opened space for a more constructive exchange.

This is the practical side of mindfulness in cross-border business. Your breath and heartbeat often register tension before your mind does. With practice—whether through meditation, yoga, or simply checking in with yourself during the week—you learn to observe the emotion rather than become it. In fast-moving or high-stakes situations, this gives you a crucial advantage. You can name the feeling, set it aside, and respond with clarity instead of instinct. Mindfulness will not tell you whether your gut instinct is correct, but it will keep you from confusing emotion with intuition. And in unfamiliar cultural terrain, that distinction can be the difference between escalating a conflict and navigating through it.

Suspend Judgment

Never assume that a practice or belief is wrong just because it differs from yours.

Marco Polo famously described seeing "unicorns" in Asia, only his unicorns were nothing like the graceful creatures of European myth. What he was almost certainly looking at were rhinoceroses. His mind reached for the closest category it knew and forced the new reality to fit an old story.

We do the same thing in business. When we see unfamiliar practices in another country, our first instinct is often to compare them to whatever we're used to at home and then quietly label them "wrong," "backward," or "risky" because they don't match. The truth is that even the fundamentals can vary greatly across borders.

Business decisions in some cultures tend to be made top-down, by a small executive team, and there is an emphasis on implementing them rapidly. Elsewhere, the presence of hierarchy does not always produce swift executive action. Japan is a notable example, and at first glance it can feel paradoxical. The national culture fosters respect for rank and authority, a trait that's embedded in the Japanese language, with its multiple forms of address that vary depending on who is talking to whom. Yet despite this, decisions are reached by long processes of deliberation and consensus-building. To a Westerner itching for an answer, the Japanese approach can feel agonizingly slow.

But that doesn't mean it's wrong. Nor would a Japanese person be justified in saying it's the right way to go and the top-down/rapid model is wrong. Each has pros and cons. One approach can move you to market faster, while the other can help to assure that when you move, everybody is aligned and the proper pieces are in place.

Furthermore, the methods reflect what the cultures value more highly. Silicon Valley, a hotbed of top-down-rapidness, has been the birthplace of slogans like "Move fast and break things" and "Don't worry, be crappy" (an exhortation to release software early, relying on user feedback to guide the finishing work). This type of thinking doesn't exactly square with the Japanese emphasis on constantly striving for perfection. One of the great achievements of Japanese industry is the Toyota Production System, which calls upon everyone involved with production to engage in carefully articulated, deliberative exercises aimed at rooting out waste and errors.

Of course, we are speaking in generalities. There are exceptions in each culture, such as Silicon Valley projects done with meticulous collaborative care and Japanese projects pushed forward in a blitz. Still, the fact remains that the cultures aren't the same—and the world has profited from the fruits of each. So again, it's hard to say that either is right or wrong. Just mind the gap, wherever you are, and don't let your stereotypes and preconceptions cloud your judgment.

We interviewed one executive who had been an advisor for a European private equity firm when it bought a company that had secured a sports entertainment rights deal in Turkey. The buyers immediately suspected the Turkish company may have done something dodgy to secure their rights, solely based on their bias and on their perception of Turkish manners, even though the business and process were actually legitimate. Had the deal been in Switzerland, it would have been viewed without suspicion, despite being the same. The deal fell apart, while the Turkish business ultimately proved successful, demonstrating how cultural biases can cloud judgment and lead to missed opportunities. The issue wasn't the deal, but the inability of the Europeans to move past surface-level preconceptions.

Sharpen Your Intuition

Intuition is a hidden tool and the first step to deciphering unfamiliar exchanges.

Often, you'll need to sense when something is wrong—when you meet a person who shouldn't be trusted or when someone offers a proposition that shouldn't be. And reading nonverbal cues can get tricky, because you're looking through the veil of a culture you don't know very well.

On the other hand, something that looks wrong may be perfectly OK. For example, in some cultures (and in some subcultures within countries), people avoid making eye contact when speaking to a person they perceive as their superior. That person could be a boss, a teacher, an elder—or a newcomer like you, if you are perceived as someone important. The thinking is that returning your gaze would be a sign of insolence, whereas looking away is a more courteous gesture. It's a nonverbal way of saying "I will let you inspect me, and I do not presume that I have the authority to inspect you back." People who hold this belief will look to the side or even cast their eyes down, especially when they're answering questions. The trouble is that the habit can easily be misinterpreted by outsiders. Many cultures say eye contact is good, a sign of paying attention and wanting to connect, while people who shift their eyes away are seen as being not interested or, worse, evasive and dishonest.

In our cross-cultural work, we've often stumbled over other forms of crossed signals. Not only have we misread what others were trying to convey, we've sent the wrong messages ourselves. This happened to Vinnie over what may seem an irrelevant matter: how many people should you bring to a meeting? When he was an entrepreneur in Silicon Valley, pitching start-ups to investors, he learned that pitch meetings should be kept small. The culture of fast-moving busyness dictates that you must not waste people's time by bringing a multitude of voices into a conversation. So Vinnie walked into pitches alone, which was appropriate, as he'd typically be talking to just one or two people at a VC firm.

The same worked well in places where the culture is similar. Now Vinnie had become the VC, and he assumed it was fine to go solo into talks with organizations that might put money into a fund: they too would have only one or two reps at the table. But the same did not work so well when he first tried pitching to the investment divisions of multinationals in Japan. There, he'd walk into a room and find himself facing a platoon of people. And being outnumbered wasn't the main problem. Vinnie soon sensed that showing up alone created a poor impression. It could lead people to wonder: Is this guy's "company" just a one-man show? Can he not even afford to have a couple of colleagues traveling with him? On subsequent trips, Vinnie brought team members, which helped to smooth the bumpy tone of the meetings and allowed for exchanges that felt more natural.

The question for you is how to minimize these mix-ups. Our first answer, again, would be to work on sharpening your intuition. Every human has this capability, but not everyone uses it often enough to trust it. It's the sixth sense that can alert you to red flags (or green lights) regardless of the culture. For us, intuition is also a tool that helps us learn from our mistakes—an essential skill, except it doesn't happen automatically. If we are able to sense, intuitively, the nature of the mistake we've just made and why it was a trigger for trouble, we have a big head start toward correcting it the next time.

Further assistance lies ahead. Chapters 7 and 8 delve into the art called cultural code-switching. Together, those chapters present an all-around guide to detecting and dealing with cultural mismatches. For now let's stay with building the foundation: an intercultural mindset.

Be Humble

As you enter a new culture, try Stefano's mantra: "I know nothing." Granted, it's not strictly true. You know a lot about a lot of things. But you don't know much about the culture, which means you may not know how well your knowledge applies. The can-do attitude that works at home might run up against "Oh, but you can't do that here."

In a pair of well-known cases that occurred a couple of decades apart, two major US-based companies failed at expanding into countries that had seemed to be fertile markets for them. Walmart's venture into Germany and Airbnb's into China were each hampered, to a significant extent, by leaders thinking their tested-and-proven practices would apply in the target countries. In each case, part of the problem was cultural mismatch. Airbnb's home-sharing model struggled in a culture where many householders felt wary of opening their homes to strangers to begin with, and apparently it didn't help that hosts and visitors had to vet each other and interact through a platform that operated counter to the ways many Chinese like to do things. Earlier, Walmart's practice of having store employees do team-spirit activities before work got a chilly reception in Germany, and customers didn't like the resulting atmosphere in the stores. Nor was cultural misunderstanding the only issue. Surprisingly, both firms also ran into problems complying with various laws and regulations. Working out compliances in advance may seem an obvious step to take, but we too have seen companies fail to give it sufficient thought.

Bottom line: In cross-cultural business, thinking you know the game is dangerous. Too much that you don't know can lie hidden. Starting from "I know nothing" is safer. This humbler mindset leads to making checklists of factors to check out scrupulously. And, we find it equally important to carry a humble mindset into relations with local people. Listening more than you talk is valuable. So is a classic bit of advice that helps to form genuine bonds of understanding with people anywhere. Put yourself in the other person's shoes.

And ultimately, it all comes back to staying humble inside your head. Overconfidence and over-assumptions are your enemies. Speaking of which . . .

Reality over Roadmaps

Do your assumptions about a new market match with what you see playing out day-to-day? Step back and make adjustments to the structure or strategy of the business for a well-prepared take-off, even if this takes a bit longer.

Sometimes a company forms an expansion plan for rolling out to multiple countries across a region. Although it's helpful to do master-planning of this type, the risk is that the plan will devolve to a cut-and-paste operation. When a particular business model and strategy add up to a winning formula in country A, and maybe also in country B, there's a strong temptation to believe that the roadmap to riches has been discovered, and all that's needed is to follow it in countries C, D, and so on. Stefano once found himself in the midst of such events. Fortunately, simple reality-checking told him to throw out the map and do what would fit the market.

In 2019 he joined an emerging fintech in the SME lending space (lending to small and medium-sized enterprises). Stefano's title was

"Co-founder and Country Manager for Vietnam," one of the next countries on the expansion list, and he'd be setting up the business there from scratch. The fintech had prospered thus far by making unsecured microloans of $5,000–$10,000 each to small businesses, in high volumes and at high interest rates. Stefano, informed by his prior experience as a finance lawyer based in Vietnam, decided his corporate duty was to step hard on the brake pedal.

High-volume/high-margin microlending had worked well in Singapore and in other places with relatively well-developed economies. In those places, even most small companies used good accounting methods. Transparency was the norm, and reliable credit-reporting systems were in place. Thanks to these conditions, the fintech had enjoyed low default rates. But in emerging-market countries like Vietnam, where such conditions were still far from universal, Stefano figured that flooding the market with unsecured microloans would invite a tsunami of delinquencies and defaults sufficient to flatten the business.

So he proposed an alternate lending strategy for Vietnam: fewer loans in larger amounts, at lower interest rates, made to midsize companies with established credit records. He even knew companies that fit the profile. HQ said, in effect, why try to fix what doesn't look broken? Stefano persisted . . . and soon built the Vietnam business into the fintech's most profitable.

That outcome then prompted a change of mindset among the company's leadership team. They migrated the new lending strategy to other markets where defaults had become a pain point. Eventually the fintech wound up with a portfolio of roadmaps tailored to various business landscapes—a fitting arrangement that fully reflects an intercultural mindset.

Dropping preconceived roadmaps and adapting to local realities is essential, whether you are running a start-up or a multinational company. Federico D'Amico, who served as CEO for India of a Fortune Global 500 company, observed this at scale. He notes that foreign investors sometimes arrive in India with operating models shaped by other markets, assuming that exhaustive planning and process discipline guarantee success. In practice, India often calls for a more flexible and adaptive approach. As Federico puts it: "If you wait for perfect visibility in India, you may struggle to move forward. As in many entrepreneurial settings, progress depends on acting with imperfect information and refining plans as conditions evolve. Execution needs to be more iterative, and planning must be continuously adjusted to on-the-ground realities."

For example, if you are developing a solar power plant, the typical Western approach would require you to wait for all the contracts to be signed, the financing to be ready, and the land to be acquired—after which you can reach your final investment decision and then start construction. In India, it is common to have a final investment decision when the main contract (called a PPA) is almost ready to go, but not signed yet, and when you have only half of the land ready for the project. This is something that would be unacceptable for any international lender but is very much accepted within India. "And so you have these two parallel tracks where process is important, but then you need to execute it and adapt it day by day in order to achieve success."

Venture with People Who Know the Culture

Multiple minds are better than one, and obviously people who have lived and worked in a culture—ideally, who were born and raised in it—know it better than a newcomer. It's simply common sense to surround yourself with such individuals, right from the start of a cross-cultural business.

When Vinnie launched Golden Gate Ventures in Singapore, one of his founding partners was Jeffrey Paine, a Singaporean who already had extensive experience working with Southeast Asian entrepreneurs. Stefano's team at his Vietnam-based firm, Aquila, is broadly multicultural, and he also makes a point of scouring the region for "super-connectors," people embedded in local cultures who have strong networks. They can help to orient new arrivals and provide introductions that move the business forward.

Your in-country associates don't all have to be certified experts. When you explore a new country or region, just bringing along an intern who's native to it would be an excellent move. That person knows the language and much more. That person will literally expand your mind.

The concept holds true at scale. Federico D'Amico emphasizes the importance of choosing the right local partner. While operating models may adapt to local conditions, standards of transparency and compliance should not; they remain foundational principles of responsible leadership. Beyond technical capability, integrity and adherence to standards are essential to avoid long-term risk. This is not about lowering the bar, but about translating clear expectations into an operating framework that reflects local regulatory and institutional realities.

When Federico selected a business partner to expand operations in India, he adopted a deliberate strategy to avoid costly mistakes, informed by earlier market missteps. He appointed highly experienced non-executive directors to advise on partner selection and governance. He recognized that paper-based due diligence has limits - documents provide structure; lived experience provides judgment. In any ecosystem, institutional memory matters, and those who understand it operate with an advantage. Senior advisors aligned with your interests and able to guide you toward—or away from—specific partners provide a clear strategic edge.

Now we have two final notes to add. They are meant primarily for students and recent graduates—but anyone can apply them at any stage of life, to build a global mindset and prepare for an international career. When you are young, you have leverage you'll probably never again possess to the same extent. You have time, freedom, mobility, and room to make mistakes without catastrophic cost. These are advantages you can convert directly into learning, growth, and global experience. Early risk-taking and exploration are not side pursuits. They are the fastest ways to accelerate your understanding of yourself, the world, and what it means to work across cultures.

So, the two practices we recommend here will serve you throughout your career. They are simple but powerful. By embracing them early, you build the foundation for a global business life that becomes easier, richer, and more fulfilling over time.

Take Risks Early

Make the leap of starting something when you are young, to get your hands dirty and learn everything it takes. It can be, and most of the time will be, full of mistakes. You'll pick the wrong market, wrong timing, wrong customer, wrong product, wrong partners, or wrong employees. But the good news is that the know-how you gain will be phenomenal.

If you fail but learn market entry, product launch, hiring, management, or how to motivate and lead a team, then failure will be more than worth the cost. Books like this can offer valuable insights. People who've done what you want to do (like us) can help you get aimed in the right direction, better equipped than before. But trying and learning along the way is the only way to actually learn how to build and do things properly.

Risks taken early are rarely wasted. They either lead to unexpected breakthroughs or leave you with the kind of resilience and intuition that serve you for decades.

Expand Your Horizons

Out of all the reasons it's great to be young, be sure to take advantage of a big one: freedom to explore the world. We urge you to exercise this freedom whenever you can. You'll see many chances for adventure, so pick any you like and say yes to them.

For openers: fly. Flying to distant places should always be a top choice. It's a low-risk investment with high payback. Do it now. It doesn't matter where you fly—to New York or New Delhi or Chile or Qatar or Vietnam. Once there, take time to roam around and meet people. Good things will flow your way, just as they did for Vinnie on his Asian adventure, even if you have only a week or two instead of a year.

You will get an intro course in navigating across cultures, in situations where it's fun and the future of a business isn't at stake. Serendipitous meetings will open up new opportunities as you build a growing global network. And you will gain the inner strength that comes with venturing out on your own. Travel also trains your ability to stay calm under pressure and improvise solutions when plans fall apart.

A small example from Vinnie illustrates the point. Many global cities have more than one airport, and on a business trip he realized too late that he had gone to the wrong one. With his connecting flight at risk, he approached two airport staff members for the fastest way across town. They immediately started arguing in front of him. Both agreed the metro was faster, but one was adamant about taking a taxi, convinced he would get lost in an unfamiliar system. The other insisted the metro was the only realistic option if he hoped to make his flight.

Vinnie had never taken that particular metro before, but he had taken metros across North America, South America, Asia, India, and Europe. Years of accumulated travel experiences gave him an internal library to draw from, even under stress. He trusted that experience, chose the metro, navigated the transfers, and made his flight with minutes to spare. The point is not about metros or taxis. It is that each new place you explore builds a reservoir of experience you can rely on when the stakes rise.

People we know who dared to fly young are among the most successful and fastest-growing. The experiences they've had and the level of autonomy they attain seem to create a momentum that carries them wherever they aspire to go.

That is why we urge you to apply what you read here, including in the chapters ahead.

Key Takeaways

- **Expect the unexpected.** No amount of reading prepares you for the cultural surprises that only show themselves on the ground.

- **Practice mindfulness.** Inner awareness keeps you steady in environments full of ambiguity, pressure, and social signals you may not yet understand.

- **Suspend judgment.** Different isn't wrong; every culture optimizes for what it values, and you must learn to see the logic beneath the surface.

- **Sharpen your intuition.** It's your early warning system in unfamiliar settings, helping you read cues correctly and recover faster from mistakes.

- **Stay humble.** Starting with "I know nothing" opens the door to genuine learning and protects you from dangerous assumptions.

(continued)

- **Reality beats roadmaps.** Strategies that worked elsewhere must be revalidated in each new market, no matter how confident you feel.

- **Frequent reality-testing keeps you aligned with the market.** Does what you're thinking and doing correspond to what you actually see playing out day-to-day?

- **Lean on locals.** Surrounding yourself with people who know the culture accelerates your learning curve and prevents rookie errors.

- **There's no better education than a start-up.** Launching or joining one when you're young can be a great move. The risks you take will pay off later.

- **Go where other cultures actually live.** Time spent in a distant country rewires your intuition, giving you the mental fluency needed for real business interactions.

3 Getting Ready to Expand

Why, Where, and How Will You Go?

"**B**e prepared" is the Girl Scout motto. It applies to scouting out the terrain for cross-border expansion, where the upsides are great—and pitfalls can be deadly. We think a failure story will set the proper tone.

Private, high-end social clubs have been part of the business world for centuries, because they offer an attractive combination: focused networking opportunities, plus a place to relax and unwind without the hubbub of a public restaurant. Recently there's been an explosion of these clubs in new forms. Operated as for-profit enterprises, they have modern amenities like co-working spaces and gyms, along with a variety of dining and lounge areas.

One of the hottest venues in Singapore was a club called 1880, a magnet for entrepreneurs and other mover-and-shaker types. Then one day, seven years after its launch, members—many of whom had already paid their yearly dues—were stunned to receive an email out of the blue. The club 1880 was closing immediately. Don't even try coming today, the email said; the doors are locked.

The culprit was a failed international expansion. Flush with initial success, 1880s cofounder and CEO—a Canadian expat—had expanded into two international locations, Hong Kong and Bali, the previous year. Bali hadn't even launched yet, and 1880 Hong Kong capsized within months. The expected swarm of new customers paying high membership fees didn't materialize. As the founder Admond Lee of The Runway Ventures observed, "Hong Kong's market dynamics, costs, and culture were completely different" from Singapore's. The competitive landscape in Hong Kong was extremely tough, with a long history of traditional members-only clubs, plus many newer entrants like the global operator Soho House—each with a business model tuned to exploit particular niches in the private-club market, such as pricing structures targeted to attract younger members or a huge wine list to draw in wine lovers.

Worse yet, 1880 had chosen a super-risky form of the expansion strategy Reid Hoffman dubbed *blitz-scaling*. The CEO poured resources into building lavish facilities in two new international markets, which saddled the company with high up-front rent and build-out costs from the start and which divided the focus of the CEO and leadership team. Given the capital and credit available to 1880, the expansion amounted to a bet-the-company move—a heavy launch from a short runway. The result was a cash drain that sank the Singapore flagship as well. An investor swooped in and bought the company for pennies on the dollar.

Scaling across borders is risky no matter how or where it's done. The key, as with any business venture, is to minimize risks while maximizing the chances of high returns. Justin Hall, a partner at Golden Gate Ventures, has spent years watching start-ups expand across borders in Southeast Asia. Here is what often makes the difference between success and failure, in his view:

"The best founders over-engineer their expansions. They spend months, sometimes the better part of a year, deciding which market to enter first. They study the regulatory landscape, map out distribution channels, identify local talent, stress-test their unit economics for that specific geography. By the time they move, they know exactly what the playbook is. The best founders are not building their car while driving it."

Three major components go into getting properly ready: choosing the right reasons to expand, selecting the right target country, and deploying an expansion strategy that fits the market. The following sections explore the nuances of each.

Why Expand Across Borders?

There can be many solid reasons for going international. Usually, in cases that work out well, more than one is present:

- You are armed and equipped to expand. Your existing business has proven to be profitable and scalable. You have sufficient resources in your pocket.

- The opportunities are too promising to ignore. A cross-border market offers significant growth potential *for your kind of business*, without red flags that could be deal-breakers.

- Your existing market can't provide the future growth you need.

- Competitors are expanding or threatening to expand across borders. They could get the jump on you in new markets; they could eventually grow to a size that lets them dominate you wherever you are.

Are there wrong reasons to expand into a cross-border market? Probably the worst would be "Because it's there." The mountaineer George Mallory reportedly spoke those famous words when asked why he was fixated on becoming the first to climb Mount Everest. The answer has echoed through history as an inspirational quote. What's little noted is that Mallory and his climbing partner died "there." Nobody reached the top of Everest and lived to tell the story until a better-prepared team was able to do it years later.

The CEO of the 1880 club was lucky. At least he survived to tell the story of a business death. To his credit, Marc Nicholson issued an apology taking full responsibility for an ill-advised decision to expand: "Call it hubris, arrogance, capitalism, or stupidity, I am solely to blame for the failure."

Key Takeaways

- **Preparation is everything.** "Be prepared" isn't just a motto; it's the foundation for cross-border expansion. Success abroad depends on readiness, not just ambition.

- **Success at home doesn't guarantee success abroad.** What works brilliantly in one market can fail fast in another. Each country has its own culture, economics, and competitive dynamics.

- **Focus is a finite resource.** The 1880 CEO's attention was divided between multiple launches, draining leadership bandwidth and weakening oversight—a common pitfall in global expansion.

- **Choose expansion for the right reasons.** Go international because it's strategic, not simply because "it's there." Expansion should serve growth objectives, competitive positioning, or market opportunity—not ego or impulse.

- **Study market fit and cultural alignment deeply.** Differences in consumer behavior and competition can easily blindside even experienced executives. Understanding local context is just as critical as getting the financial model right.

> - **Be realistic about capital and capacity.** Even good ideas fail if the expansion burns cash faster than it builds value. Each new market should be approached with clear runway, ROI targets, and contingency plans.
>
> - **Own your mistakes and learn from them.** Marc Nicholson's public accountability for 1880s failure is rare but admirable. Honest reflection turns a failure story into a learning story.

Scaling across borders can be a great decision, as long as it looks viable for your company. Be sure to make the assessment before you leap.

Choosing a Target Country (It Might Not Be Obvious!)

A simple rule of thumb can go far in evaluating places to expand. Don't rely solely on broad market-research indicators like the country's population and market size or GDP growth or demographics. A country can look phenomenal by these measures and still not be fertile ground for the type of business you want to bring in. The best choice(s) are best judged by looking at *business-specific criteria*.

For example, here is a basic checklist:

- *What does the market for your goods or services look like?* Do you see sufficient demand, or the signs of emerging unmet needs?

- *What about the competitive environment?* Are strong players moving in, or perhaps already established? If so, can you offer a competitive advantage? Is there a neglected niche you could fill—either in terms of market segmentation or geographically?

- *Consider cultural barriers and cultural fit.* To what extent would you need to adjust your product, business model, marketing, and/or other factors? Is this doable? Would it be worth doing, given the likelihood of projected returns?

- *Take a hard look at the legal and regulatory environment for your industry.* Here again, consider the adjustments you'd have to make. When Stefano's green finance firm expands across borders, the critical factors are regulatory specifics—such as rules on how sustainable funds can be used, how assets can be used as collateral, and how ownership or loans must be officially registered. Other industries may need to consider import duties, local content regulations, data localization rules, or product certification requirements. These technical details determine whether an expansion can succeed.

- *What is the status of the infrastructure you'll be using?* E.g., for a manufacturing business, consider access to industrial zones, power and water stability, transport links, and the availability of local suppliers and technical talent. In Vietnam, for instance, the pool of technical talent is large and affordable, but international manufacturers have complained of power restrictions during the summer months, when air conditioning puts extra strain on the national grid.

- *How stable is the government? And how reliable?* Think about this in business-specific terms, not just in general terms like the possibility of a coup or sudden turnover of the government. Business-specific terms might include the government's friendliness to your industry (especially regarding "foreign-owned" companies, if it's an industry seen as one that should be built up domestically). The risk of corruption impacting your business might be a factor in some cases, too.

- *Go in with a plan for forecasting your rollout, and test your assumptions along the way.* Executives leading expansion often overestimate how quickly they'll be up and running in a new market. The 1880 example shows how easy it is to mistake enthusiasm for readiness. In reality, international rollouts almost always take longer than expected; 12 to 18 months is a safe baseline. Key hires take time, local demand builds gradually, and unexpected costs inevitably appear. The best teams set quarterly checkpoints to test assumptions and, most importantly, plan ahead for when to pull the plug. Flexibility dominates discipline here. A good plan adapts when reality doesn't follow the spreadsheet.

- *Last but definitely not least, consider timing.* Is this the right time to enter? Or should you wait—or has the window already closed? Even the right market can be the wrong move if you enter too early or too late. Sometimes the signals come from outside your own business: a shift in economic growth, new regulations, or a change in how consumers adopt international brands or tech platforms. The venture capital world treats timing as a decisive factor in success. If you are the only player in a market, it may mean you're too early and demand hasn't yet materialized. If you're entering late, you will need to find your niche and push through existing competition. Timing often comes down to intuition, something that only practice and mistakes can teach.

Vinnie believes that his Singapore-based venture capital firm might not have succeeded if it had launched just two years earlier, or a couple of years later. Two years too soon, and Southeast Asian markets wouldn't have been ready for his business proposition; two years later, and the wave of local VC firms starting in the region might have squeezed out a newcomer. Vinnie and his co-founders came together at a rare moment of opportunity, but even then, early traction was hard-won. Timing is everything when entering a new market.

That's why being forced to move on someone else's timeline, often under pressure from investors or board members, can lead to suboptimal outcomes. Between 2015 and 2022, launching or expanding into Indonesia became almost mandatory for tech start-ups across Southeast Asia. The country was home to the largest population in the region by far (and the fourth largest in the world). This made it seem, at least on paper, the most promising market and opportunity. Investors demanded the move, shareholders expected it, and founders complied. Yet many companies discovered that Indonesia was not the right fit for their model, and several stumbled from inadequate preparation.

Stefano saw that supply-side pressure firsthand while leading regional expansion for a fast-growing start-up. As he recalls, other countries were delivering much better results than Indonesia but were still being de-prioritized by top management in the product roadmap compared to Indonesia. The decision appeared to make little sense from a numbers-and-data perspective, but to US-based investors, no Southeast Asian success story felt complete without Indonesia. A first attempt to drive expansion in Indonesia from scratch had failed within 18 months. A second attempt, based on the acquisition of a local player, also struggled to take off, mainly because it was being directed remotely from HQ rather than in the field. Eventually, Stefano—who had been driving remarkable growth for the company in other countries—was asked to push Indonesia's growth directly on the ground. He flew to Jakarta every other week until the company could recruit a strong and experienced local general manager. The reality is that strategy and timing were wrong and that it would have been better to enter the market a few years later at a cheaper cost and with a stronger product-market-fit.

Key Takeaways

- **Timing is everything.** Entering a new market too early risks unmet readiness; too late, and competition closes the window. Base expansion timing on data and real market signals, not external pressure or hype.

- **Choose the market, don't let it choose you.** Picking the right country for expansion isn't simple or obvious. Evaluate it through business-specific metrics—customer readiness, operational feasibility, and local talent fit—rather than assumptions or narratives.

- **Resist supply-side pressure.** Investor or board expectations can distort priorities. Move when your company is operationally ready, not when others say you "should."

- **Avoid the Fear of Missing Out.** FOMO-fueled expansion often leads to half-built operations and costly retrenchment. Sustainable growth comes from strategic conviction, not fear.

- **Trust ground truth over spreadsheet theory.** Expansion decisions made from afar often miss the nuances that determine success. Spend time on the ground, test assumptions locally, and let firsthand understanding guide the plan.

Push versus Pull: Two Paths to International Expansion

Every expansion is done under unique circumstances. Nobody else has solved the puzzle of matching your company's particular goals and qualities with the characteristics of the country you are entering, in a situation that exactly matches the one prevailing now. Therefore, every expansion is also likely to take a unique form, shaped by how you decide to proceed and by the team that will implement it. Every time you expand, it is an experiment shaped by timing, team, and the realities on the ground. Yet when you strip away the details, most international rollouts fall into one of two patterns: pull and push.

Pull happens when genuine market signals draw you in—customers asking for your product, local partners inviting collaboration, or trusted contacts opening doors.

Push, by contrast, is when the company drives expansion from the top down—often under pressure from investors or competitive fear—before those signals exist.

"Go where the signals already pull you." That's how Fernando Fabre, CEO of Kauffman Fellows and previously president of Endeavor Global, described how his team at Endeavor chose new cities—"push versus pull." When they mapped more than 150 cosmopolitan metros globally as potential expansion targets, they resisted the urge to push their way in. Instead they managed for pull, by looking at several factors:

- Strength of invitation. Were those cities calling them to come meet? Could they find a credible local champion inviting, convening, and opening doors?

- Proxies for purchasing power. Borrowing a trick from an education-tech platform (and echoed by a Deloitte mentor), they used quirky but revealing indicators—such as global high-end retail chain density—as shorthand indicators for a growing local purchasing power and professional depth.

- Pull decides sequencing. "Out of 150 potential locations, we decided the next launch by the amount of pull from whichever city was calling us stronger," Fernando recalled.

- Time on the ground. The team typically visited 10–15 times before launch. By then, a referral network for hiring had formed organically. They noticed who the locals suggested as targets for the Managing Director role, often ex-consultants, investment managers, or entrepreneurs with global experience—so no search firm was needed.

Anyone choosing expansion markets can apply this method. Score each market's pull—invitations, inbound leads, local champions, early customer meetings. Layer in proxies for customer quality, and don't commit until repeated visits and warm referrals signal readiness. Build your first hires from that same pull network.

Organic Expansion: The Pull Approach

Pull-driven or organic expansion is slower but safer. It follows real demand rather than forecasts. Ideally, you grow by serving existing clients who invite you into a new geography. This leverages proven relationships, reduces risk, and limits waste.

For example, in one of Stefano's tech start-ups, a long-standing client in the Philippines asked for support on a new project in Thailand. That single request became a springboard into a new market—with minimal speculation. Further, it offered several advantages. Risk was significantly reduced. Learning was highly targeted to the specific legal, technical, and operational requirements necessary to execute that specific project, and resource use was tightly controlled. Most importantly, cash flow was predictable. Working for an existing and trusted customer reduced the risk of not being paid upon successful execution (which can be a common problem when launching in a new market). Once the project ended, the experience became a blueprint for winning similar work, progressively building a stronger market presence in Thailand as volumes increased. That's how organic expansion can pay off.

As demand in a new market grows and more contracts are signed with customers, a time may come when you'll need to ramp up your on-the-ground presence. But that sort of resource commitment is justified, not purely speculative. Altogether, the step-by-step organic approach is a mode of *slow* expansion. However, it's a relatively easy, safe method that avoids waste. While the timing and initial scale of growth are determined by the existing client and its first project, the choice of partner remains yours—and building on top of a trusted, proven relationship makes this path highly recommended.

Blitz-Scaling: The Push Approach

At the other end of the spectrum lies *push*, or blitz-scaling. This path suits companies with ample funding or where speed is essential to capture a fleeting opportunity. It's aggressive, resource-intensive, and risky by design.

A decade ago, the Samwer brothers' Rocket Internet epitomized this model. In the early 2010s, their firm launched dozens of global start-ups in record time—e-commerce, food delivery, classifieds, travel, and ride-hailing—each led by polished ex-McKinsey operators. The strategy was to move faster than anyone else into cities across the globe—clone proven models, and flood local markets with capital.

For a while, it worked. But over the next decade, results told a different story. In verticals where capital itself created advantage—warehouses, fleets, logistics—their companies held ground. In others where success depended on local adaptation—classifieds, home-sharing, fintech, ride-hailing—Rocket's ventures lost to nimbler local competitors. Blitz-scaling bought reach, not resilience.

For blitz-scaling, you need to put boots on the ground ASAP. As we emphasized in Chapter 2, you must also be ready to re-assess your progress and pull out of the country if reality testing says you have made a wrong choice. A quick mercy killing is better than slow death by bleeding cash and wasting the company's attention.

Stefano saw that happen to a competing fintech company during expansion into Indonesia. The competitor was well-financed and took off spectacularly at first, sprinting ahead and chasing customer growth before building the foundations to sustain it. For months the numbers looked spectacular, but the surge turned out to be a classic case of hare-and-tortoise. The company had hurried to market without putting firm foundations in place. Rushing the process seemed to work for a while, because the emerging market was in flux, and early-adopting customers were grabbing the first products they saw. But was the fintech's business model sustainable? Was it truly scalable; had the necessary business support structures been laid out; were looming roadblocks anticipated? The answers were no, not sufficiently, all around. Within a year, the expansion collapsed. The fintech withdrew from Indonesia, which left an opening for the second mover—Stefano's firm, Aspire—to scoop up all the customers left behind.

The lesson: moving fast does not mean moving wisely. Blitz-scaling demands constant testing, rapid learning, and the humility to stop when reality disagrees with the plan. A quick exit is far less damaging than a slow, cash-burning retreat, and if it's not working, remember that stopping early is a sign of maturity, not failure.

Whether your growth is pulled by genuine demand or pushed by strategic urgency, the real question isn't how fast you move, but why. Expansion succeeds when timing, readiness, and local traction align. Move with conviction, but only when the market is truly *moving in your direction.*

Key Takeaways

- **Let pull guide your path.** The strongest signal for expansion is not a spreadsheet forecast but real, on-the-ground demand—customers asking, partners inviting, champions opening doors. Follow where the pull is genuine.

- **Time "in" market beats time "to" market.** Visiting repeatedly, listening, and observing reveal whether a market is truly calling you in. Don't launch until local traction and a hiring network start forming naturally.

- **Organic growth compounds trust.** Expanding through existing clients or referrals reduces uncertainty, lowers costs, and builds knowledge you can reuse in future markets.

- **Push carries power—and risk.** Blitz-scaling can capture short windows of opportunity, but capital and speed alone rarely create staying power. Without local foundations, early wins evaporate fast.

- **The best companies balance both.** A mature expansion strategy blends pull and push: pulled by authentic demand but supported by the resources and urgency to seize it at the right moment.

4 You Have to Be There

Build Trust and Knowledge on the Ground

We've gotten used to doing almost everything remotely, whether it's meeting with team members or earning an MBA. Launching a business in a new country should not be on the list. On-the-ground presence *before* launch is essential for two reasons: to build the trust and relationships your company will need and to gain the knowledge needed for structuring the expansion properly.

We have experienced the rewards of "being there" more than once. For openers, consider a pair of parallel cases from the growth of Vinnie's venture capital firm, Golden Gate Ventures (GGV).

Based in Singapore since its founding in 2011, the VC firm had flourished by tapping into the rich networks of Singapore's highly open, international-oriented business climate. By the early 2020s, GGV had a portfolio of start-ups in several Southeast Asian countries as well as an Indonesian office in Jakarta. However, it was becoming clear that one country was under-represented in the portfolio: Vietnam. With a rapidly growing tech economy and a well-educated population of more than 100 million, Vietnam showed many signs of being a prime growth market for venture investing. Yet further expansion there had proved challenging. Vietnam was (and still is) an outlier among the region's emerging nations in several respects.

It's one of the few countries in the world that combines a communist government with a market economy. The ethos and spirit of Vietnam reflect this unusual mixture: you'll meet many people who are entrepreneurial and collectively-minded at the same time. Business regulations are strict in some ways while being unclear and/ or frequently changing in others. Vietnam is a highly dispersed and fragmented country, and this fragmentation is rooted partly in its geography and history.

Both geographically and culturally, Vietnam has long had stronger ties to East Asia than many of its Southeast Asian neighbors. Its territory stretches in a narrow ribbon for more than 2,000 km (1,200 miles) along the coast, a shape that historically connected it by sea to the wider East Asian world. Those maritime links helped shape its cultural traditions, social values, and emphasis on education. Finally, although many Vietnamese speak English and more are learning, English isn't a universal business language to the extent that it is elsewhere. And perhaps most importantly, Vietnam's business culture remains strongly domestic and relationship-driven. Even regional firms headquartered in Southeast Asia are still viewed as outsiders unless they have a true presence on the ground. For Golden Gate Ventures, all these factors added up to one conclusion. The firm couldn't properly take part in Vietnam's growing start-up ecosystem merely by relying on periodic site visits and video chats.

This prompted a radical move. Vinnie, GGV's founding partner, relocated with his family to Ho Chi Minh City. With the firm solidly established in Singapore and trusted partners managing day-to-day leadership there, he could handle his HQ responsibilities from afar. But tapping into Vietnam required face-to-face presence. He spent major parts of each day meeting individually with start-up founders, co-investors, and a variety of influential people in the country's business hub. To grow his network, he hosted small gatherings and went on "double dates" with his wife, while his children often joined community events—quiet reminders that he wasn't passing through but settling in. By spending time in the streets and small sidewalk cafes of Ho Chi Minh City, he began noticing how everyday business actually worked. Urban logistics ran almost entirely on motorbikes, and cash remained the preferred mode of payment.

Gradually, the results of this on-the-ground presence added up. Casual friendships tightened and deepened. Informal meetings evolved into serious business discussions and then into deals. Investments in Vietnam grew. Before Vinnie's move, Vietnamese start-ups had accounted for less than 10% of GGV's portfolio. Within a few short years they made up more than one-third of the firm's most recent fund.

Meanwhile, a second expansion was under way at Golden Gate Ventures. Though originally focused solely on Southeast Asia, GGV had begun building relationships in the faraway MENA (Middle East-North Africa) region as early as the mid-2010s. The Gulf states in particular presented an intriguing new market. Nations like the United Arab Emirates and, more recently, Qatar with its surge in LNG exports had built vast wealth from hydrocarbons and were starting to expand their ambitions beyond energy. Now they were looking to diversify into newer tech-based industries. The start-up ecosystem, though rudimentary and by no means fully formed, was opening up to outside participants. GGV—already armed with skills in working with emerging-market start-ups—saw the potential for a good fit.

Early scouting efforts consisted of short-term visits to network with financial executives, entrepreneurs, and others in the Gulf region. Golden Gate's executives also made formal "guest appearances," such as when Vinnie and a colleague spoke at a Saudi chapter of the Young Presidents Organization (YPO) in 2018. These early visits built initial familiarity with the region's emerging start-up ecosystem and got the VC firm's name known.

Then in 2022 a partner at Golden Gate Ventures, Michael Lints, established a base in Doha before relocating with his family full-time. The move placed him in the heart of Qatar's financial sector and its growing university complex. It furthermore gave him a central base along the shores of the Gulf region, just a short-hop flight away from several other major metro areas: Muscat in Oman, Dubai and Abu Dhabi in the UAE, Riyadh in Saudi Arabia, and Kuwait City in Kuwait. Over the next year and a half, Michael developed face-to-face relationships with key players in all of these places—start-up founders, financiers, government officials, and more. During that time, Michael also deepened a friendship with Hussain Abdulla, a Qatari-born and educated investor who was then CEO of Qatar's largest private investment bank. Hussain became a trusted guide to the region, invested with GGV, and eventually joined as a partner.

Finally in 2024, GGV announced its first early-stage MENA investment fund, based in Doha, and managed by Michael and Hussain. This represented an expansion built on nearly two years of full-time on-the-ground activity, preceded by seven years of exploratory visits. The trust and knowledge acquired throughout that period enabled GGV's MENA Fund to draw major anchor investors including the Oman Investment Authority and a member of Qatar's royal family. By 2025, MENA was no longer just a new frontier for GGV—it had become a steady pipeline of new investments.

Start-up investing is often perceived as a fast-moving, get-it-done business, which in many ways it certainly is. Keen foresight and prompt action are essential at every step from identifying high-promise start-ups to nurturing them as they grow. What tends to be overlooked, though, is the foundation that allows trust and relationships to form quickly. Silicon Valley's dense, interconnected networks act like highly conductive circuits, on which reports of good actors travel fast and those of bad ones even faster. Reputation is the currency, reinforced by shared norms that reward integrity and punish breaches. People in Silicon Valley also can move fast because many of them have been living, breathing, and working within the region's business environment for years. *Their lives are woven into what's happening on the ground.* They know how things need to be done, and the system is held together by its shared norms. Silicon Valley's dense, interconnected networks make speed possible. But the underlying principle is universal: relationships built in person compress time and reduce uncertainty.

The need to build trust and knowledge on the ground doesn't apply only to start-up investing: it is a must for every company that intends to expand cross-border, either by direct investment, partnership or acquisition. Ricardo Melaré shared two cross-border M&A cases that showed how decisive in-person engagement can be. In the first, a long-standing family-owned fertilizer business in rural Brazil received an acquisition offer from a major Russian company. The family spoke only Portuguese and had never handled an M&A process. Ricardo acted as their advisor and as a cultural bridge between the Brazilian sellers and the Russian executives. The parties met in person in Brazil, and spending time together allowed trust to develop and helped bridge the cultural and communication gaps. The Russian buyer later told Ricardo that he believed the Brazilian family would not have proceeded with the transaction without the personal connection and the time spent face to face.

The second M&A case failed precisely because those in-person moments never happened. A large Western European group attempted to acquire a Brazilian petrochemical business, but the parties relied almost entirely on remote communication. The sellers had a financial advisor, but the valuation logic was never translated in a way they could relate to, trust was never formed, and the negotiation eventually broke down. As Ricardo put it, intangible elements (relationships, reputation, confidence) cannot be conveyed through spreadsheets or emails. One deal worked because people sat together; the other collapsed because they never did.

For Brave Capital's Ernestine Fu Mak, the bottom line is simple: "Nothing beats selling in person." What hasn't always been simple in her case is finding the time to always get onto the scene in person. Based in California, she once did a complex deal with an international company that involved flying between Asia and the Unites States as often as twice per month, oftentimes for only two or three days per trip, over an extended period. She traveled so much that she qualified for United Airlines' elite Global Services status, reserved for the airline's most frequent flyers. She insists that all the effort was worthwhile because "the trust that's built in person cannot be replaced by simply Zooming or phoning." And that's precisely what got her international deal through the finish line.

Building Trust and Relationships

Mutual trust is a prerequisite for doing business with anyone, anywhere. In some places, it comes so naturally it's almost taken for granted. The challenge comes in cultures that require a lot of foundation-laying before one can even ask a partner or investor to get onboard.

In Silicon Valley, trust forms fast because the ecosystem is built to support it. There and in places like Singapore, New York, and London, networks are porous—trust circulates quickly, and reputation follows close behind. Winning trust in these cultures is relatively easy. If you show up with an admirable track record and recommendations from a couple of reputable parties and you come across well in an initial meeting, you are likely to be trusted at least provisionally. You'll still have to make a persuasive pitch to get what you want. But you will be pitching from a basis that says your word is good and you're worth listening to.

In other cultures, newcomers find that it's far from quick-and-easy to be trusted. Your track record and recommendations will only buy an entry ticket: they qualify you to be a potential candidate for eventual consideration as someone whose business pitch is worthy of a listen. The guiding principle is that solid personal relationships must be formed before an outsider can propose a specific business relationship.

This more deliberate approach to building trust can be found in countries including the Gulf states, Japan, and Korea. Although they welcome outside business entrants much more than in the past (and in the Gulf's case, actively court outsiders), they remain places where *personal* transparency isn't the norm. People are not in the habit of opening themselves up to persons they have recently met. Nor do they consider a newcomer to be "part of the gang" after a few getting-acquainted sessions. Trust is built over time and ongoing presence. To put it analytically, people want to evaluate a lot of data points before they're ready to judge you as a trustworthy business associate. They and others in their network will want to observe you being a good actor across a range of situations.

The same dynamic appears in many other markets. How, then, can you best proceed to win trust? Our first suggestion is simple: be yourself. Go in with the core attitudes and behaviors that have led people to trust you in your career thus far. Trust is a complicated tapestry. It's not an arena where play-acting is likely to succeed. You would be perceived as straining to make a good impression or, worse, perceived as an inauthentic con artist. Conversely, by being yourself, you naturally come across as honest. And honesty is the ingredient everybody looks for, in every culture.

There is a caveat to our suggestion. You do need to temper your behavior in accordance with local customs. To give a simple example: if formal bows and handshakes are the customary form of greeting, you won't win friends by greeting business prospects with a big American-style hug or a French-style double-kiss on the cheeks. It's also helpful to be aware that signals you are sending—both in your manner of speaking and in your nonverbal mannerisms—can have an impact quite unlike the impact they have in your home culture. For more about this topic, see Chapters 7 and 8 on "cultural code-switching."

But the fact remains that your best self is the self to bring. Vinnie, for instance, does not try to suppress his innate "Americanisms." When he arrives in a new place, people are *expecting* to meet an American, and they'd find it disturbing if he acted as though he was trying to hide his identity. However, he'll show respect and courtesy to others at all times, and he does refrain from the American-ish habit of assuming instant familiarity with someone new to him.

Maintaining balance is an important attribute for winning trust. If you are inclined to speak openly and directly about sensitive subjects, then you should do so—but not in an aggressive or obnoxious way, *especially* if you're in a setting where the norm is to dance delicately around such a subject. Your directness must be balanced with a courtesy that others will find appropriate. And it should be balanced, too, with the common sense to save your directness for use on subjects that truly matter.

Likewise, we find that showing vulnerability can be an authentic way to win trust. Of course, this isn't natural in every culture. Where formality or hierarchy run deep, vulnerability may take longer to be understood as strength. But if, at an opportune time, you share a story about a mistake you made in the past and a lesson you learned from it, or an aspect of yourself that you're still trying to improve, that transparency will usually be well received. By opening up in this way, you signal trust in the other person. You are giving them a peek behind the veil, granting them access to information that isn't widely known. But here again, balance is important. An exhaustive confession of your faults will not be well received at all. Selective confessions—along with occasional, humble admissions that you've just made a mistake—need to be balanced with a natural projection of self-confidence and self-control.

Above all, in cultures where winning trust is a gradual process, proceed gradually. It's fine to be clear up front that you hope to explore a possible business relationship; the other party knows it.

But don't jump the intermediate steps and rush into a pitch. In many meetings across Asia and the Gulf, even when Vinnie has been an investor in a company for years, half the discussion may revolve around personal stories before business begins—a rhythm very different from that of Silicon Valley. Also, as you go along the path of trust-building, watch for occasions when you can move the process forward. On more than one occasion, Vinnie has brought his *children* to meetings with potential Gulf partners. Coming from a culture that prizes family relationships, they appreciated the gesture and saw it as an authentic picture of who he is as a family man.

Finally, we should mention a possible way to accelerate the winning of trust: hire a high-level person who's already known and trusted. If you can find someone who fits your staffing needs and is well-connected within the local industry, or with the government, that person becomes a bridge-builder. This isn't a substitute for making yourself (and your company) trusted. Nor does it replace the relationships you can form on your own. But we have seen cases where it augments those efforts considerably. When Stefano managed Aspire's expansion into Vietnam, one of his key hires was a person highly regarded in the country's e-commerce space. They effectively brought a market segment with them, as Vietnamese e-commerce companies soon began signing on as clients for Aspire's financial services in money transfers and working-capital loans.

Now for the other side of the trust coin. In a country and culture new to you, how can you best judge when others are trustworthy? We have a couple of suggestions. The first is to use your intuition. If you have gotten to the point of expanding a business across borders, even as a first-time start-up founder, you've probably developed a keener intuitive sense than you realize you have. Learn to listen to it. Sometimes intuition calls out from your mind's background, begging to be heard above the analytical weighing of pros and cons that might qualify someone as a business partner or not. Vinnie recalls pitch meetings at his VC firm, in which a start-up founder has said all the right things and yet didn't get an investment—because he, Vinnie, sensed intuitively that something felt wrong. He later learned that in some of these cases, the start-ups failed, due to unsound or unethical practices, though he also admits there were cases where those founders went on to succeed—a reminder that intuition sharpens with hindsight and experience.

And experience shows that intuition can work across borders. It can help you see beyond the words that others are saying. Further, it can help you look beyond habits of dress or local customs that may seem unfamiliar, to discern the human qualities behind these facades.

Our other suggestion is to screen out dubious partnership candidates by looking for obvious red flags. When reading case studies of international fraud, it's amazing to find how often experienced businesspeople have ignored red flags in the rush to be part of an attractive-looking deal. One such case is the scandal that befell Wirecard, the Germany-based financial firm and payment processor. From the early 2000s into the 2010s, Wirecard grew faster than the industry average, mainly through a series of overseas acquisitions. Red flags included large portions of revenue from obscure "partner" firms in Asia, and multiple auditors having flagged missing documentation and cash balances. Yet Wirecard's (apparent) growth triggered high share prices for the publicly traded company, until its fraudulent accounting practices were publicly exposed.

Another high-profile example is Luckin Coffee, in China, which admitted to fabricating hundreds of millions of dollars in sales to inflate performance. Similar patterns have appeared elsewhere—charismatic founders, aggressive expansion, and financial numbers that seemed too good to question. The warning signs were visible, yet excitement often silenced skepticism. Whether in Munich or Beijing, the lesson is the same. Red flags rarely hide; they're simply ignored.

Key Takeaways

- **Mutual trust is the foundation for everything else.** To succeed across borders, you must signal credibility early and earn enough trust for people to engage with you—while also learning whom to trust in return. Relationships, not credentials, open doors.

- **Be your best self, with local awareness.** Honesty and authenticity build credibility, but so does respecting local customs. Cultural fluency strengthens relationships and prevents unnecessary friction.

- **Deep trust takes time.** First impressions help you get in the door, but meaningful trust develops gradually. Some cultures move quickly once reputation is proven; others need repeated interaction before business begins. Patience earns far more than pressure.

- **Use intuition—and don't gloss over red flags.** Instincts can reveal character where words fail, but they sharpen only with experience and reflection. Trust your read of a situation, especially when something feels slightly off, and follow up rather than dismissing the signal.

- **Trust removes complexity, which creates speed.** As Carl Fritjofsson, general partner at Creandum, explains, "The benefit of Nordic culture is that it's incredibly trust-heavy, which allows for speed and removes complexity. That can actually be an advantage compared to Silicon Valley–style aggressiveness."

And this brings us to the second reason why you have to be there: to gain the highly detailed, situation-specific knowledge your expansion will need.

Building On-the-Ground Knowledge

Fact 1: Online research, especially now with AI-enhanced search, is an extraordinary source of business information. It can surface patterns, data points, and insights you might have missed even a few years ago.

Fact 2: A lot of what you need to know cannot be learned from a screen.

Think of a town just an hour's drive from where you live—a place that's growing, with new shops, new housing, and more people moving through its streets. Now imagine you want to open a restaurant there. Will online research tell you everything you need to know? The best street corner? Which dishes locals actually crave right now, as tastes and trends shift? Whether you can hire good chefs? How to position yourself against existing eateries—and the ones that will emerge as the market evolves?

AI will give you useful data and maybe even some sharp predictions. You'd be negligent not to start there. Your prior experience will help a little, and so will calls with people who know the area. But before investing real capital, you would still spend time in the town itself—walking the neighborhoods, watching how people move, talking to business owners, suppliers, and potential customers. That is where real understanding comes from.

Launching a business in a new country is the same—only more so. There will be new customs, unfamiliar business practices, different expectations, and cultural signals that don't match your instinctive reading. These intricacies can lie hidden in

seemingly simple things, as seed investor Maciej Małysz of Inovo.
vc told us.

Maciej had invested in the Polish start-up Booksy, now a global
hair-and-beauty booking platform. On paper, Booksy was addressing
a universal set of needs: people want to book appointments with good
barbers and beauticians, who in turn want to manage their bookings.
But Booksy's multicountry experience showed how this simple idea
splinters into different products across markets.

- In Poland, salons are owner-operated with small teams. Owners
  want to *limit* employee use of an app like Booksy and access to
  client lists, for fear that they may one day poach the clients.

- In the United Kingdom, barbers operate as independent
  freelancers, with high visit frequency and irregular schedules.

- In the United States, many barbers are micro-entrepreneurs
  renting chairs in barbershops; they expect *full* access to their
  customer base and contact history.

The result: the same product category produced conflicting
feature requests, incompatible permission structures, and divergent
customer journeys. Country managers struggled to agree on priorities
because each market behaved like a different industry altogether. Says
Maciej, "Even a haircut looks different in every country." Booksy
couldn't localize its business just by translating the language on the
app—it had to localize by reinventing workflows at the core of
the product.

As Stefano puts it, the safest assumption is that you "know
nothing" at the start. This is why directing an international expansion
from a distant HQ—in London, Singapore, or anywhere else—is a
high-risk move. There is no substitute for proximity.

Knowledge gained remotely is bound to be incomplete. The
portions you do get may turn out to have little relevance to your

company's specific expansion needs. Much of the material on the Internet has been filtered through the motivations of people posting the content, and despite our current age's emphasis on immediacy, much of it reflects a rearview-mirror perspective. News reports and business analyses dwell mainly on what has happened. For a smart launch, you need a deep dive into what's happening right now and, more importantly, where the trend is going. That kind of knowledge can only be acquired through on-the-ground presence.

Of course, you would start gradually. The best occasions for initial networking in a new place are conferences held by industry groups and regional development orgs. Vinnie's VC firm has used industry events and regional forums to pave the way for building relationships across the globe. If you can get a spot on a conference agenda as a speaker or panelist, that's better yet. The host groups are usually eager to have an international presence at their events, and securing a featured-guest spot in advance offers multiple benefits. It puts your company's name in front of everyone. It gives you a chance to publicly praise your target country, explaining why you want to do business there. People will then approach you afterward, wanting to meet *you* instead of vice versa.

But even as a simple attendee, one can make useful contacts and learn a lot. Some conversations lead to direct business prospects; others uncover hidden opportunities or local pitfalls to watch for. The key is curiosity. Keep asking, "As someone looking to bring in this kind of business, who else should I be talking to?"

One interesting example of this comes from Adeo Ressi, founder of the Founder Institute. When his team convened a small dinner in Bogotá, they discovered that the 10 most influential founders and investors in the city had never all been in the same room before. A few hours of conversation did more for the ecosystem than months of passive observation. Once people met each other, deals, collaborations, and investments began to appear on their own.

Nothing in the macro data had changed, only the human connections. For leaders entering new markets, it is a reminder that showing up is not just about gathering information; it is also about convening people who might otherwise remain disconnected.

Periodic on-the-ground visits come next. By this stage you should have appointments to meet with specific people—prospective partners, potential clients, or government officials. These visits allow you to gain a fine-grained understanding of the markets you hope to enter, rich in details that directly affect your business. During the time Stefano worked for the fintech Aspire, the company was developing a range of financial products and services beyond business loans. He quickly learned which offerings would resonate in which markets. For example, spend-management software (tools that help companies track and control their corporate expenses) wasn't a strong fit for emerging markets like Vietnam. There were plenty of potential clients, but most were not yet large enough or structured enough to benefit from such systems, and the emergent nature of the country's financial framework complicated the picture. By contrast, spend management tools were a natural fit for Hong Kong, where the financial infrastructure was highly developed and client companies were ready to use the tools. *For any business, insights like these can make the difference.* On-the-ground visits give you the earliest and clearest view of what will actually work.

If you inquire across the networks that you're starting to build, you may also arrange to meet former employees and existing clients of competing firms. These people can be great sources of inside knowledge. In addition to knowing local markets, they'll often provide insights into mistakes that competitors have made. (See the next chapter for a story of what Stefano learned from a predecessor company's mistake.)

You don't always learn about mistakes made by other companies just by searching the Internet. Although high-profile blunders by big firms will attract news coverage, the lessons to be learned from them may or may not apply to your expansion into a new country. Some online sources do dive into failure-and-lesson stories that fly beneath the level of major headlines, and it's helpful to read them: For instance we previously mentioned Admond Lee's e-newsletter *The Runway Ventures*, which analyzes the misadventures of Asian start-ups. Similar observers can be found who track other regions of the world. And in some cases it's useful to look at online forums or employee review sites, especially when workers share insights about companies in your target market.

But market-specific and business-specific relevance matters greatly. People you meet on the ground, who have been in the loop for decisions made by companies in your new market, can be unfiltered sources of information that does not make it into news stories or press releases. If they're willing to talk—either directly to you, or to a credible contact person—they can shed light on what happened behind the scenes: the decisions that flopped, the under-the-radar moves that paid off.

Stefano profited from this kind of groundwork when he managed Aspire's expansion in Vietnam. Fintech start-ups in the country typically partner with existing banks to do licensed lending. From conversations on the ground, Stefano learned that one competitor had been treated badly in its partnership with a certain bank. And that another had been let down by another partner bank. This warned him to avoid both banks. It also armed him with detailed knowledge of how those partnerships went wrong, which helped him negotiate better terms with the banks he eventually chose.

Timeliness of information matters, too. A business approach that failed a year ago, when the market wasn't ready, might be a promising approach for the years ahead. (And conversely, what worked in the past might be a hopeless effort now.) Clients and others who are in the market day-to-day can share timely firsthand knowledge.

Queried by a newcomer who shows interest in serving them, they may be inclined to tell you things they like about the products and services they're getting, things they *dislike* about their current supplier companies, and things they wish they had but cannot obtain.

Data from periodic visits should then prepare you to put boots on the ground in a more ongoing, long-term manner. Every pilot venture into a new country does not require a full-time field office, but many do, and those that grow will require it eventually. The more you can learn before committing substantial resources, the better your chances of success are likely to be.

In markets that are new to you, uncertainties abound. You'll never eliminate all of them. The purpose of establishing a presence on the ground, step by step, is to progressively narrow down the uncertainties and unknowns. Gradually you replace many of the "un"s with verified knowledge, giving your company an ever-firmer platform for expansion—and more resilience for navigating the new uncertainties that are sure to arise.

Key Takeaways

- **Online research is a starting point, not a strategy.** AI-enhanced tools and data can help you map the terrain, but they can't show you how a market actually feels or functions day to day.

- **Learn through proximity.** You can't understand a market from a screen. Being on the ground reveals the signals, systems, and human nuances that remote research can't.

(continued)

- **Expand step by step.** Start with industry events and regional forums to build familiarity, then follow up with repeated visits and local meetings. Gradual presence leads to deeper insight and stronger networks.

- **Local conversations uncover truths the web can't.** Talking with former employees, clients, or even competitors can surface hidden pitfalls and behind-the-scenes lessons that never appear in press releases or reports.

- **Groundwork reduces uncertainty.** Every visit replaces assumptions with verified knowledge. Over time, local presence transforms ambiguity into clarity and builds resilience for future challenges.

Being on the ground does more than build trust and detailed knowledge—it also reveals the under-the-radar forces that shape how business really works. You start to see where written rules meet lived reality and how deals depend as much on human understanding as on legal structure. Once trust is in place, the next challenge is turning that understanding into agreements that last.

5 How to Get the Deal Done

Different Systems, Different Finish Lines

Emerging markets can be excellent places to grow a business, but many businesspeople tend to overlook a challenge they present. Very often it's not just the market that is "emerging." The country's legal and regulatory systems, as well as the business practices that are common there, may be in an emergent state as well. This can make them unfamiliar—and potentially treacherous—to newcomers who enter the market expecting these things to work pretty much as they do in more fully developed environments.

An emergent and uncertain business context doesn't mean you cannot scale there. It *does* mean you need to be mindful of the risks and how to tackle them. So we'll now lay out a mental map that can serve as a helpful guide.

What Exactly Does It Mean to Close a Deal?

The meaning can vary from one culture to another. In the United States and Europe, it normally means to find commercial alignment with another party and then crystallize it into one or more contracts to make it binding and enforceable. Contract signed = deal done. Stefano remembers clearly his first M&A deal as an attorney in Europe. Months of due-diligence work, commercial negotiations, and drafting of terms all culminated in the signing and closing of the transaction. In a room crowded with lawyers and representatives of the two parties—two large European funds, which were respectively buying and selling a portfolio of a dozen commercial malls and outlets across three European countries—the CEOs of the two groups signed the closing of the main contract, and the CFO of the buyer immediately instructed the bank to wire the purchase price. The executives smiled, patted each other on the back, and went out for a celebratory lunch. A long period of back-and-forth negotiating was over at last.

But this is not the case everywhere. In certain countries and cultures, a signed contract means that negotiation is only just starting. This may sound surprising to businesspeople who come from mature markets, where a contract is a legally binding agreement that can be quickly enforced in court, and where breach of contract can result in swift judgment to pay damages. There are places—especially in emerging markets—where the judiciary system is still underdeveloped, slow, inefficient, and sometimes even nontransparent. In these places you cannot rely on a signed contract as a binding agreement that can be properly enforced against a breaching party. Enforcement is possible, but it may take years, cost a lot of money, and have an uncertain outcome. Hence, a signed contract is not the finish line, but just one of several milestones in a much longer journey. In these contexts, the level of uncertainty is much higher, and milestones worth celebrating are more real. For example, players in these markets are used to celebrating when payment from a customer is received in the bank account, not when the customer's signature is scribbled on a piece of paper.

And it must be remembered that norms are not divided neatly between emerging and mature markets. In the Gulf region, for instance, an investor sending over their identification documents—a photo of their passport, say—can give an entrepreneur real peace of mind that the deal is closed. Not so in the United States, where that gesture would mean little. And in parts of Asia, whether in fast-growing Vietnam or established Japan, the true deal-closing moment may come over late-night drinks, karaoke, or a family-style dinner, where a verbal commitment signals that the partnership is real and the work can begin.

As Wee Liang Chua told us, many foreign investors enter China believing that once an agreement is signed, the deal is "done." But in practice, that signature may simply formalize a moment of understanding, not a binding commitment. "I've seen it so many times," he said. "You reach consensus, shake hands, sign the MOU— and then a week later you discover they've gone with someone else. Signing doesn't necessarily mean anything."

In the West, the act of signing carries legal and moral weight. It's a declaration: I will honor what's written here. But in China, the signing ceremony serves a different purpose. It represents goodwill—a step toward cooperation—rather than a final, enforceable promise. "If you treat it like a Western contract and threaten legal action," Wee Liang Chua added, "you'll destroy the relationship and get nowhere." Instead, the real work begins after the signing—maintaining the relationship, understanding shifting circumstances, and being ready to return to the negotiation table when the terms inevitably move.

He gave the example of managing investment funds in China. "You agree on a 2% management fee, and both sides sign the documents. Six months later, they tell you they'll only pay 1%. And what can you do? Sue them? You'll lose the investor. So you sit down again, try to explain your perspective, and renegotiate."

The Western instinct is to treat such behavior as a breach of contract; the Chinese instinct is to treat it as a continuation of dialogue. To succeed, you have to accept that "closing" a deal doesn't mean the discussion is over—it means you've reached a temporary equilibrium that must be maintained through ongoing trust and flexibility.

When a Signed Contract Won't Hold a Partner in Place, You Must Maintain a Win-Win Relationship

In emerging-market countries, where highly effective legal systems have not yet fully formed, every partnership must remain a commercial win-win for all parties involved—negotiations are continually ongoing. You can't rely on written contracts, or on the implicit threat of legal action, to keep the partnership held together. To a local partner, a contract signed at the outset may be perceived merely as a starting point—a snapshot of today's understanding, open to revision as conditions change. In fast-moving or less predictable economies, detailed long-term planning can feel unrealistic. When the unexpected happens, the contract isn't treated as a binding liability for the local party but as the basis for a new round of negotiation: a chance to rebalance the deal so that everyone keeps winning.

In some markets, business operates like a professional football match: the rules are clear, referees are consistent, and everyone knows what counts as a goal or a foul. But in others, it's as if the rules are still being written. After every score or penalty, a new conversation begins about what's fair. Local players see this not as bending the rules, but as keeping the game balanced in a landscape they can't fully predict.

There is nothing inherently unethical about such a view. Think of the professional sports stars who ask for (or demand) a renegotiation of their contract with a team, after they've had an outstanding season or two. Then think of a local business partner who faces the opposite situation. The partner has signed a contract that grants a certain share of revenues for several years. But then business conditions change, leaving the partner short-changed. Partners in that predicament are likely to want a boost, or they'll walk. It doesn't help to try holding them to the contract, because that will only create further ill will and because the country's courts may be painfully slow and/or ineffective in moving to protect you.

Your best choice—indeed, your only practical choice—is to find a solution that rebalances the win-win equation. The same applies to employees. If an employment contract is no longer a win for them, they're not going to think, "Oh, too bad I signed an agreement. Now I need to stay for another two years." They'll be gone the next day. Just like the sports stars who opt to sit out a season rather than playing for less than they believe they're worth.

This doesn't mean contracts do not matter in emerging markets. Christopher Beselin, managing partner at Endurance Capital, shared that before moving to Southeast Asia, he kept hearing the same warning: "You can sign a contract, but good luck enforcing it." But then he discovered that the opposite is actually true. As he explained, businesses in the region often treat commercial agreements with deep respect, but rely less on formal enforcement and more on what he calls "natural leverage."

"Contracts are taken seriously, but they work through a different mechanism. Because formal enforcement can be slow, companies design agreements so both sides are fundamentally incentivized to follow the contract without ever needing the courts."

In practice, this means structuring deals so that money, goods, and obligations move in carefully sequenced steps. Deposits are paid before work begins, prepayments are made before goods are released, and delivery is tied closely to staged payments, with clear rules about who holds the product and who holds the money at each point in the process. The contract is respected not because it might be enforced someday but because it is designed to function in real time.

"By building natural leverage into the contract, both parties create a pragmatically focused system where the agreement can be respected in practice."

What struck Beselin most was that this approach can produce more reliable commercial behavior than in markets that rely almost entirely on formal enforcement mechanisms.

"In many ways, this works better than systems where people assume the courts will handle everything. Take Sweden as an extreme example of the opposite, where it's common to give thirty days of full credit on services or goods with minimal background checks. That approach comes with its own dire recurring consequences (as the suppliers of Northvolt recently discovered)."

From the outside, this system can feel unfamiliar, even risky. In reality, it reflects a deeply practical understanding of how to protect agreements in environments where time, liquidity, and trust matter more than legal theory. Contracts remain central in Southeast Asia. They are followed because the commercial structure is designed to make them workable. Once investors understand this logic, the region becomes far easier to navigate than many assume.

We actually have found the win-win requirement to be beneficial. It keeps us sharp, ever vigilant to see that our business associates are kept happy and working to full capacity. Unhappy partners, vendors, and employees don't usually give you their utmost. They are more apt to slide along in a state of middling mediocrity or in worst cases create a toxic work environment. We urge you to enter a new country with excellence as the goal—and with the understanding that you'll have to be creatively flexible, constantly re-adjusting your terms, if you want to have a team capable of reaching the goal.

In one Southeast Asian case, a private equity fund bought 40% of an F&B company while the local founder retained control. Tensions soon emerged. The investors wanted to accelerate an ambitious growth plan that had been pre-agreed, while the founder, already wealthy and under little pressure, was reluctant to move forward. The investors asked Stefano how they could "legally convince" the local partner to move forward with the agreed growth plan. Stefano's answer was simple: they couldn't. Although the contract clearly outlined their rights, enforcing it would have been slow, costly, and ultimately self-defeating. Using legal pressure or punitive tactics would only breed resentment.

Instead, Stefano advised the private equity fund to create a new opportunity that would make cooperation worthwhile. The fund brought in a strategic investor whose capital and expertise could multiply the company's value. Faced with this prospect, the local founder saw a chance to win again—and willingly supported the plan. The lesson was clear: in markets where the rule of law is still emerging, success depends not on enforcement but on alignment. You must continually re-create win-win situations.

This also applies to China. As Wee Liang Chua, a renowned technology investor based in Shanghai, reminded us, agreements on paper are only part of the equation; what sustains collaboration is the informal layer of human connection built around them. "You have to approach it not head-on," he said, "but from the side—through the relationship with the person across the table. It's rarely solved through formal channels. You build trust in the informal way first. Then the formal communication follows."

In other words, even when contracts exist, progress often depends on the strength of personal rapport. Without it, no legal clause will keep both sides aligned when interests diverge.

This also applies to how joint ventures operate in China. As Wee Liang Chua has observed, Western and Chinese partners often set up 50–50 structures, believing that equal ownership guarantees fairness. In reality, it often guarantees deadlock. "I've seen so many

50–50 joint ventures fail," he recalled. "Everything must be decided together, but when both sides hold equal power, nothing moves—because nobody is in charge."

One of his early experiences illustrates this well. The joint venture he helped manage rotated leadership every three years—the local partner appointed the chairman, while the foreign partner appointed the general manager; then after three years they swapped. It sounded fair in theory, but in practice, no one truly led. Every major decision stalled in endless discussions, and the partnership eventually broke down.

"Not Enforceable!"—How to Navigate Situations Where Going to Court Is Not an Option

Stefano learned a hard lesson in Thailand, where a digital bank he was advising had accumulated, under the previous management, a lending exposure of about $800,000 toward small and medium enterprises. Some of that exposure resulted from scammers who had entered into multiple financing contracts with the digital bank. The identities of the scammers were known. There were IDs, addresses, even company records. But enforcing claims against them proved nearly impossible.

The first obstacle was technical, inherited from the previous country manager of the digital bank. Many financing contracts had been signed electronically, relying on digital signatures not yet recognized by Thai courts at the time. Other financing contracts, though properly executed, failed on minor formalities that easily could have been prevented by a local lawyer's review. Even for the subset of contracts that were fully enforceable, the judicial process itself became a dead end. Each claim was small, court costs were high, and hearings were repeatedly postponed—sometimes with less than 24 hours' notice and delays of six to nine months each time. After two years, the digital bank still had not a single enforceable court judgment.

And in certain emerging-market jurisdictions, even a favorable court judgment guarantees little. In another country where Stefano had practiced law, a multinational client obtained a court decision entitling them to seize the warehouse of a distributor who had defaulted on their contract. Yet when the enforcement officers were called to act, they simply refused—claiming they were too busy, that the site was too far, that "next week" would be better. It later became apparent that these officers expected to receive an illicit payment, equal to half the value of the goods they were supposed to seize, before doing their job.

Gustavo Rugani, M&A partner at a prestigious law firm in Brazil, shared a similar experience from Latin America. After its dictatorship ended in 1984 and democracy was restored, Brazil enacted a new Constitution in 1988. Because the country was still reacting to the abuses of the previous regime, the constitutional framers deliberately made access to the judicial system extremely open. As Gustavo explained, anyone can file a lawsuit for virtually any reason, with almost no procedural barriers. Combined with a highly complex appeals system—there are more than 10 different kinds of appeals that you can file over the life of a lawsuit in Brazil—this openness completely flooded the courts system.

This structure makes it easy to start a lawsuit but extremely slow to finish one. A case may reach a judge quickly, but reaching a final decision takes years, not months. Litigation is cheap, further encouraging people to take disputes to court for even trivial matters. As Gustavo put it, the system is so accessible that someone might file a lawsuit simply because "someone stepped on their foot."

Brazil is also another example of a country where even a court order or final judgment may be difficult to enforce in practice. Gustavo shared the case of one of his clients, a real estate pension fund that owned a newly renovated commercial building. On Independence Day, a group of protesters invaded and occupied the property. Gustavo and his team moved swiftly and within 24 hours managed to obtain a court injunction ordering the authorities to remove the occupants. But enforcement proved far more complicated. Multiple agencies had to be notified, coordinated, and prepared, and some of the authorities refused to act immediately despite the court order. The process stretched on for more than a year and moved only after a fatal accident in a similarly occupied building elsewhere pushed officials into action. Even then, the injunction itself was never executed. The occupants left only after the government offered them benefits such as temporary homes and the promise of permanent housing.

These experiences underline a truth that many discover only after costly lessons. In some emerging markets, you cannot rely on the judiciary to deliver justice or to enforce a judgment once rendered. The legal victory on paper often remains just that: a piece of paper.

For that reason, international lawyers working across such environments spend considerable effort designing structures that avoid the need to go to court altogether. Arbitration clauses are a common first step, providing an international forum outside the local judiciary. Yet even arbitration awards require recognition and enforcement by local authorities, which brings one back to the same fragile system.

The real art lies in structuring agreements so that enforcement happens contractually, not judicially. For instance, parties may sign in advance certain conditional agreements—pre-signed transfers of ownership, admissions of liability, or assignments held in escrow by a trusted third party. Upon default, these instruments can be released and executed immediately, without having to wait for judicial intervention.

In project finance, similar logic often applies. A lender financing a rooftop solar installation may stipulate that, in case of default, the host factory redirects its electricity payments to the lender and that the solar-as-a-service agreement automatically transfers to the lender's sole discretion. The lender thus immediately gains control of the cash flows and access to the site, with the cooperation of the host factory—no lawsuit required.

Such arrangements make remedies immediately enforceable, sparing years of litigation and uncertainty. If challenged, a local court will likely uphold them, but by then the lender has already secured the outcome in practice.

Ultimately, this is the mindset required to do business where the rule of law is still evolving. You must design contracts that can stand on their own, operating through consent rather than compulsion. This is not lawlessness. It is law adapted to the terrain. Like driving on a winding mountain road without guardrails, it demands skill, caution, and respect for the limits, but it is entirely possible. And in the process, you realize that guardrails, while useful, are not always necessary.

These considerations are not limited to emerging markets only. Even in China, the legal system exists, but enforcement is weak. As Wee Liang Chua explained, filing a lawsuit may be possible in theory, yet in practice it's a long, exhausting process that drains attention from the real work of building the business. "You can sue," he said, "but by the time you finish, you'll have lost far more than you'll gain." Foreigners, in particular, face an uneven playing field. The judicial system tends to favor local parties, especially state-owned enterprises. As a result, taking a dispute to court rarely ends well.

The only viable option is often the practical one: preserve the relationship, renegotiate, and move forward. In places where enforcement cannot protect you, trust—however fragile—becomes the real contract.

How to Deal with Local Business Partners More Powerful Than You

"Everyone is equal before the law." This basic principle, embedded in most constitutions worldwide, explains how a working legal system tends to provide companies with a fair and objective way to handle conflicts and disputes. It is a major step beyond the mere "law of the jungle," where the strongest player prevails. But how do you deal with a disparity of power when you don't have a legal system that works well enough to provide a level playing field?

When Stefano was practicing law, he advised a fintech company in Vietnam whose business model depended entirely on a partnership with a local bank. Because the fintech lacked a license and could not obtain one as a small foreign-owned entity, it relied on the partner bank's infrastructure to onboard and serve its customers. While this arrangement enabled rapid growth—eventually reaching hundreds of thousands of paying users—it also created total dependency on the partner bank.

Under the partnership, revenues were to be shared equally after deducting the bank's infrastructure costs. However, the fintech had made a fatal strategic mistake. The company's leaders had accepted an exclusivity clause, binding them to work with that single bank. Over time, the bank simply inflated its declared infrastructure costs, eroding the fintech's margins and leaving it perpetually unprofitable. Worse, after several years, the bank launched its own copycat application, capturing much of the fintech's market. Having no alternative partners due to exclusivity, the fintech was forced to terminate the partnership and start over from scratch, losing valuable time and market share.

When Stefano later managed Aspire's fintech venture in Vietnam, he faced a similar challenge: finding a local bank willing to partner and operate under the umbrella of its license. He signed a 50–50 revenue sharing agreement but insisted to not include any exclusivity clause. Anticipating that if things were to go well, the bank might try to increase its slice of the profits, he negotiated in parallel a second banking partnership. Sure enough, once Aspire began to grow, the first bank demanded 70% of revenues—threatening to shut Aspire down if it refused. Stefano immediately began redirecting customers to the second partner. Within weeks, the balance of power shifted. Aspire continued serving clients, while the first bank watched its "bigger slice" turn into smaller returns. It didn't take them long to calculate that 50% of something was better than 70% of nothing. They restored the original equal-sharing agreement and gladly kept to its terms.

In markets where an established local entity can try to dictate changes in a partnership and is much better positioned than a newcomer to battle any issues in court, legal recourse offers little protection. What matters is maintaining commercial leverage. Then you can use the leverage to pry the relationship back to a win-win. Here again, the underlying fact is that contracts will be honored only as long as they remain advantageous to both sides. The key is to stay continually relevant and beneficial to one's partners. It's more like an ongoing courtship than a settled marriage.

Similar scenarios of unbalanced partnerships are becoming more and more common also in countries like China. As Wee Liang Chua explained, "In the last few years, the state-owned companies have taken center stage. The government's presence is growing, and the private sector is slowly taking a back seat." This creates a paradox for any foreign business trying to scale in China. On one hand, working with a company backed by the state can open doors—faster permits, access to funding, easier introductions. On the other, it comes with a weight of bureaucracy and decision-making processes that aren't always guided by market logic.

"When you work with a company that has government behind it," Chua said, "you gain resources, but you also inherit their pace and their politics."

This duality defines the challenge. You cannot compete head-on with a system that powerful, nor can you fully depend on it. The art lies somewhere in between—cooperating without surrendering control, aligning interests without losing autonomy.

Key Takeaways

- **Contracts travel differently.** In some markets, a signature closes the deal. In others, it only starts the conversation. Learn to read which kind of field you're on before you play.

- **When the law can't protect you, alignment must.** If a country's legal mechanisms are less than fully effective, you cannot rely on a signed contract to preserve a business relationship. Keep it a commercial win-win instead.

- **Win-win cuts both ways.** This holds true when your partners, suppliers, or employees feel they're losing out—and it holds just as true when you're the aggrieved party. In either case, whether you need to help out the other side or apply leverage, keep coming back to balance.

- **Flexibility is the real protection.** Build optionality—secondary partners, backup licenses, alternative paths—so leverage never depends on one contract.

- **Anticipate the renegotiation.** Assume success will trigger new demands. Plan for it early, as Stefano did with Aspire, and you'll stay in control when terms start to shift.

- **Alignment beats enforcement.** When rules evolve midgame, those who adapt with fairness and foresight keep both partners—and progress—intact.

Dealing with Opposite Extremes: Total Defiance and Hyper-Compliance

Thus far, we've been talking about countries where the legal system isn't yet reliable enough to offer the protection you might want. This kind of business context must not be confused with contexts where *illegality* is the norm. Think, for example, of places so lawless that a disgruntled business partner might threaten you with personal harm—even put a gun to your head. Such conditions still exist, typically in countries that have been disrupted by wars or violent internal unrest.

One person who has faced them firsthand is Dr. Mark Thaller, a risk-management advisor who has spent two decades working with multinational firms and governments in some of the world's most unstable regions.

During his time in Baghdad in 2005, Dr. Thaller learned that "business meetings" could look very different in unstable regions. At one lunch with a local business syndicate leader, the host calmly set a large caliber handgun on the table before the conversation began—a wordless show of authority, as the meeting was occurring outside the Green Zone and without any US oversight or special security. The Coca-Cola served came from a bottling plant owned by the same man, one that Dr. Thaller had just toured and knew was grossly unsanitary. Still, he drank it, knowing that he was liable to be violently ill but that refusing would have been seen as an insult. Around the room, 10 armed assistants stood silently, listening without understanding a word of English.

The meeting was very successful and included friendly interaction as well as business discussion . . . and most importantly, involved neither party purposely insulting or criticizing others. "That meeting and my overt display of respect, which is not to be confused with weakness, set the stage for why I was safe when other foreigners were targeted, even though I lived out in town and travelled in my own car without US security," Dr. Thaller later reflected.

Dr. Thaller explains that in volatile environments, trust often has to come before proof. As he puts it, you must "sail toward the horizon before proving the world is round."

During a project in Juba in 2010, as South Sudan moved toward independence, a simple act changed how a local General saw him. Dr. Thaller was leading a group of senior advisors assisting the Southern Sudan Ministry of Defense (MOD) Generals for post-sovereignty as Southern Sudan was preparing to separate from Sudan. Dr. Thaller was with a group of SPLA (Sudan People's Liberation Army) MOD generals when he noted that there were very few operable lights in the entire building. The generals stated that the building had been recently built by the United States, but the past contract had failed to provide for lights or labor to change the bulbs. Dr. Thaller didn't criticize or point fingers. Instead, he purchased lights in town, grabbed a ladder, and replaced the bulbs himself. One of the generals, surprised, asked why someone of his rank and education was doing such work. Dr. Thaller replied, "It's dark in here, and nobody can see what they're doing. I'm just trying to help." The general then held the ladder for him and helped finish the job. That moment of humility built the foundation of a lasting relationship. Today, this general is now a government minister and responsible for drafting the country's new constitution—and he credits that small gesture for his decision to work with Dr. Thaller as he continues to rely on him as one of his most senior and trusted advisors.

For every story like Dr. Thaller's, where trust and humility build lasting goodwill, there's another that starts the same way but ends very differently. You enter a country where institutions are shaky and corruption is common. A local partner greets you warmly, promising to take care of everything. But when conditions turn difficult, so does the relationship. What once looked like hospitality becomes hardball.

That is an "error" sign flashing in your face. It means you never should have gotten into the situation in the first place. And usually, the fault lies not with the partner but with your own fact-finding. Red flags that should've been caught by due diligence were either missed or ignored. Now you have only bad options, the least bad of which is to extricate yourself as soon as possible and write off the losses. No attempt to re-balance the equation by presenting new opportunities can guide you to a win-win outcome. The partner will simply learn that you respond to pressure by yielding. In such contexts, no gain can be made without compromising ethics, integrity, or safety.

Of course the best option is to exercise extreme caution beforehand. Having seen how difficult expansion can be, even in relatively tame countries, we ourselves would not consider a business entry in a highly lawless place. Our advice is: just don't go there. And if you go anyway, *please* be careful whom you choose to work with.

Conversely, we also have a milder (though still important) caveat to consider. One should know that adjustment may be necessary when dealing with hyper-mature and hyper-regulated legal systems in highly developed countries. These systems can slow down your growth by imposing strict compliance with rules that are not required in your home country. A start-up in Vinnie's portfolio experienced this firsthand in Japan. When the company tried to recruit through a local recruiter, that person refused to contact any candidates until a domestic Japanese legal entity was formally established. From the start-up's perspective as an international company, accustomed to operating through employer-of-record structures in multiple countries, this seemed unnecessarily rigid. Yet it reflects a deeper cultural and structural difference in how "readiness" is defined.

A similar contrast surfaced in Stefano's personal experience. When his wife accepted a position in the Southeast Asia office of a Japanese law firm, she was told she could not begin working until her work authorization was fully approved—a process that took more than six months. During that time, she was technically hired but practically stuck in a limbo: not permitted to enter the office and not receiving any salary. Meanwhile, Stefano's employer at the time—also an international law firm but from Australia—took a more flexible approach. Once he signed his employment contract, he was invited to start working right away while the paperwork was being prepared and accepting that a proper work permit would follow later. Both approaches were technically compliant with the local regulations. It's just that the Japanese firm took a more conservative approach, reflecting the strict attitude toward compliance that often characterizes the country's business and legal culture.

These employment stories highlight how different cultures may interpret the concept of a "deal." In some, it signifies a commitment to proceed only after every procedural requirement is met. In others, it marks the beginning of collaboration, trusting that compliance will catch up.

Key Takeaways

- **Trust begins before proof.** In volatile environments, you often have to extend a small act of trust first to invite reciprocity. As Dr. Thaller puts it, you must "sail toward the horizon before proving the world is round."

- **Ethics travel, but the definitions shift.** What looks like corruption in one culture may be considered loyalty or survival in another. Learn the local frame without abandoning your own standards of legality and integrity.

- **Integrity is your strongest defense.** In places where the law can't protect you, your conduct often determines whether you're targeted or trusted. Never trade ethics for convenience.

- **Be wary where order breaks down.** If you must operate in highly unsettled or violent contexts, use extreme caution in vetting partners—and know when to walk away.

> • **Expect friction at the other extreme.** In hyper-regulated, risk-averse systems, strict compliance can slow growth but also signal reliability. Adapt your pace and paperwork to match the local definition of readiness.

The Roles of Local Governments, and How to Interact with Them

How a country's government could impact your business should be an area of primary concern. It probably won't deserve the bulk of your planning time when you are preparing to expand, but it definitely needs diligent attention. Laws and regulations will frequently determine how you are able to operate, as well as what you shouldn't even try. Government policies can help or hinder your business—and those policies are liable to change. Moreover, when it comes to dealing with the government of a place that's new to you, you may not know what you don't know. That is why we strongly recommend finding partners who can help you navigate the maze.

Start with a basic fact. Depending on the nature of your business, a country's government can be either a huge asset or a force you must reckon with. Often it's both. On the asset side, many governments offer incentives to international businesses. These go well beyond tax breaks and so-called enterprise zones. Often they consist of hard money. At the time we're writing, Australia has a multibillion-dollar set of government programs for investing in cleantech R&D and related business ventures. Given the country's relatively modest domestic population of about 28 million citizens—of whom only a fraction are involved in cleantech—it seemed likely that international players would reap a substantial share of these cash incentives.

Similar incentives in Southeast Asian countries hold promise for aiding the expansion of Stefano's green finance company, Aquila. In 2011, Vinnie's launch of Golden Gate Ventures was fueled for lift-off by US$10 million in matching investments from the government of Singapore.

Another thing to keep in mind when operating in emerging markets (or in any market, really) is that *government policies aren't carved in stone. They can change in ways that influence your business dramatically.* Especially in emerging markets, but really anywhere, government decisions may very quickly reshape the business landscape. Consider what happened in the United States after the 2024 election: a new administration came in and, with it, sweeping policy reversals. Tariffs were reintroduced, renewable energy funding dried up, and entire industries saw the rules rewritten in their favor—or against them.

Policies can change even when a nation's government doesn't. Even when the political power structure stays the same, a law that impacts your company can literally appear overnight. This happened to Gojek, the Indonesian start-up that became the country's first unicorn and later a decacorn. Gojek began as a ride-hailing service to link passengers with motorbike drivers. Growth took off when the company replaced its initial call center with a mobile app. But then conventional taxi companies complained about losing business, and in 2015, Indonesia's Ministry of Transportation suddenly announced a ban on all app-based ride services. Of course the ban could have wiped out Gojek. Fortunately for the firm, there was an immediate public backlash including a #SaveGojek campaign, and, more importantly, the start-up's lead investor privately lobbied government officials to reconsider. The ban was reversed within a day. Gojek went on to build a payment app and an entire suite of services around its core business. Meanwhile, Indonesia's government embarked on a more careful, iterative course of regulating personal transport services.

Yet plenty of controversy ensued over the evolving regulations—and the banning incident remains as a reminder to be ever aware of how government laws and policies can affect you.

Also keep in mind that when dealing with government officials, you may need to recalibrate the pace and rhythm you are accustomed to—in any established system, understanding the tempo matters as much as the strategy. Federico D'Amico, who closed several energy infrastructure deals in complex markets, recalls experiencing extended waiting times before meetings with senior civil servants in India. He came to recognize that such delays typically reflected layered administrative responsibilities rather than personal factors. Senior officials operate within structured hierarchies and shifting priorities— much as leadership roles anywhere require constant reprioritization. The key is to remain patient and adaptable, recognizing that every environment has its own internal logic and unwritten rules.

Unclear Local Regulations—and How to Deal with "Gray Areas"

Now consider a complicating factor. In a number of emerging-market countries, laws and policy documents remain unclear on many points. This is not a mistake. Gray areas are left on purpose, because unclear legislation requires interpretation, and with interpretation comes power and opportunity.

A recent example came in a Southeast Asian country. New legislation was introduced to promote technological innovation and support start-ups. On paper, it promised generous incentives for companies driving digital transformation. Yet the criteria for what constituted an "innovative start-up" remained unwritten, existing only in bureaucratic limbo.

Stefano's team at Aquila spent months trying to resolve this uncertainty, chasing phone numbers and names, until they finally identified the one official who held the authority to decide eligibility. The team invited her for a coffee, hoping to understand how Aquila might qualify. What became clear was that the law itself offered no definitive guidance. The decision ultimately rested on the woman's personal judgment.

That single official, through discretion alone, wielded immense power over who received financial incentives and who did not. This pattern is common across many countries where regulation is intentionally vague. It grants policymakers, from ministers to provincial officials, the authority to decide on a case-by-case basis whether a project is approved, encouraged, or prohibited.

When this discretion is used wisely, it allows governments to adapt quickly and make context-driven decisions for the public good. But when misused, it opens the door to personal gain, favoritism, and corruption. In such systems, progress often depends less on the written law than on the interpretation—and the interpreter.

The situation has consequences for companies entering the market from outside. If a "gray area" that's created by vague legislation happens to be an area in which you hope to operate—for example, if it's not clear whether you will need a license to conduct a certain aspect of your business—we would advise proceeding with great caution. Stick to business models and product offerings that are clearly OK, at least until you can gain clarity on the gray area. Even huge multinationals such as Uber have run into trouble when some of their business practices were deemed not-OK in particular markets. For a start-up or smaller company that doesn't have the resources of a major MNC, misunderstandings of this type can do more than cause costly hassles. They can be fatal to expansion plans.

A mental tool for navigating unclear legislation has been suggested to us by Kieran Donovan, CEO of k-ID. His company helps businesses create and scale online content for children and teens, by scanning markets worldwide for standards on what's deemed to be age appropriate in various places. Kieran says every legal or practical standard that k-ID discovers is put into one of five categories, from the strongest to the weakest.

1. *A law that a court has enforced.* There is no lack of clarity in this category. Legal precedent has been established, and if you violate the law in question, you are inviting trouble.

2. *A clear statement of a rule in regulations.* The rule may not have been enforced yet, but it constitutes a legal requirement. Whether or not it *will be* enforced is an open question, and a risky one for businesses.

3. *An inferred legal obligation.* A requirement of this type is not strictly spelled out in the law, but when you consider market practice and how regulatory enforcements or court decisions have gone, you can infer how you should operate in a given jurisdiction. Inferred obligations are often found in emerging markets.

4. *Regulatory guidance.* This is not a legal requirement *per se*, but a government authority may issue guidance saying, in effect, "Here is how we believe you should behave." These too are common in emerging markets. It is usually much easier for an agency to issue guidance than for a parliament to pass a law.

5. *Best practice.* Aside from looking at laws and regulations, it's possible to rate companies by how conservative they are in terms of "playing it safe" with their business practices. Kieran's firm performs the ratings, and clients can then benchmark themselves against the most conservative on the scale.

This five-part framework could be helpful to any company entering a new market. It's an analytic basis for understanding an often-hazy aspect of the business environment.

Advisors and How to Use Them

Everything we've covered so far leads to a final point—the need to *engage with people and firms that can help you navigate the local landscape*. The people don't have to be members of your company. They can be trusted external contacts who live and work on the ground in your target country. They can receive some form of *quid pro quo* for guiding you through the maze of confusing or conflicting regulations. Ideally they have connections within the government, or with people close to the government. This enables them to give you a heads-up on impending changes and to intervene on your behalf if possible. They should also be able to advise you on how to handle gray areas, because they know the ways that interpretations of the law are likely to lean, and they probably know which boundaries can be safely pushed to which extent. Having a well-informed local advisor of this type is extremely valuable.

But it's not a total solution. We also strongly recommend engaging an international firm that has proven experience in understanding and dealing with business-facing systems in the country you plan to enter. These firms can bring outside leverage and expertise to the table. They are much more likely than a local individual to understand business conditions in the wider world that affect your company and to which you must also be responsive while entering a new country's market. The international firm could be a law firm, an accounting firm, a consultancy, or some combined hybrid.

Depending on your business, you may need more than one type of international firm. Their services will be expensive. To a fledgling start-up, they may seem prohibitively expensive. But compliance with every requirement that a new country will place on your business is vital for ensuring the survival of the business itself. It merits being treated as a priority item in your expansion budget.

We've seen many firms that employ both savvy local partners on the ground, and major international service providers able to respond with boots on the ground as well. We engage both in our own firms. It's a winning combination.

And winning combinations, on the ground, are what you need before you launch anywhere.

Key Takeaways

- **Government policies can make or break your expansion.** Incentives, restrictions, and regulations all shape how you can operate. Whether you're entering Singapore or São Paulo, staying aware of how government policy impacts your sector is critical.

- **Policies change—sometimes overnight.** Even stable governments rewrite rules that affect industries. A new administration, a new minister, or sudden public pressure can shift the playing field dramatically.

- **Use frameworks to clarify gray areas.** Operating in gray areas without certainty of how the rules will be interpreted is a gamble. Always aim for proper structure and reputable partners. As shared by Kieran Donovan of k-ID, his team developed a five-part framework that classifies each business requirement as either an enforced law, a formal rule, an inferred obligation, regulatory guidance, or best practice. This approach helps executives see which rules are absolute, which depend on interpretation, and where cautious behavior is the smarter move.

(continued)

- **Local insight is your best defense.** Success depends largely on the people around you. Choose local partners who understand the landscape, maintain credibility, and have the influence to guide you through shifting regulations.

- **Blend local expertise with global guidance.** The strongest approach combines local advisors who know the terrain with international firms that ensure compliance and global alignment. Budget for both. It's not optional— it's insurance for your expansion.

6 The Power of Transcreation

Working Where Tech and Culture Intertwine

When a company crosses borders, new requirements arise—and new possibilities open up.

This chapter takes a wide-ranging look at the options available when you enter a new market. If you enter with cultural awareness—observing how people live, gauging how they might respond to your product offering—you get a clearer picture of how you will need to adapt the product for them. And if you can grasp the underlying cultural currents, you will get ideas about what *could* be done to take the business to new levels.

In fact, a core purpose of this chapter is to invite broader thinking about how products and companies can evolve in new markets. The chapter was co-written by a brilliant observer and thinker we've had the good fortune to know.

Professor Savanid "Nui" Vatanasakdakul of Carnegie Mellon University is a cross-cultural traveler. Born and raised in Thailand amid a rich mix of Asian cultural influences, she developed an early interest in how people, technologies, and social norms shape each other. Nui's career has taken her across four continents as both an academic and an entrepreneur. Today she teaches information systems at Carnegie Mellon's campus in Qatar.

Nui's research explores how culture affects technology adoption and how it *should* shape design.

As she says, "Many people try to build machines that work like humans. I tend to look from the human perspective to build machines that will work for us."

Nor is that all. Nui's studies go further, delving into how tech and culture evolve together over time. This is where her thinking moves into complex territory. It's also fertile territory, where one can see blue-sky visions turning into practical opportunities. But it would be best to start with concepts more easily grasped.

Moving from "Task Fit" to "Culture Fit" to "Transcreation"

Academic researchers have a term for how tech design typically proceeds: the goal is *task-technology fit*. Software developers or machine designers look at a task that people do—whether it's searching through data or carrying loads. Then they build a machine that will perform the task, except faster-cheaper-better than humans could. And they judge the results mainly by how well the technology fits the task. If it does a good job of that, then the product is good, and the main human concern is to make the product easily usable—with a good UX, good ergonomics, or whatever applies.

Nui has expanded on this by insisting that culture has to be factored in. She says you have to consider how people of a particular culture would like to use a product and the features they would value . . . and what kinds of tasks they would want to have done to begin with. One of her chief contributions to research has been proposing a new model of tech design, task-technology-*culture* fit.

As for what this all means in practical terms: a product won't transfer well across borders, into another culture, unless you give it a solid culture fit. And that process is called *transcreation.*

If you just port a product across with some standard, necessary adaptations—such as translating interface text into the country's language and making the product comply with local regulations— you are not doing enough, Nui says. You're essentially using a "one-size-fits-all" approach, dressed up with cosmetic touches. And you will lose to players who transcreate. Transcreation means taking an existing product or model and re-creating it in some fundamental ways so it aligns with the preferences and habits of people in the culture.

One of Nui's favorite examples is the introduction of ride-hailing service to Southeast Asian markets during the 2010s. Uber entered from its base in the United States, while some SEA start-ups launched to compete for the business. These included Grab, expanding across the region from a base in Singapore; Indonesia-based Gojek; and others.

Uber versus the Transcreators

When local ride-hailing companies entered Southeast Asian markets, they did not simply copy Uber. They inverted many of Uber's underlying assumptions about what a ride-hailing service should be. In its early years, Uber positioned itself at the premium end of the market, beginning with luxury black cars—and then went on treating the car as the natural unit of urban mobility. That logic worked in cities where many people owned cars and nearly all were used to riding in them.

In Southeast Asia, the starting point was the opposite. The motorbike is the backbone of daily transportation across the region. The lean two-wheeler is the fastest way to navigate through chronically congested cities, it can reach narrow alleys and informal neighborhoods that cars cannot, and it matches the spending patterns of most riders. Local platforms understood this and built their services around motorbikes from day one, creating an entirely different mobility model rather than a small variation on Uber's.

They also kept cash at the center of transactions, reflecting local payment behavior, and designed systems that paid drivers at the end of each workday rather than every two weeks. For workers who plan their finances daily, this was not a convenience. It was a prerequisite.

Uber did not adapt quickly enough to these dynamics when entering Southeast Asia, and its model remained misaligned with how people moved, paid, and worked. The company eventually withdrew from the region. The transcreators stayed and won.

How Culture Rewrites the Playbook

These differences are not limited to ride-hailing. Across industries, when products cross borders, they rarely behave the way their creators expect. What looks like a straightforward global model frequently requires deep reconstruction when it lands in another market.

The need for local judgment shows up in how products behave across borders. Clip, now one of Mexico's largest fintechs with a valuation that exceeds $2 billion, is often mistaken for a local replica of Square: the product is a small card reader plugged into a phone. But as VC Santiago Zavala of 500 Global explains, that surface similarity hides a completely different reality.

In the Bay Area, if you showed up at a farmers market with Clip's very first Square-style prototype—a homemade reader plugged into a phone's audio jack—early adopters would line up to try it. Trust in digital payments was established, card penetration was high, and curiosity outweighed skepticism.

But Clip's leaders knew that breaking through in Mexico would be tougher. At street markets there, many merchants assumed the unbranded reader was meant to clone their cards and steal money. It wasn't seen as innovative. It looked suspicious. And aside from trust being a barrier, Clip confronted a fundamental challenge: many consumers didn't have credit or debit cards. The problem was not just perception. It was infrastructure.

What seemed like a simple "copy of Square" required a completely different approach to building a business. Instead of launching quickly with a sleek device and onboarding flows, Clip had to help the market evolve, in terms of both merchant demand and consumer readiness. Through a process that involved design tweaks along with vigorous advertising and marketing, the company gradually built its presence in Mexico. Cultural awareness was the key. A product that could've gained instant traction in some markets had to win trust and acceptance in another. In Silicon Valley, the question would have been, "Does this work?" In Mexico, the question was, "Can I trust you?" Clip recognized these realities and redesigned its go-to-market strategy around them. It built a business that fit the market rather than forcing the market to fit the product.

Alexandre Lazarow of Fluent Ventures adds another layer by providing the example of Careem's expansion in Saudi Arabia. While Careem was often described as a regional Uber, its success came from decoding the cultural nuances that global playbooks overlook. One of its biggest breakthroughs was around women's mobility, at a time when local norms were shifting but still restrictive.

Instead of treating ride-hailing as a generic service, Careem reconfigured everything from driver availability to location coverage based on women's actual daily movement patterns—even increasing supply around school hours and exam times. These hyper-local operational details, Lazarow notes, mattered far more than any top-down strategy.

Across Clip, Booksy, and Careem, the pattern is unmistakable: localization is not translation—it is *transcreation*. Assumptions that hold in one market collapse in another. The same product behaves differently not because of technology, but because of people—their habits, trust levels, cultural norms, and lived realities. Global founders who understand this build resilient companies. Those who don't never leave the launchpad.

And the same human forces that shape products also shape communication. Once a company enters a new market, success depends on understanding not only what people do but decoding how they speak, commit, and build trust. These cultural patterns do not just influence operations. They also determine how quickly new forms of technology gain acceptance.

Culture Influences Adoption: Livestreamed E-commerce

Nui offers a clear illustration of this with livestreamed e-commerce. The selling is done by online influencers—individuals who sell products in bursts of live performance to people who follow them on social media platforms.

This form of e-commerce has become an industry in its own right throughout Asia. Sometimes, pop-music stars or other celebrities cash in on their fame by becoming live marketers and pulling their fan base along with them. But the players include legions of young people, many of them women, who don't have prior fame to propel them. Many audition for product-pitching roles at companies formed explicitly to profit from live e-commerce. Others jump into the market freelance, aiming to build a wider audience from an initial group of their friends, families, and neighbors. They pitch a wide variety of products to their followers: lots of fashion and beauty goods for women, plus foods, health-and-wellness products, and more.

What's amazing is how huge the Asian markets have become. According to recent figures as we were writing this book, live e-commerce accounted for 30% of *all* e-commerce in China. And perhaps equally amazing is the influencers' ability to sell products online, which really seem to call for in-person sampling and purchase. "Perfume!" says Nui. "How could you smell it online?

Why do people even buy it online?" The most likely answer Nui sees is that the influencer has formed trusted social relationships with her followers, who then are inclined to believe what the influencer shows them and tells them: "They are selling belief."

By contrast, this form of belief has been slow to gain traction in the United States. While livestreamed e-commerce has a foothold in the US market, it's nowhere near as popular, and not nearly as large a share of total e-commerce, as in China and other Asian markets. Nui attributes this to Asian cultures being more collectivist, as sociologists call them. Seeing oneself as part of a larger group, and wanting to partake in group activities, is a highly prioritized part of life. Thus, groups form easily around online influencers, attracting others to join. Watching and shopping together becomes a sort of virtual social activity, fueling purchases in big group-sized volumes. By contrast, although there are many groups and group activities in the United States, the culture leans more to the individualistic end of the scale. Online shopping remains more of an individual activity and a mainly "functional" activity, Nui says: you browse for what you want, then find and click, and you've got what you came for.

Finally, an even greater contrast exists in the culture where Nui now lives, in Qatar. The live e-commerce model has only made minimal inroads compared with the explosive growth seen in Asia. Adoption remains modest rather than widespread across the Gulf region. Nui points to cultural and social norms as additional headwinds in this market. The culture for the most part follows conservative Islamic values and social standards—including constraints on public visibility and influencing roles.

In an interesting footnote, Nui notes that *becoming* an influencer has strong historical roots in Asian societies. For centuries, right up into modern times, a lot of trade has been centered around micro-entrepreneurs selling fresh foods and other goods on the streets or in open-air markets. Now that new technologies exist, moving from a streetcorner stall to an online platform feels like a natural move—just a step up to a different and much more wide-open spot along the street. So it's not surprising, Nui says, to see a new generation of microentrepreneurs emerge.

Cultures Aren't Static. They Can Change

A given culture's attitude toward a tech product can evolve over time. Nui cites this example from her home country:

"When mobile banking first came to Thailand, people were not used to it. 'Why should I transfer my money online? Money should be in physical paper. I need to see the bank manager in front of me at the counter, then I feel safe.' So at the beginning, nobody used mobile banking very much."

"But culture can change. The fit of culture is not static, it's dynamic; it's variable." In the case of mobile banking, it changed gradually over time. So the real question to ask is: "How will your technology fit with the task and the variations of culture over time?"

That is a good question indeed. It's been proven time and again in international business that timing your entry to a new market is critical. In a lot of cases, timing is literally everything. But usually, when people think about timing their entry, they look at business factors like the state of the competitive environment. They'll also look at how ready the market is for them. So now, per Nui, add another consideration to the list. Is culture change afoot? If so, how can you leverage it, and when should you move?

Leveraging Cultural Change

In 2018, Saudi Arabia lifted a long-standing ban on women driving cars. This was seen as part of a growing trend in Gulf countries toward liberalizing the restrictions placed on women, in part to draw more of them into the workforce. And well before the Saudi ban actually was lifted—as soon as the upcoming policy change was announced—the ride-hailing company Careem started recruiting Saudi women as drivers. Careem, based in Dubai in the United Arab Emirates, had been hiring female drivers in a select few other Muslim-majority markets.

There was no shortage of applicants in Saudi Arabia. Various observers noted why driving for the company had broad appeal:

- Many women customers there prefer women drivers—it feels more secure—and the Careem app lets them request a female driver.

- In a region where female participation in the workforce had lagged, a gig as a ride-hailing driver could be an attractive entry route for women. You didn't need a degree. There were part-time and flextime options for women with children or household duties.

- In a culture where women traditionally had only limited degrees of autonomy, driving one's own vehicle—while being essentially one's own boss, as the person at the wheel—offered a significant leap in autonomy compared to many other jobs. Women applying for jobs with Careem often mentioned this in news interviews.

Another interesting footnote, business-wise: Uber also moved to recruit female drivers in Saudi Arabia. And had success doing so, as Careem did. But eventually Uber took a different approach to markets in the Gulf region by simply buying Careem's ride-hailing business and continuing to let it operate under the Careem brand. This was similar to Uber's exit strategy in Southeast Asia. There, Uber acquired about a one-fourth share in Grab. See Chapter 10's analysis of M&A as a vehicle for entry into international markets.

Living in the "Now-Future"

When companies roll out a new state-of-the-art product, they'll often have a marketing campaign that says something like "The future has arrived" or "The future is now."

Nui's perspective is a twist on that statement. The future isn't actually now. The future is the future, and now is now. But Nui points out that we're living in an age when potential *prototypes* of the future are here now and are even being sold on the market. It's possible to notice them, and the great challenge is to anticipate them and move toward where they are headed, if you can.

Because we're immersed in potential future prototypes, Nui says we are living in a time she calls the "now-future." In both timeframes at once.

For example, with progress in AI and robotics, we're now on the path to having highly capable mass-market humanoids—robots that look, think, and act like humans. That old sci-fi vision from the past now seems within reach. At the time we are writing this book, dozens of companies in China are selling humanoids—typically at very high prices, for specific commercial or industrial uses. But technologies have a habit of improving while coming down in price, as demand grows and more skills are applied to design and production. At the time we are writing, a Buddhist monk named Mindar preaches the Heart Sutra in a temple in Japan, and Mindar is a humanoid— limited in movement and scope, definitely, but he's a humanoid. And when Nui spoke at a recent professional conference, she shared the stage with a separate-but-similar secular version of Mindar: a humanoid who not only lectured the audience but fielded questions from the audience and made up jokes.

So Nui asks, as humanoids develop more fully, what cultural traits should *your* humanoid be imbued with? Can they be installed consciously and deliberately, or will they just sort of happen? How can you build cultural adaptability into a humanoid?

Maybe your company has nothing to do with advanced robotics. But it probably has growing potential for using advanced AI. And maybe, just maybe, in the verticals you inhabit, something is happening in the now-future that's worth paying attention to.

Nui thinks that this is very likely the case.

Key Takeaways

- **Transcreation outperforms translation.** Examples such as motorbike-based mobility, cash payments, and daily driver payouts illustrate how genuine transcreation outperformed global incumbents. And many products can't succeed across borders without fundamental adaptation to local habits, expectations, and cultural norms.

- **Technology adoption depends on cultural acceptance.** Trust, hierarchy, time orientation, and user behavior vary substantially across markets.

- **Culture is dynamic.** Effective market entry requires understanding current norms and anticipating the direction of cultural change.

(continued)

- **The "now-future" is already visible.** Early prototypes of emerging technologies exist in the present. Thinking ahead to how you might use them is better than letting them make you obsolete.

- **Winning globally means thinking locally.** The companies that scale effectively are the ones that rebuild their models for each market rather than assuming a universal fit.

7 Cultural Code-Switching

The Way to Evolve and Thrive

Darwin's theory of evolution is described as "survival of the fittest," which more precisely means "survival of the most adaptive." Creatures that persist are those that adapt best to competition and changing environments. The same holds true in business, so this chapter presents a method of self-evolution that will help you fly smoothly across cultures, just as Darwin's finches evolved differently to thrive on different islands.

Cultural code-switching is not new. Throughout history there have been people who've done it. (And people who didn't, to the disadvantage of many.) Yet the label is new, and it seems that each person has to learn the practice anew. For a bird's-eye overview—which should accelerate the learning process—let's start with a simple step-by-step explanation.

The term *code-switching* is borrowed from linguistics, where it refers to the practice of shifting between languages or speaking styles depending on the social context. For example, a young American might greet a friend with "Hey, what's up?" but moments later take a business call by saying "Hello, Mr. Madison. How are you?"

The speaker switches from a casual/friendly code to business code to fit the context.

Linguistic code-switching can be used for dramatic effect. Former US President Bill Clinton, an eloquent public speaker, often did it in the midst of a speech or a press conference—switching from policy-wonk style to the style of the rural, small-town area where he had grown up. Sometimes, to dismiss an idea he didn't agree with, Clinton would say "That dog won't hunt."

This old saying refers to a useless hunting dog, one you might feed and nurture without ever getting results. It's a perfect metaphor for a bad policy idea. Whenever Clinton said it, he'd get a sympathetic laugh from the audience. Furthermore, he used this kind of language as a positioning statement. Despite his elite-school education and his polished presence, Clinton wanted to be perceived as someone who came from the ranks of the common people—a perception that could help him win trust. Given his high popularity ratings, perhaps the code-switching did help.

That's an example of how *linguistic* code-switching can work on multiple levels. Now consider what *cultural* code-switching consists of and what it can do.

Cultural code-switching goes deeper. It involves changing not only your communication style but also your mindset, your tactics, and your general behavior in order to adapt to a culture other than your own. In short:

Cultural Code-Switching Touches Everything You Do in a Culture New to You. And It Is a Make-or-Break Skill for International Business

Fluency in cultural code-switching enables you to understand what's going on around you and to *be* understood. Once you learn to switch fluidly, you become much more able to build trust and relationships . . . to close deals more effectively . . . and to scale across borders successfully.

On the other hand, failure to learn cultural code-switching will often mean failure, period. When you miss the need to switch, it's literally like a railroad train jumping a switch that should have routed it onto a safe track. You will tumble off the rails and crash.

Vinnie once learned this lesson the hard way when pitching an investment deal to potential partners in Japan. As a former entrepreneur in Silicon Valley, he was used to an assertive, direct style: you show confidence, make your case quickly, and don't waste anyone's time.

But Japan was different. In that boardroom, people expected a more humble, deferential approach. Slowing down, reading subtle cues, and leaving space for silence would have been the wiser course. Instead, when a senior person—older than Vinnie and clearly respected in the room—expressed an opinion he felt deeply to be wrong, he jumped in to correct them. Even though he was speaking from experience, not just floating a counteropinion, it was the wrong move. It came across as a stranger publicly contradicting an elder. The atmosphere turned icy cold, and the deal collapsed.

The incident underscored how much cultural expectations can shape the outcome of a negotiation. What would have been standard practice in Silicon Valley was a costly misstep in Tokyo.

Looking back, Vinnie says he could have handled that moment very differently. If he had paused, listened more carefully, and repeated what was said to show that he was trying to understand, the classic "mirroring" approach might have defused the conflict. That would have allowed him to keep trust in the room and steer the conversation in a safer direction. Even a simple response like "Thank you, let me think about what you said" would have signaled respect and a willingness to find common ground. Sometimes the smartest move is to show deference, not prove yourself right. In other settings, the reverse is true—an assertive opinion signals strength. Knowing which approach to take is the essence of cultural code-switching.

But in Japan or Korea, you will often find four or more team members around the table. Showing up solo can signal a small, under-resourced company. Mirroring the local approach by bringing colleagues strengthens your presentation, especially in those first-minute decisions where perceptions are formed.

Key Takeaways

- **Credibility is cultural, not universal.** Behaviors that signal confidence and competence in one context can undermine trust entirely in another.

- **Hierarchy changes the rules of engagement.** In cultures that value seniority, publicly challenging someone above you is interpreted as disrespect rather than rigor.

- **Mirroring buys trust and time.** Active listening, reflection, and restraint can defuse tension and keep negotiations on track.

- **Assertiveness and deference are situational tools.** The skill is knowing when to push forward and when to step back.

- **Team presence sends a signal before words do.** In some cultures, showing up with colleagues signals seriousness and resources, while going solo suggests weakness.

> • **Cultural code-switching is adaptation, not
> performance.** It is situational awareness that allows you to
> stay aligned with your goals while adjusting how you
> pursue them.

Code-Switching Is an Art, Not an Act

The art of cultural code-switching lies in adapting to the social
context while staying true to your goals and messages. You need to fit
in without caving in. And done properly, it is not merely an act, not
performance art. If you do it as an act, people will sense that you're
trying to play games with them. The motivation has to be authentic.
It must come from a genuine desire to understand others, reach across
the gaps, and connect with them.

Learning the art takes time. You will make mistakes, as we did.
But with practice and reflection, it starts to come naturally.
Furthermore, as you grow proficient at cultural code-switching, you
develop an ability to recover from mistakes on the fly. (For example,
by noticing that you've offended someone and promptly taking steps
to restore rapport.)

There's a lot to learn. Gaps between one person's culture and
another may exist in a variety of ways. Adapting from Erin Meyer's
book *The Culture Map*, we've experienced these across five
dimensions:

Communication styles: Whereas one culture is grounded in
communicating directly, with no dancing around the subject,
another might have an indirect style. Cultures can also differ in
having a formal versus a casual style.

- **Direct cultures:** Netherlands, Germany, United States
- **Indirect cultures:** Japan, China, India

Decision-making and hierarchy: Some cultures are hierarchical: respect for authority is valued highly, and the person at the top pulls the trigger. Others are consensus-based and more egalitarian.

- **Egalitarian cultures:** Sweden, Denmark, Netherlands
- **Top-down cultures:** Japan, South Korea, UAE

Orientation to time: People of some cultures adhere strictly to schedules and deadlines. Others tend to be flexible.

- **Flexible cultures:** Indonesia, Brazil, Nigeria
- **Punctual cultures:** Germany, Switzerland, Japan

Trust-building: Some cultures respect outcomes and tasks to build trust; others are heavily relationship based.

- **Task-based cultures:** US, Germany, UK
- **Relationship-based cultures:** China, Saudi Arabia, Mexico

Risk tolerance: There are cautious cultures and entrepreneurial cultures. None is entirely one or the other, but the direction in which they lean can vary significantly.

- **Cautious/risk-averse cultures:** Japan, Russia, Germany, South Korea
- **Entrepreneurial/risk-taking cultures:** US, Israel, Singapore

Chapter 2 of this book has already mentioned a key point to keep in mind. When it comes to cultural variances, no culture—not yours, not Vinnie's or Stefano's or a Luxembourger's—can be judged as doing things "right" or "wrong." Every culture has evolved to suit the conditions that people are facing and what they value.

For instance, why does Silicon Valley culture favor direct communication? One reason is that the tech industries move fast and everyone's busy. Conversely, a culture that uses the indirect style may have evolved that way to minimize conflict. (Anthropologists have noted that in some traditional communities of the Arctic, cooperation was a primary value—necessary for surviving in the frigid climate—while selfishness and conflict could quickly turn fatal. Therefore, a proper person wouldn't even ask for food by saying "I am hungry," which is a selfish statement. The correct, indirect form was "Somebody is hungry": an appeal to the communal values.)

The main challenge in building a cross-cultural business is knowing when and how to code-switch. Drawing from the previous bulleted list, the following are two examples to jumpstart the learning process.

"Communication Style" Includes Dress and Body Language

A person can say all the right words but still fail the intercultural communication test. How you carry yourself often speaks louder than verbs and nouns. Vinnie learned early in Silicon Valley that confidence could be expressed by dressing down. In a world where billion-dollar founders wore hoodies and jeans, looking casual was a way of signaling power: *I don't need a suit to prove myself. I'm too busy building the future.*

Body language can convey a power statement, too. If you're familiar with HBO's *Silicon Valley*, you may remember Erlich, the brash entrepreneur who would stroll into meetings, lean back, and sprawl out as if declaring: *See how relaxed I am? Nothing rattles me. I've done big deals before, and I can handle this one.* That kind of posture and style made perfect sense in the Valley, where casual confidence was read as credibility.

But when Vinnie first arrived in Asia, the same style sent the opposite message. For one investor meeting, here the Silicon Valley standard T-shirt and jeans. Arriving first, he sat in the designated room to wait. Then the investor opened the door, glanced at him, and immediately shut it again, assuming this was the wrong room. He thought Vinnie was a bicycle messenger waiting for a document to be signed!

It was a jarring but important lesson. What looked like confidence in Palo Alto looked like disrespect in Singapore, Tokyo, or Seoul. Instead of projecting ease, casual dress and body language came across as laziness or even arrogance. People assumed he wasn't taking the meeting seriously.

Vinnie realized he had to code-switch. Instead of jeans and a T-shirt, he wore a suit. Instead of leaning back, he mirrored the people across the table—upright, attentive, and focused. Over time, this became second nature, a subtle but powerful way of signaling that he respected their expectations and values.

These shifts—in posture, dress, and team composition—might have seemed small, but they shaped the first-minute impressions that reflected deeply held cultural perceptions and often determined whether a business relationship could move forward.

Key Takeaways

- **Signals don't always translate.** What looks like confidence in one culture can look like arrogance or disrespect in another.

- **Dress codes are cultural codes.** A hoodie may signal power in Silicon Valley but immaturity in Muscat or Tokyo.

- **Body language speaks volumes.** Mirroring posture and attentiveness shows respect and builds trust.

- **Team presence matters.** In East Asia, bringing colleagues signals seriousness and resources. In Silicon Valley, the same move can look like wasted resources.

- **First impressions are fast and sticky.** Small cues in the first minute can reinforce deep cultural perceptions and decide whether business moves forward.

Keep Time to the Clock of the Culture You're In

For some of us, moving from one of the world's time zones to one on the opposite side of the globe is a major adjustment. But for all of us, there's a more important time adjustment. We'll do best when we move to the daily ticking of the clock in ways that acknowledge the local culture's view of schedules and deadlines.

Stefano grew up in Italy, where time was treated with a relaxed flexibility. A meal could last for hours, allowing time to enjoy both the food and the company. From his work across Southern Europe, he also learned that being five or ten minutes late to a meeting was rarely a problem. People would accept it easily—they might even be late themselves and welcome him warmly when he arrived.

In parts of Southeast Asia, including Indonesia, time operates more fluidly in business settings. Arriving exactly on time does not necessarily create a problem, but status is often reflected in who waits for whom. Senior figures may arrive later, and visitors are expected to accommodate that hierarchy. The higher the rank, the longer the delay you may encounter.

But that logic does not apply everywhere. In the United States, in Northern Europe, and in many Asian countries such as Japan, lateness is seen as disrespect. It suggests arrogance, as if to say, I am so important that you should wait for me. In those cultures, even arriving a few minutes late to a meeting can draw hostile stares.

When Stefano began working for an American law firm, he had to retrain his own habits. Punctuality became a form of code-switching, and it is still an ongoing exercise. With family and friends who share his Southern European background, his natural inclination is to remain flexible. But when wearing his hat as a founder and CEO, he tunes into the expectation of being precisely on time.

Key Takeaways

- **Time is culture-bound.** A "few minutes late" may be acceptable in Southern Europe but deeply offensive in Northern Europe or Japan.

- **In some places, lateness signals status.** In parts of Southeast Asia, arriving late can imply importance, while punctuality may be read as desperation.

- **In others, punctuality signals respect.** In Northern Europe and Japan, being on time shows professionalism and courtesy.

- **Code-switching is ongoing.** Leaders often juggle different cultural expectations—relaxed at home, precise in global business.

Juggling time standards isn't only a cross-border challenge. Within every culture people distinguish between situations where punctuality is non-negotiable—catching a flight, taking your seat before a performance begins—and those where flexibility is expected. At some social events it may be fine to arrive fashionably late. But at a wedding or a ceremony, lateness can mean missing the most important moment or, worse, interrupting it.

Scaling a business across borders multiplies the complexities. What looks like a fixed project deadline to you may be seen as an approximate target by your local counterparts. The real questions become: how will you plan for the range of possible outcomes? And how can code-switching help you manage expectations while steering the project toward the outcome you prefer?

To prepare you for weaving through the maze, the next chapter explores details and further mini-case studies of cultural code-switching.

8 When "Yes" Means "No"

Some Fine Points of Code-Switching

Scaling (or starting) a business across cultures can feel like entering an upside-down universe. Something that happens automatically in your culture might be a laborious grind elsewhere. People in some places really will say "yes" when they mean "no." To cope, getting your head right-side-up is paramount. The experiences shared in this chapter may help.

We have tried to avoid calling cultures other than your own "different." The word carries a somewhat pejorative connotation—different can come across as meaning lesser-than, so we don't write it. But we'll make an exception here. As a cultural code-switcher, you really do need to think differently. The practice will empower you to bridge gaps like those described in this chapter, starting with perhaps the toughest.

Learn to Decipher the Codes in Which "Yes" Means "No," or Meanings Are Otherwise Scrambled

Why would some people say a yes that means no? Because the culture frowns on creating disagreement and conflict. Because they want to leave a door open for the future, but just aren't willing to walk through it now. Because they worry that a no will be perceived as disobedience. Or because they want to get business from you (as in, "Yes we can meet your deadline," when in fact they can't. The yes in this case means "We'll try our best."). And a big disorienting factor is that all such reasons may seem to defy reason.

Vinnie once gave a speech at a conference in the Persian Gulf region where he remarked, "Nobody around here ever says no." The audience broke into laughter; they knew it was true. The moderator quickly added "Inshallah"—"If God wills it," a term often used to mean agreement, as in "May it be so"—and the crowd roared with laughter again. This was a clever wordplay, because people in the culture also use "Inshallah" as an indirect substitute for saying no: They're declaring that God, not them, is the real decider.

The trouble, of course, is that none of this helps you discern when you are actually being played. There are guides that try to map out which countries use "yes" to mean "no," but they don't solve the problem. Sometimes yes really does mean yes—and the hard part is knowing when it doesn't.

Many East Asian cultures share a similar trait with the Middle East: they are relationship-based and place a high value on saving face. In many East Asian languages, refusal is wrapped in polite agreement. The real answer often lies not in the literal word "yes" but in the tone, hesitation, or follow-up phrase.

For example, in Korean culture there are more than five different ways a "yes" can actually mean "no":

- **"Yes, but . . ."** (네, 그런데 . . .)—Often used to soften disagreement. The "but" that follows usually means "no" or "I can't do it."
- **"Yes, I'll look into it."** (네, 한번 알아보겠습니다)—Polite deferment. Usually means the answer is no, or very unlikely.

- **"Yes, I'll review it."** (네, 검토해 보겠습니다)—Sounds positive, but often a polite way to close the conversation without intention to proceed.

- **"Yes, let's do it next time."** (네, 다음에 하죠)—Functionally a no; "next time" often means never.

- **A simple "yes" (네) with a hesitant, drawn-out tone**—The delivery signals discomfort or unwillingness. Locals hear it as "no," but foreigners may miss it.

One approach to figuring out what "yes" really means would be to judge by the circumstances. If the situation allows for evasion, you are looking at an increased likelihood that "yes" means "no."

When Federico D'Amico led a global firm's investments in India, he occasionally encountered ambitious timelines set despite clear constraints. In many professional environments, declining a request directly can be uncomfortable. The adaptation is simple but essential: build prudent buffers into timelines and reinforce commitments through disciplined follow-up. "You cannot change the environment," Federico says. "You can only adjust how you work within it."

Other cultural-communication quirks are too numerous to examine them all. You might even use them yourself, when you're code-switching. When you tell a person across the table that you'll think about what they have said, it's often a polite evasion—a signal that you actually disagree but aren't going to let that stand in the way of collaborating on a deal.

This brings up a vital point. Most of the time, an evasive or disguised statement isn't meant to deceive you or take advantage of you. It's just people communicating in a manner shaped by their culture. And every culture is loaded with communication trickery: over-zealous encouragement, meant to build up morale ("We can do it! We can do it!"); flat-out fibs ("You look great."); false modesty ("What I did isn't very special. Credit should go to . . . .").

And how do you know when things like these are trickery? You sense it by intuition. You're open to nonverbal cues, like the tone and cadence of the voice. These skills can be learned at home. They ought to be, and often are. Then, when you reach out to do business across cultures, remember to use the skills instead of being paralyzed by attempts to analyze. Chances are they'll work equally well there.

When "Yes" Means "Not Yet" How to Interpret Silence and Delays During Negotiations

Federico D'Amico—today at EQT Group leading the Transition Infrastructure strategy in APAC—went through similar experiences during his years as CFO across East and South Asia. He learned that many challenges in cross-border business stem from misinterpreting how trust, consensus, and decision-making processes operate in different institutional settings.

In his view, misunderstandings often arise when silence is interpreted too quickly. He recalls a negotiation in which a local partner went quiet for weeks, leading headquarters to assume disengagement. In reality, the state-owned counterparty was aligning internally across ministries and stakeholders before taking a formal position.

His takeaway: understand how your counterparty's decision process works. Efforts to accelerate negotiations by engaging only top decision-makers may not be effective. In many institutional settings, groundwork precedes executive endorsement, and major commitments require internal consensus before confirmation. Leadership often requires adjusting pace rather than increasing pressure.

Federico also learned that "yes" does not always mean immediate commitment, particularly in parts of Southeast Asia and Japan. Often it signals acknowledgment rather than contractual intent. What may initially appear inconsistent can reflect a more deliberative or consensus-driven decision process. At times, the counterparty genuinely supports the transaction but must navigate internal reviews and hierarchical approvals before confirming agreement. These internal dynamics are typically not visible to external stakeholders.

Patience, then, is not about waiting politely. It is about recognizing that your counterparty may be solving complex internal dynamics that you're not aware of and are not supposed to be aware of. Becoming confrontational simply because the process is slow is counterproductive. If you cannot adapt to this rhythm, you should probably do business somewhere else.

Federico learned this lesson while closing one of his first deals in East Asia. Everything had been negotiated; every term agreed. From his prior experience, nothing appeared to remain but the signature. Yet at the time of signing, the counterparty stepped away for several hours without explanation. Concerned, Federico escalated the issue, calling senior leaders to understand what was happening.

"I reached out directly to the highest levels but couldn't get clarity," he recalls. "I later learned that, before signing, the counterparty required final endorsement from a senior individual who was unavailable that day. My escalation was perceived as impatience rather than urgency. There was an internal protocol to follow, and all that was missing was formal clearance. Greater transparency would have helped in the moment—but as an external counterparty, you are not always privy to internal governance processes."

A Gap in Core Values Between Cultures Can Be Profound

One story from Stefano's legal career illustrates just how profound such gaps can be. He omits the names of the countries involved, because the dynamics he observed could happen between many different cultures, not just these two.

During his lawyer days, Stefano represented a company from a nation that had grown very wealthy by exporting natural resources. Its executives wanted to partner with a firm in a developing country—one that was only starting to emerge from decades of turmoil, war, and poverty. The two sides met at a neutral site, in a city both knew well. Stefano's clients, coming from a culture that equated hospitality with credibility, hosted the event lavishly: a luxury hotel suite, extravagant meals, music, and dancers. To them, displaying wealth and generosity was part of proving they were serious partners.

When negotiations began, the wealthy-nation clients expected to propose a slightly unequal split—60% of earnings in favor of the developing-country partner. But the lead negotiator on the other side, a man in his sixties who had lived through years of scarcity, pushed far harder than they anticipated. When 60/40 was put on the table, he demanded 80/20. When the hosts countered with additional benefits, he escalated to 90/10.

Stefano called for a timeout. He explained the situation to his clients approximately as follows:

"You have to understand how this man thinks. In his country, people have lived with the fear they may not eat tomorrow. So they push for as much as they can get right now. Unless you stop him, he'll walk away with 99.9% and your underwear! When he says 80/20 and then 90/10, he doesn't expect to get those exact terms—he's testing your walk-away point. You have to push back or he'll keep going. You need to say, 'The deal is off,' walk out, and wait for him to call you back. Only then will the real negotiation begin."

When they returned to the room, Stefano's clients still hesitated, reluctant to risk offense. Finally, Stefano stepped in and took the lead, steering the discussion back toward a more balanced 60/40 conclusion.

Note that this kind of hard bargaining at the beginning of the negotiation isn't the same as the "last-minute add-on" we described in Chapter 1. In that case for the Australian client, a small extra demand came after both sides believed the deal was done—which for some cultures feels like "moving the goalposts" and is a breach of trust. In this case, by contrast, some unreasonably exorbitant requests were made at the start, as a way to test the other party's determination and bargaining stance. The lesson for global founders is to learn the difference: is the ask a tactic to test your walk-away point or a change after agreement? One can be handled with patience; the other may require walking away.

In our experience, similar cases of clashing cultural values abound. In a scenario we've seen repeatedly, one side goes into a partnering deal with the view that it's all about the money. That is how they measure value. They are baffled when people from the other side turn out to have multiple priorities: family, reputation, whatever.

To Stefano's surprise, as a lawyer mostly assisting American and European multinationals doing business in Southeast Asia, he realized that his main role in a negotiation, if he wanted it to succeed, had to be that of a cultural mediator. If you choose to take on the role, no plug-and-play solution is available. The task becomes like solving any complex problem. Divide the problem into manageable pieces, bring people as close to the ideal as they can go, deal with new pieces when they arise. Eventually, as the case-by-case approach takes hold, it may add up to an overall harmony with a momentum of its own.

Key Takeaways

- **Extreme demands can be signals, not expectations.** In some cultures, asking for far more than is realistic is a way to probe limits, not a literal position.

- **Scarcity shapes strategy.** In societies with histories of insecurity, negotiators may push until they're stopped; knowing this helps you hold firm without overreacting.

- **Global founders must read intent, not just numbers.** Learn to ask: is this a test of limits, or a breach of trust? The answer determines whether you push back, concede slightly, or walk away.

- **Distinguish the stage of negotiation.** An aggressive counter bid (like 80/20) can be a tactic to test your walk-away point, whereas changing terms after an agreement risks breaking trust.

- **Remember the human baseline.** We share the same species and many universal traits—but culture, history, and external events often produce contrasting behaviors that are not easily made to converge.

- **Code-switching is your edge.** By being conscious of these cultural dynamics, you can play a pivotal role in bridging gaps and creating convergence where others cannot.

In Some Cultures, Trust Is the Default Setting. In Some It's a Hard-Earned Prize

As we stated earlier, it's absolutely essential to build trust when entering a new culture. Typically you have a prospective partner or partners in mind, with whom you want to do business. And they won't be your actual partners until they trust you.

The tricky thing with this subject is that talking about trust gets complicated, for several reasons, which we will now unwind.

First of all, trust is a two-way street. Before you set out to win the trust of potential partners, how do you know you can trust them? The answer to that is fairly straightforward. Choose them largely on the basis of personal recommendations from people you already trust. It's the classic networking approach. While it doesn't always work perfectly, we have found it more reliable than targeting partners by other means, in which case we would at least seek personal recommendations to vet the choice.

A second complexity is that trust is defined and understood differently across systems. In an interview with Roman Kniazev, a biotech entrepreneur with deep experience on both sides of Russian and American business cultures, Roman put it plainly: trust in Russia is personal and tested through *pressure*, while trust in the United States comes from consistency within the process. Some teams look for how you behave in uncertain moments. Others look for how reliably you follow the agreed steps. How people grant trust often reflects how they navigate risk. Roman described one system as driving at night on an icy road and another as flying a plane with a checklist. Some cultures trust leaders who act decisively when the road gets slippery. Others trust leaders who show structure, preparation, and alignment. Both approaches can work, but only if you recognize the environment you are stepping into.

Understanding which expectation you are walking into helps you frame your intentions clearly and avoid misreading signals of confidence, caution, or commitment. Trust also shapes how agreements form. Roman shared that in Russia, deals hinge on the person, not the document. In some markets, trust grows through personal reliability and informal conversations. In others, trust grows through clarity in terms, timelines, and written commitments. Founders need to know whether they are in a relationship-driven environment or a structure-driven one, because the path to yes looks very different in each.

Cultural differences shape how trust is earned, but they do not change a simple truth. The most dependable first step in any market is finding someone you already trust who can bridge you into the new environment. Stefano once found a cluster of clients for a new lending service among renewable energy companies he already knew and trusted from his earlier days as lawyer. Sure enough, they repaid their loans regularly and never once defaulted.

A third complication is that trust comes in many forms and levels. Even within a culture, what "trust" means can vary widely, and across cultures it's even trickier. Some possible meanings:

- **Can I trust your honesty?** Are you telling me the truth?
- **Can I trust your intentions?** Are you here for mutual benefit or just to take advantage?
- **Can I trust your ability?** Do you actually have the skills and resources to deliver?
- **Can I trust your consistency?** Will you act tomorrow the way you do today or shift when it suits you?
- **Can I trust your discretion?** Will you protect confidential information?
- **Can I trust your resilience?** Will you stay engaged when things get difficult or walk away?
- **Can I trust your network?** Who stands behind you, and can I rely on them too?
- **Can I trust your fairness?** If you gain the upper hand, will you use it responsibly?

- **Can I trust your respect?** Will you adapt to our norms or try to impose your own?

- **Can I trust you when things go really well?** If success comes, will you share fairly, or will you try to take more than your share?

- **Can I trust you with the long term?** Will you look out for our collective interests so this partnership can endure?

Trust is never a single question. It's a layered calculation, and the layers change depending on history, culture, and context. Put this issue on hold for a moment—we'll return to it soon.

The fourth and final complication is inherently cross-cultural. Some cultures are generally more open and trusting than others. They also vary in terms of their conditions for bestowing and withdrawing trust. For example, the United States has long been a relatively open, noninsular society, with large numbers of immigrants and internal migrants. That kind of society needs to be one where trust is granted easily. So it has long been customary in the United States for people to trust others from the first time they meet, *unless* they see a compelling reason not to. You can see this in the porous networks of major American business centers—Silicon Valley, Hollywood, Wall Street—where young and ambitious newcomers are often welcomed quickly and judged on what they can contribute.

Of course, there are exceptions. Like people anywhere, Americans can find "compelling reasons" not to trust neighbors who differ from them or disagree with them or appear to pose a threat. But business-wise, it's possible to be trusted (and funded) rapidly. Vinnie did it twice in start-ups within a few years. One caveat to the quick-trust model: In the United States and in similar cultures where the model prevails, people tend to have zero tolerance for breaking trust. One breach and you're done. (Remember the

Australians in Chapter 1, who stormed out of a deal when they thought their trust had been violated?) In places like Silicon Valley, networks are hyper-connected, and reputations move fast. Doors may open quickly, but they slam shut even faster when a founder or investor missteps.

Meanwhile, at the opposite end of the spectrum are cultures where trust is granted slowly. Asian and Middle Eastern cultures are among these. Usually you will need to grind for years to reach the long-term partnership stage. But we've discovered a few excellent tips for paving the way.

Start with the first varieties of trust. Be honest and open about your intentions. Put yourself in the shoes of the person(s) in front of you—so you can understand *their* needs and desires—and then, within that context, make it crystal-clear what you hope to achieve with them. If the culture favors indirect communication, you can't just blurt out "I wanna be your partner!" Circling a path around to the proposal will work best. But as you land on opportune moments, state your goals unmistakably.

Jonathan Lynch, an American M&A lawyer who practiced in South Korea, Thailand, Singapore, and Saudi Arabia, was able to experience all this firsthand across these different cultures. He explains how trust in those countries is earned differently. What outsiders often perceive as slow or opaque is, in reality, a deeply structured process built around hierarchy, social bonding, and rituals that sit outside the formal workday.

In much of East Asia, Jonathan tells us, the real substance of a deal rarely unfolds between 9 a.m. and 5 p.m. Business moves forward in saunas, over long dinners, in izakayas and karaoke rooms, on golf courses, or through late-night drinks. These informal moments create vulnerability, intimacy, and a sense of shared experience that formal meetings cannot replicate. "In the United States, trust is built during office hours. In Asia, trust is often built after hours," he says. From this he has derived a golden rule: if you want to do business in Asia, never reject an invitation.

South Korea is where this dynamic becomes especially pronounced. Loyalty shapes every layer of interaction. The sense of belonging is pervasive and is reinforced in young adults by the country's mandatory military service. Once someone begins calling you *brother*, you have earned a powerful and enduring bond—but reaching that point takes time, patience, and humility. Korean society is rooted in long-standing traditions and relationships, so foreigners cannot expect to "shake things up" quickly.

When it comes to formal business meetings, Jonathan explains that often in South Korea the person with real decision-making authority is not even present at the negotiation. If they are, they tend to be the quietest in the room—listening, observing, avoiding anything that might cause a loss of face.

As a result, meetings often end with polite nods and an appearance of alignment, even when there is none. Foreigners may leave feeling optimistic, only to receive an email days later that contradicts everything they believed had been agreed. This is not deception; it is protection. Koreans prefer to listen, gather information, and then discuss privately with the true decision-maker, who frequently remains behind the scenes. Very few decisions are made in real time.

Incidentally, it's important to identify the true decision-maker(s) on the other side in any kind of deal, anywhere. The decision-making authority can vary even among similar companies in the same culture. Ernestine Fu Mak of Brave Capital recalls being party to a deal in which a Silicon Valley tech start-up was up for acquisition. The bidders included two larger Silicon Valley companies. At one, the CEO made all M&A decisions; at the other, the product team decided what would be a good fit to acquire.

Jonathan saw another distinctive rhythm in Saudi Arabia, though shaped by different cultural forces. Hierarchy there is more vertical than almost anywhere else. CEOs are deeply hands-on, issuing instructions across departments, and their word cascades down through the organization. Negotiation also blends seamlessly into hospitality. Jonathan was often invited into private homes before any business discussion began, taken on tours meant to signal status, values, and identity. Meetings that might last an hour in the United States easily stretch to three in Saudi Arabia. Personal chemistry comes first; the deal follows later.

He recalled one negotiation with a buyer purchasing three $10 million villas. Jonathan arrived expecting to settle two minor contract points in under an hour. Instead, he spent more than two hours drinking coffee and listening to the man's life story before any part of the deal was addressed. As he put it, "In the Middle East, anticipate that any meeting will last three times longer than it would in the United States."

Across Korea and Saudi Arabia, Jonathan arrived at the same conclusion shared by many leaders in this book: trust is slow, relationship-driven, and built far outside the formalities of the meeting room. "Foreigners who push for speed or directness often break the very trust they are trying to build." Those who listen more than they speak, respect hierarchy, and embrace the social dimension of negotiation eventually enter the inner circle—where real decisions finally happen.

Building on those after-hours settings, another essential tool for trust in these contexts is food. In much of the Middle East and across many Asian cultures, meals and social gatherings are not just hospitality—they are part of the trust-building process itself. A dinner is often where the real groundwork for a deal begins. Sharing food signals generosity, sincerity, and respect, and it provides space for the personal connection that formal meetings alone may never create.

Over a meal, for example, you might say in simple terms that signal commitment: "I would like to build a long-term business relationship with you, and I know that takes time. I'm prepared to invest the time. After today, I'd be happy to visit you for the next conversation and then host you afterward so we can continue exploring what a partnership might look like."

Clarity about your goals (and a roadmap for reaching them) lets the person know exactly where you stand. It can head off misunderstandings that might derail the trust-building later. And, since you're not making a big ask—just offering an invitation to talk further—the person shouldn't feel unduly pressured.

There was a hot start-up in Indonesia that Vinnie was trying to land an investment in—and it was a very competitive round. When a founder offers to meet you in person, you book the next available flight, sometimes the same day. So when this founder invited Vinnie for lunch, he flew out the next morning. Only after arriving did he realize the meal would be at the founder's family home. The founder, in his early twenties and still living in a multigenerational household, was not just offering hospitality. He was setting a test. Lunch with the founder led to an invitation to stay for the afternoon, which stretched into dinner with the entire family: parents, siblings, nieces, and nephews.

Vinnie quickly shifted gears. This was no longer about spreadsheets and valuations; it was about winning trust, favor, and respect. He shared personal stories—his own trials and triumphs, his journey to Asia, the lessons learned along the way. Around the dinner table, the founder's parents lit up at his anecdotes. Vinnie felt less like he was pitching for a deal and more like he was courting a family. The next business day, the call came: they wanted his firm's investment. In a round crowded with suitors, what tipped the scales wasn't just money. It was the values he revealed, and the trust he earned, by passing each layer of the test.

Is this approach needed to build trust in Silicon Valley? Or in any fast-moving business culture? The notion is ridiculous. That is why we present it as an example of cultural code-switching. We've learned that we build trust when we trust a process that fits the culture we're entering.

Key Takeaways

- **The speed of building trust looks different across cultures.** In some places it's granted quickly; in others, building trust can take years (time well spent).

- **Start with who you know.** The most powerful shortcut is doing business with entities you already trust. Beyond that, personal recommendations from your existing network are the most reliable path to new partners.

- **Trust is layered.** People may test your honesty, intentions, ability, discretion, resilience, fairness, values, and long-term alignment.

- **In open networks, speed cuts both ways.** In the United States, trust can be won quickly but lost instantly when broken.

> - **Match your directness to the culture.** Trying to push the process forward too quickly, or being overly direct in a relationship-driven culture, can close doors instead of opening them.
>
> - **In relationship-driven cultures, process matters.** Meals, social settings, and family connections are not side activities—they are where deals actually move forward.
>
> - **Code-switch to fit the culture.** The way you build trust in Silicon Valley won't work in Jakarta or Riyadh; adapt to the process that fits.

Honesty

When presenting your company to potential investors, partners, or clients, always present what the company's real situation is. "Fake it till you make it" is a poor tactic anywhere. In a culture where you're already viewed with some skepticism, because you are an outsider, such dishonesty can be deadly.

Just remember that you can be strategic about the company details that you reveal, and those you can keep close to the vest unless you're pressed for them. People *expect* you to highlight your strengths and gloss over your weaknesses. It's a pattern that has traveled across cultures since time immemorial.

And be honest everywhere, in every respect. Honesty travels better than wrinkle-free clothing. Finally, if you need a scrappy practical reason for being honest, this should do the job: you are not nearly familiar enough with the culture to succeed at lying.

Even in a world full of polite evasions, half-truths, and cultural disguises, one principle travels across every border: honesty. It's the one signal that is almost never scrambled.

Key Takeaways

- **Beware of death by politeness.** A "yes" is not always a yes. In many cultures, agreement may mask hesitation or a polite escape.

- **Context is your compass.** The setting, stakes, and relationships often reveal whether words mean what they say.

- **Match your pace to theirs.** Silence or delays rarely mean disinterest, they often mean your counterparty is navigating internal processes, politics, or hierarchy that are invisible to outsiders.

- **Spot the actual decider.** Influence often sits with the person others glance at for approval. Build trust with them. Sometimes the real decision-maker may not even be in the room, and that is perfectly normal in the early stages.

- **Lead with patience, not directness.** Trying to push the process too quickly, or being overly direct in a relationship-driven culture, can close doors instead of opening them.

- **Study the culture where it lives.** Restaurants, cafés, and local hangouts teach you more about norms than any briefing.

- **Look for everyday signals.** Watching sports events, entertainment, and even TV commercials show you what people find funny, respectful, or offensive—insight you can't get from meetings alone.

- **Always be honest.** Highlight your strengths, but never misrepresent. In a culture where you're already an outsider, dishonesty can be fatal.

- **Listen between the lines.** Tone, cadence, hesitation, and body language often carry more truth than the literal words.

- **Code-switch your ear.** Develop intuition for reading signals in your home country—then apply it abroad with humility and patience.

9 Deals Are Human

Align the Human Factors, or You'll Fail

No country shaped the video-game industry more than Japan. Seminal companies such as Nintendo, Sega, and Sony are Japanese. Franchises like *Pokémon*, originated by Tokyo-based Game Freak, are global phenomena. It would be fair to say that gaming is embedded in Japan's national culture. Japan long excelled at designing games and it's also home to players who care deeply about how those games feel and function. So the story we heard from a Japanese VC, Shin Iwata, had strong undertones of irony.

He told us about a European gaming company that tried to enter the Japanese market. The product was proven in basic design, with success elsewhere. But the company failed to tailor other aspects of its standard playbook to the Japanese audience. The user experience didn't fit the players' preferences. A marketing campaign that had brought in big sales back home came across as clumsily off-target and the pricing structure didn't help. It was as if the company's leaders had walked into a music hall where experts and aficionados were singing their harmonies and annoyed them by chiming in with a discordant cascade of wrong notes. Without cultural resonance, the company managed to ring itself right out of the market.

One might ask, how could anyone be so foolish? The truth, however, is that many of us have sometimes ignored the human aspects of doing business. It's too easy to get caught up in numbers and spreadsheets and technologies, without paying enough attention to the deciding factor: the people you're dealing with. Cross-border expansions can be sabotaged in this way, and so can partnerships and internal relationships. Let's delve into some cases where companies failed the human test . . . and some countercases where they aced the test.

The False Consensus Trap (and a Naked-Truth Solution)

Olivier Tonneau has spent years watching the world's smartest scientists and engineers learn that intelligence does not protect you from misunderstandings. As founder of Quantonation, a Paris-based venture fund dedicated to quantum technologies, he invests at the frontier where physics meets business. Yet even in that world of rigorous logic, cross-border partnerships often falter on something much less precise: assumptions.

One company in Olivier's portfolio, a European quantum-hardware start-up, signed a high-profile collaboration with an Asian telecom operator. The tone was upbeat. Engineers exchanged specs and schedules, and everyone celebrated a shared vision for piloting new quantum technology.

But when the agreement reached the legal teams, progress froze. The Europeans assumed that any intellectual property created during the pilot would remain theirs, as was standard in their home market. The Asian telecom's lawyers expected joint ownership of all IP. Weeks of tension followed, and the partnership nearly collapsed.

Tonneau calls this the danger of *false consensus*—the belief that globalization has erased difference. "Both sides think they're aligned on ownership or governance or timelines," he said. "But in reality they are operating from very different rulebooks."

The pilot-project conflict was resolved only when both parties went back to first principles. They defined background IP, foreground IP, and licensing terms. Once clarity replaced assumption, trust returned. The pilot succeeded, and the experience became a model for how to structure future collaborations.

In retrospect, the problem wasn't legal. It was cultural. Each side thought it understood how the other worked because business now feels borderless. Yet beneath that illusion are national systems, norms, and incentives that still shape how people negotiate, regulate, and define fairness. The cost of false consensus is time: months of lost progress and frustration. The cure, Tonneau says, is radical clarity. Partners must over-communicate early, translate not just language but logic, and never mistake politeness for agreement.

Marek Kiisa knows that lesson. He applied it from the start when he founded an intercontinental, intercultural VC firm. A European border-crosser himself, Marek is from Estonia but earned an engineering degree at KTH in Sweden and became a serial successful company founder and operator in the Nordics. During that time he was given an award for "angel of the year." A team of Japanese investors came to the event and asked to talk with Marek. They were amazed that small-to-tiny Northern European nations like Sweden, Estonia, Norway, and Finland managed to outpace Japan in start-ups and unicorns per capita—and they wanted in on the action.

In 2018 Marek partnered with them to start NordicNinja VC, based in Stockholm. The idea was to invest in a range of new-tech start-ups across Northern Europe, combining Marek's regional expertise with the Japanese partners' ability to raise funding from large Japanese corporations. NordicNinja was structured for equal input on decision-making, with two managing partners from Europe (Marek plus a colleague) and two from Japan. As Marek notes, some ingredients for a good match were present. The principals on both sides were all savvy founders and/or engineers turned investors. More importantly, both the Swedish and Japanese business cultures are grounded in decisions made by consensus, which was how NordicNinja planned to operate.

But Marek saw a potential danger flag. He was the oldest member of the managing team—late middle-aged, while the Japanese partners were younger. He knew that Japanese culture emphasizes showing deference to one's elders. And since he, Marek, also had deep on-the-ground familiarity with European tech ecosystems, he worried that his Japanese counterparts would hold back from challenging his opinions. "Holding back can be disastrous," he says. "Each person has to express it if he feels uncomfortable with something. You have to try to sell your own ideas to the team." Marek believes that energetic back-and-forth is essential for reaching a true consensus. Otherwise, there's a risk of the process devolving into a yes-man exercise.

So Marek urged his mates at NordicNinja to align around basic ground rules: "From day one we agreed that we are all equal. And that we will be *brutally honest* with each other." Marek has a Nordic metaphor for such an agreement. He calls it "sauna culture"—creating an environment where "everybody's naked in front of each other" and nobody wears a king's regalia or a general's hat.

We were impressed to learn that the Japanese partners accepted these terms. That approach runs counter to what's typically imagined about doing business in Japan. Yet it seems the NordicNinja partners have gone beyond merely "accepting" the shift in mindset. They've bought into it heart and soul—challenging Marek to the point where he admits, with a laugh, that "sometimes I think brutal honesty isn't such a good idea." But it works. With an initial investment pool of 100 million euros, NordicNinja hit the ground running. The VC firm has racked up consistent growth ever since. And false consensus hasn't been a problem.

> ## Key Takeaways
>
> - **Cultural fit beats product strength.** Even world-class products fail when they ignore the tastes, habits, and expectations of local users.
>
> - **Clarity beats confidence.** Over-communicate early, define every term, and surface hidden expectations before they turn into conflict.
>
> - **Create a culture where dissent is safe.** True cross-border collaboration requires environments where all partners can challenge, question, and push back without fear.
>
> - **Assumptions kill deals.** What feels "standard" in one country may be unacceptable in another, so never assume shared definitions of fairness, ownership, or process.
>
> - **Politeness is not agreement.** Silence, nodding, or soft language often signal deliberation or discomfort, not consent.
>
> - **Equal partnership must be explicit.** Don't rely on goodwill or intuition—set shared rules for how decisions are made and how disagreements are handled.

The Stereotyping Trap: Africa and Europe Are Continents, Not Cultures

When Western investors talk about "the African market," Hisham Halbouny can't help but smile. As the managing partner of P1 Ventures, which invests in places across the continent, he has seen that misconception mislead many.

Expansion into Africa may begin with a slide deck titled *Africa Strategy*—a single line loaded with over-generalization. Has the author traveled, say, the 8,000+ kilometers from Algiers to Lagos to Cape Town? "Africa is 54 countries," Hisham says. Within those 54 live more than 1.5 billion people using vast varieties of different currencies, regulatory systems, and languages. They include thousands of ethnic groups, each with particular cultural norms. Their business practices and speeds of doing business don't always match.

Worse yet, sometimes the Middle East region, including the Gulf states, gets lumped together with North Africa as MENA. Says Hisham, "The culture is different; the economy is different. In the Middle East, you have sovereign wealth funds. You have things that are funded more easily, you have dollar-pegged currencies and very stable reserves. That obviously doesn't translate when you look at North Africa." And then, he notes, things change very significantly when you go into sub-Saharan Africa. Economies there tend to be cash-based, regulations fragmented, and local relationships indispensable. "You can't copy a model from Dubai or London and drop it into Nairobi," Hashim says. "You have to rebuild it from the ground up."

One Middle Eastern fintech, flush with capital, tried to replicate its Gulf model across East Africa. The playbook looked sensible on paper—same product, same marketing, same dashboards—but the reality was harsh. Local banking partners demanded trust built over time. Digital signatures weren't legally binding. Payments still relied heavily on cash. In parts of Africa, Hisham noted, as many as 80% of transactions are still physical. Companies must build collection systems that blend online and offline operations, sometimes even sending staff in person to complete wet-ink documentation. What had been a fast-moving digital business in the GCC became a slow-motion experiment in adaptation. Within a year, the Middle Eastern company pulled back to its home market.

"The mistake wasn't ambition," Hisham Halbouny says. "It was assuming the context would adjust to the company, instead of the other way around."

Similar cautionary tales can be found in Europe. Olivier Tonneau: "One of our portfolio companies entering Europe assumed that the same sales and partnership approach that had worked in the United States would apply. Instead, they ran into delays with national compliance requirements and fragmented public funding programs." The company could only gain traction when its leaders pivoted to a strategy of "building relationships country by country."

In an email interview, Olivier made a series of points. "Europe is not one unified market but 27 different ones. Deeptech expansion here demands local adaptation: tailoring go-to-market strategies to each national ecosystem, securing local champions, and aligning with regional public funding mechanisms." And last but not least, "A 'one-size-fits-all' mindset risks burning time and resources."

The same holds true in Latin America. Uruguay and Paraguay are not alike. Argentina and Brazil are LatAm neighbors, but they differ in language, ethnic makeup, industrial profiles, societal assets and issues, and more. A map isn't a model. Where the map may say "Here's a big block of land waiting for you," the business model needs to go fine-grained.

One catch: "fine-grained" doesn't mean localizing everything. That would only bog down your ability to go global, says Ashley Lundström, partner at the Swedish-based investment firm EQT Ventures. Ashley offers practical advice on the global-versus-local dilemma: "Decide and clarify what's non-negotiable globally, for your company/product/brand/values, and then localize everything else," she told us in an interview. "Few companies dare to make these distinctions, but doing so provides exceptional clarity for the team."

In product design, even one-size-fits-all can work if the circumstances are right. Ashley cites the case of Toca Boca, maker of mobile video games for small children. The design team decided early not to use written-language prompts, which would need to be translated for various markets, since few kids in the target age group are able to read yet anyway. An all-visual design approach proved to be both globally scalable and popular, as Toca Boca games are now used worldwide. Designing for global scale means removing anything that slows localization.

And what's more common is a blended strategy, with some aspects of the business standardized and others localized. Ashley: "I saw one European team offer the same generous benefits packages, globally, even though they didn't need to in many markets. This was mainly done as a manifestation of the company's values around fairness and equality, but it created a competitive edge which turned out to be very helpful in hiring. However, the same company made sure to localize salary levels, so that while different markets had different headline numbers, everyone had the same spending power."

Now, there's a culture fit that does the job.

Key Takeaways

- **Global business isn't borderless.** Even in advanced tech fields like quantum, legal, regulatory, and cultural norms diverge more than people assume.
- **Regional labels hide real complexity.** Treating Africa or LatAm as single markets leads companies to overgeneralize, overlook risk, and misread opportunity.

> • **Honest debate builds real partnership.** Teams that
>   challenge each other openly—regardless of age, title, or
>   culture—create stronger, more resilient decisions.
>
> • **Global clarity enables local flexibility.** Companies that
>   decide what must stay global and what can be adapted
>   locally move faster, scale cleaner, and avoid wasted effort.

No Culture Is Monolithic—and Internal Variances May Be Nonobvious

Moving deeper, every national culture has subcultures. Professor Nui, our transcreation expert from Chapter 6, laughs as she rattles off some obvious ones: "Wealthy and less-wealthy cultures, urban and rural cultures . . . ." If you're B2B, you'll find "organizational and industry cultures" within a country's business market.

There are geographic cultures, too. Within the United States, the states in the northeast are culturally different from those in the so-called Deep South, and both are different from California. To see how this can impact a business, look at electric vehicle adoption state by state. In recent data we studied, California led with more than 3,000 EVs per 100,000 people; nearby West Coast states averaged about half that, and some southern and rural states fell below 200 per 100,000. The variations reflect not just income or infrastructure but deeper lifestyle and cultural differences.

Going further on the automotive front, in a famous study, the Stanford computer scientist Fei-Fei Li used Google Street View to sort towns and urban/suburban neighborhoods of the United States according to the types of personal vehicles spotted there. Specifically she asked, did a given area have more pickup trucks than passenger sedans, or vice versa? Then Li correlated the findings to voting patterns in elections. The pickup-truck-dominant areas voted strongly Republican—a marker of having conservative, traditionalist social views—while the sedan areas voted strongly Democratic, signifying liberal/progressive attitudes. This has business implications. It can impact what will sell in given areas, and it influences how best to market the products. (Pickup trucks tend to be marketed in the United States with TV ads linking the product to earthy, traditional uses such as ranching or farming or outdoor construction. And the ads score well even in modern suburban areas where few people actually need a pickup truck.)

The message: obviously, subcultures constitute market segments. But the subcultures that matter may be more subtly demarcated than by simple metrics such as location or income.

Consider, too, that generational shifts can make a big difference. Stefano has learned this with his green-financing start-up in Southeast Asia. When he launched Aquila, the initial strategy was to partner with major banks. The strategy seemed to make sense. Banks have money to lend or invest. At the time the start-up launched, many were mounting public-relations campaigns and internal programs that proclaimed a strong interest in going green to save the planet. So Stefano's team began pitching banks (and investment funds) with the idea that their start-up could provide the legal/regulatory expertise and technology to facilitate the funding of sustainability measures region-wide.

The results? Virtually none. Stefano found that the greentalk at big SEA banks was, to a large extent, just talk. Follow-through, other than with internal programs, was rare, and when it happened, it moved painfully slowly. "In a year-plus, we couldn't do one proper financing deal with any of these companies," Stefano recalls. "So instead we started working with what we call climate heroes."

The new strategy was to serve companies that *needed* the funding and were eager to use it. Many were young companies, in verticals from renewable energy to electric mobility. The founders and leaders were passionate about fighting climate change with greentech. Many had foregone the chance to earn high salaries elsewhere. They backed up their ideas by moving to implementation as fast as they could. And Stefano noticed that these founders/leaders shared a common characteristic. Nearly all were around age 35 or younger—a generation younger than most executives he'd met at the big banks and funds.

This was hardly surprising. Aside from work, in his roaming around Southeast Asian metro areas, Stefano had often seen groups of volunteers who spent their Saturdays picking up litter in the streets or cleaning riverbanks and beaches. And almost always, the volunteers were young adults and teens. Older people often walked past, accepting the clutter as a fact of life.

Stefano's start-up has scaled dramatically across Asia by targeting climate heroes. Aquila has built a networked community of thousands of greentech companies, winning clients among them consistently.

> His reflections: "I see a shared purpose across cultures when it comes to sustainability and climate. And what I've witnessed is a generational shift, meaning that across countries—from Indonesia to Thailand, from Vietnam to Italy, from Germany to the United States—it's primarily the young people who have an understanding of climate change and the importance of sustainability. *And are willing to work for it.* They're building gigantic electric fleets. Covering their countries in solar panels. They speak the same language across countries, they move fast, and with them, business is a breeze for us."

Stefano's parting message to cross-border enterprises of any kind: "Partner with companies that have the right mindset. A mindset that you share, and are passionate about." Another kind of subculture emerges here, one defined by alignment of values and vision. Across borders, that alignment may matter more than any other form of market segmentation.

> ### *Key Takeaways*
>
> - **Subcultures shape markets more than national labels.** Within any country, regional, urban–rural, and industry-specific cultures create wildly different behaviors and buying patterns.
>
> - **The real segmentation is often invisible.** What looks like geography or income on paper may actually be lifestyle, identity, or worldview—like the pickup-truck versus sedan divide predicting US political and cultural values.
>
> - **Generations can be different cultures entirely.** Young leaders across countries often share more values with each other than with older people in their own nation, reshaping sectors like climate tech and sustainability.
>
> - **Shared mindset beats shared nationality.** Alignment of purpose, speed, and values—not borders—is often the strongest predictor of productive cross-border partnerships.

Mind the "Scale of Values" in Your Target Country

When Queen Elizabeth II died, she was laid in state in London's Westminster Hall. Thousands of her longtime subjects then queued up in a line that stretched for miles, waiting their turn to file past the closed casket and, if they wished, say a personal goodbye. Comedian Trevor Noah felt moved to comment on the spectacle. Speaking to an American audience, well known for queuing overnight for each new iPhone release, he said he was amazed by how long some people in London were willing to wait: "22 hours in line—that's no joke.

Twenty-two hours! Because remember, there's no iPhone at the end of that line. It's just a box. And you don't even get to open the box."

Noah drew laughs by poking fun at two countries' different *scales of values*. Why would people submit to such an endurance test? For many Americans, the chance to buy a hot new product will do it, whereas for many British, it's the chance to pay respects to a dead monarch who symbolized a bygone age. The values strike radically opposite chords and hence the humor.

But it's not a laughing matter when you do business in a country where the scale of values is unfamiliar to you. During Stefano's lawyer days, he represented companies operating in Vietnam. One software company had a Vietnamese developer who entered a public coding contest. The young man won, which earned him the grand prize, a shiny new motorbike. There was only one problem. His winning entry was software that he and fellow employees had written for the company. Not only did the company own the IP, they had just made a sale that put them on the global map, by licensing the software to a big corporation overseas. And the buyer at the corporation was furious. He had paid millions for rights to the code. Now, according to the rules of the contest, it was being published as free open-source software.

Stefano stepped in. He sat down for a tough talk with the employee and then phoned the people running the contest. After more tough talk they agreed to delete the company's code. This accomplished the mission, and yet Stefano was struck by how the interactions departed from the value systems in his Western-world background.

Start with the prize the developer wanted to win. In Vietnam, a good motorbike is a necessity, not a nice toy. It's the main means of personal transport. You rely on it to help support yourself and your family. The young man had a strong incentive to go for it. When Stefano questioned him, he denied doing anything wrong. He didn't "steal" the code, which remained right there on the company's servers; he simply "published" it for a side use of his own.

On one level, that might seem like typical excuse-making. But seen another way, the developer's argument reflected his scale of values.

He didn't budge from his position when Stefano told him that his motorbike could cost the company a big contract. Although sociologists see Vietnam as a "collectivist" society—one where the value scale says people should put the interests of the group ahead of their own—the employee was displaying the flip side of collectivism: the belief that what belongs to the group belongs to each member. He was part of the company, so why shouldn't he use the company's software?

Tired of debating, Stefano reached for a book and put it on the table. It was a book of Vietnam's criminal law. Stefano showed the young man that taking the property of others for your own use, without permission, is theft—*a crime against the government*, not just a matter of civil dispute. Then he showed the man the penalty that the government could impose. Only then did the developer admit guilt and beg for mercy: *please don't call the police!* (The company didn't, though they fired him.)

The same approach was what finally swayed the contest people. Threatening a civil lawsuit didn't move them. They had specified the conditions of the contest and said they were obliged to uphold those conditions, which meant keeping the code posted on their website. But when Stefano ended the phone call and emailed, formally stating that they could be accomplices to a crime, they took down the code within minutes.

As Stefano notes, both the young man and the contest runners revealed their cultural scale of values. Both revealed what they feared most.

Key Takeaways

- **Values drive behavior,** even more than rules. What people protect, pursue, or fear reflects their cultural value system—and those values often override policy manuals or contracts.

- **"Collectivism" has two sides.** In some cultures, loyalty to the group means protecting shared assets; in others, it implies shared entitlement to those same assets. Knowing which version you're dealing with prevents costly misreads.

- **Consequences must match the local value scale.** Arguments that work in one culture (lost revenue, brand damage, lawsuits) may have little effect elsewhere. The persuasive lever might instead be social shame, legal exposure, or community consequence.

- **Never assume your logic is universal.** What looks like misconduct to you may feel justified or morally neutral to someone shaped by a different cultural framework. Diagnose the value system first, react second.

Transcreation from an International Team: Carro

While it's becoming common for start-ups to have founders from more than one country, few start-ups have leveraged their international roots as effectively as Carro has. The founders are from Singapore, Indonesia, and Thailand, and they met far from their homes, as students at Carnegie Mellon in Pittsburgh. After finishing university and returning home, their vision was to build a state-of-the-art Southeast Asian platform for buying and selling used cars.

Carro launched first in Singapore, a logical choice. The market is small but affluent, with high levels of digital trust—people are comfortable buying big-ticket items online. Carro's Singaporean founder knew there would be a plentiful supply of good used cars along with demand for them, and the company's efficient digital marketplace soon drew substantial traffic.

Expansion to Indonesia didn't go so smoothly. This was a leap from the region's smallest nation to its largest—a sprawling market with a population roughly 46 times the size of Singapore's. Although the Carro platform was designed to scale up, volume sales were not forthcoming. Carro's business model, ported to Indonesia with few changes, failed to fit the characteristics of the market. Average incomes and buying power were much lower than in Singapore and not even wealthier customers responded in droves. The missing ingredient was sufficient trust. Indonesians would gladly buy groceries, clothing, and household supplies online. But paying many thousands of dollars online for a car—for an important asset that needed to be right, sold by someone they'd never met, who seemed to exist only online? That was a notion that flew far above the trust ceiling. Other online car-market companies had sputtered in Indonesia, despite international funding, then backed out. Carro was headed down the same dead-end street.

Luckily, the founders, with an Indonesian among them, diagnosed the mismatch and saw a solution. People in Indonesia bought cars from dealerships, where they could examine the product and see the seller. Carro pivoted to a B2B2C model, building software that allowed local dealers to list and manage their inventory online. Consumers could browse a white-labeled Carro site to find cars that looked right and then visit a dealer to make the final purchase decision. This was transcreation in action. The new model created a distribution channel and a user experience that fit what people liked. It added value for each party involved, including Carro, which reaped a share of revenue from growing high-volume sales.

Carro also learned that adapting the model was not only about consumer trust; it was about dealer trust. In several markets, including Thailand, deep dealer relationships had been built over decades and could not be replaced quickly no matter how well-funded a start-up was. Carro eventually acquired Motto Auctions (formerly Manheim Thailand), which had been around for over two decades, because buying trust was faster than trying to build it.

Next came another bright idea. The founders migrated the dealer model back to Singapore. There, it became a second offering paired with the all-online model. Carro was giving people two choices of how to buy, which drew in a new tranche of consumers and funneled them to partnered dealerships. Meanwhile, in Indonesia, the dealership model gradually built trust in Carro, to the point at which all-online sales could be introduced in *that* country. The net result: a culturally agile founding team was able to learn from their first flawed expansion effort, converting it to win-wins all around.

Carro's regional expansion continued to reinforce the same lesson. In Thailand, a put option in one acquisition later created serious misalignment and cost. A put option is a clause that allows the seller to force the buyer to purchase the remaining shares at a future date, usually at a predetermined price. When it was exercised, it shifted the economics of the deal and became a costly reminder that cross-border expansion requires careful attention to structure, not only customer-facing adaptation.

And the story didn't end there. Several years later, Carro entered Japan. By then the company was a regional brand, operating in markets across Southeast Asia. Yet the founders refrained from assuming they had found the secret sauce. They hired a Japanese leader to shape the market strategy for Japan. That person knew that even in this technologically advanced country, offline trust still dominated. For years, many Japanese consumers had preferred to pay for online purchases in cash at convenience stores. To honor this preference, Carro launched a network of offline showrooms, positioning itself as a modern but familiar dealership. The company also focused on used electric vehicles, a fast-growing but underserved niche. Success soon followed.

Carro was forced to expand organically into Japan after evaluating dozens of acquisition targets, many of which came close to closing, but Aaron Tan, the CEO, watched each seller back out. Japanese founders were often willing to meet and discuss, but uncomfortable with selling domestic assets to a foreign company. (We've seen this play out with much bigger companies looking at Japan for M&A as well. Circle K gave up after one year of trying to acquire the 7–Eleven convenience store chain in Japan, known as Seven & i Holdings, specifically stating the Japanese chain presented a "calculated campaign of obfuscation and delay.")

Multiple lessons can be learned from Carro's journey—including the value of learning from mistakes, quickly enough to change course. We have the obvious lesson that transcreation works where copying-and-pasting won't. But a more fundamental fact underlies these. Good business is human business. Transcreation, as Carro showed, is the art of seeing how people actually live, buy, and trust and then using one's own human capabilities to build from there.

> ### *Key Takeaways*
>
> - **Transcreation beats copy-paste.** A model requires you to understand people's behaviors, not just market stats.

- **Trust has a price point.** Consumers may happily shop online for low-ticket items, but the moment the stakes rise, trust thresholds shift.

- **Adaptation compounds across markets.** Lessons earned in one country can be re-exported to others—but only when leaders resist the temptation to assume they've "found the formula."

10 Strategy in a Strange Land

How to Launch and Build and How Not To

Companies have dozens of ways to enter new markets, but most strategies fall into a few core patterns. These approaches range from direct launches to joint ventures, acquisitions, and distribution partnerships—each with its own opportunities and risks. This chapter examines the four most common market-entry strategies, drawn from real cases of success and failure across the world.

Direct Launch

Launching directly means entering a market without the help of a local partner. It is the purest, riskiest, and most revealing form of expansion. A company can either do it remotely—from another country—or establish a team on the ground. Both paths can work, but only one allows real visibility into what's happening in the market.

The Downsides of Launching Remotely

A remote launch is often the first idea that comes to mind in today's digital age. Founders and executives assume that because their product is online, their expansion can be, too. In practice, few purely remote launches succeed for long. Without being physically present, it's almost impossible to see or feel the market—to understand customer behavior, distribution gaps, or cultural friction.

Yet the urge to go remote persists, backed by the reasoning that everything is global these days. The logic sounds convincing: *people from another country can visit my website, so why can't I reach them from my website to their country?* The trouble is, you can't see or feel what you are reaching into. Every market hides nuances that can trip you up if you come in blind.

Example: The App That Didn't Fit

One interviewee shared that a company was blindsided when launching a mobile app in a new market for a consumer-facing business. The business didn't seem to need much deep understanding of local preferences, or tailoring to local markets, so the company started expanding remotely with very little change to the product. That strategy hit a snag in an emerging market with minimal mobile telco infrastructure and customers using low-cost Android phones. The app had been optimized for a rich browsing experience, downloading multiple images and more. This worked well in high-speed markets but strained this country's then-growing mobile networks and still-developing infrastructure. From the company's headquarters, the team only saw slower-than-expected adoption. Not until they spent time on the ground in the country—using the older phones most locals had—did the team realize that the app's feature-heavy design made it nearly unusable for many people on old processors with slower downlinks. A lightweight version of the app then fixed performance and reignited growth—but only after months of lost traction.

Lesson: Market realities cannot be seen from a dashboard.

Example: MoneySmart

MoneySmart's core product is an app for comparing financial products such as loans and credit cards. Users can click through to buy the ones they want, so partnerships with product providers are key to the business model. But the Singapore-based company's entry into Hong Kong didn't begin with a full team on the ground. MoneySmart began with a playbook that had worked well in Singapore: build organic traffic through content and then layer on partnerships. The first hire was a head of content, and the early plan was run largely from Singapore. At the same time, the founder was flying in periodically to introduce the company to banks and explain the vision.

When he started conversations with local partners, the gaps in that remote model became clear. Banks wanted to see commitment— not just emails and calls but a team they could meet regularly. Without a local presence, MoneySmart came across as an outsider. Partnership discussions moved slowly. Some stalled entirely.

The deeper issue wasn't the product or the intent. It was proximity. Managers in Singapore also couldn't see the nuances shaping financial behavior in Hong Kong. For example, Hong Kong has a seasonal "tax loan" product—a major annual lending opportunity, tied to the fact that residents pay their taxes up front, unlike Singapore's monthly installments. The dynamics, timing, and size of this opportunity were invisible from far away.

Everything changed once MoneySmart hired its first country manager in Hong Kong. That single move unlocked the traction the remote model couldn't. With a leader who understood the context, spoke the local language of the industry, and could meet partners face-to-face, trust grew quickly. Opportunities surfaced faster. The execution plan was adapted to match local realities, not assumptions from Singapore.

On reflection, the team realized their sequencing had been off. They had hired for content first and leadership later, when the opposite would have given them a much stronger start. In a new market, presence and context shape everything.

Summing up the experience, MoneySmart CEO Vinod Nair told us: "When you enter a new market, you find out quickly that the playbook doesn't travel as neatly as you expect. The only way to see what truly needs to be localized is to spend real time on the ground and listen. My advice to any founder expanding cross-border: don't try to manage it purely from afar. Even the strongest playbook needs local hands and local insight to take root."

Lesson: Even digital businesses depend on human presence.

Key Takeaways

- **Remote looks easy, but it's costly.** What seems efficient from afar often leads to lost time, missed signals, and expensive course corrections once reality sets in.

- **You can't fix what you can't see.** Without firsthand experience in the market, the data tells only part of the story—and often the wrong part.

- **Proximity wins.** Teams that show up learn faster, adapt sooner, and earn trust before their competitors even know what's changing.

> • **Local presence beats perfect plans.** The most valuable
> insights and opportunities emerge through personal
> interaction with potential partners and clients.
>
> • **Test before you leap.** Small experiments reveal what slides
> unnoticed from afar, saving months of missteps.

Launching with People on the Ground: Some Fine Points

Earlier chapters explored why presence matters. The next step is
understanding who should represent you on the ground—and how to
set them up for success.

When choosing someone to lay the groundwork in a new market,
the first instinct is often to hire locally: someone who knows the
terrain and can lead effectively from day one. That's usually the best
option. But in many emerging markets, a candidate who combines
deep local knowledge with real leadership experience can be
hard to find.

Sometimes, the right person is already on your existing team.
A strong internal leader can carry the company's values and culture
into a new environment while learning local dynamics along the way.

Another option—often overlooked—is what we call a *third-
culture* professional. This could be someone of any nationality whose
background gives them a kind of cultural flexibility; perhaps they've
studied abroad, worked in several countries, come from a
multicultural family, or grew up moving between worlds. These are
the people who learn fast, adapt instinctively, and operate
comfortably across boundaries.

How that adaptability was acquired matters less than the fact
that it's visible in action. You don't need the most internationally
decorated résumé; you need someone who shows third-culture

acumen—the ability to bridge differences, read signals, and build trust anywhere.

The executive who turned around MoneySmart's Hong Kong launch wasn't Chinese or even Asian. He was European—but globally minded and culturally curious. His success reflected not where he came from but how he listened, adapted, and built relationships.

Now let's turn to a theme raised earlier in the book that merits reiterating. Regardless of who is chosen to be on the ground in a target market, part of their mission should be to identify and understand market segments within the market. The previous chapters pointed out that no nation's culture is monolithic. There are subcultures within the culture, and it's not always clear how to draw meaningful lines between them. "Urban professionals" include people of many ages, occupations, and habits. Many may be part of a subculture that has little to do with urban professionalism, and the sorting may work out differently in Marseilles than in Lyon. The more accurately you can localize, the better.

And a final point: going in with boots on the ground doesn't always mean establishing a permanent presence from the start. It usually makes sense to explore and test before you leap. One classic way is through on-the-ground pilot ventures. A distinctive US company offers an interesting example:

While US-based fast-food chains such as McDonald's, Burger King, and others plunged heavily into international expansion from about the late 1960s onward, Chick-fil-A—a chain focused on chicken sandwiches and side dishes—clung for decades to a more cautious (and very successful) strategy of operating only throughout the United States. The sole exceptions were occasional store openings in nearby Canadian metros. That began to change in 2018–2019, and again the company proceeded cautiously, opening a select few test locations in Scotland, England, and several years later in Singapore. Testing was done with a mixture of pop-up stores, open for a few days, and months-long pilots.

Chick-fil-A also allowed ample time for evaluating test results and planning. An international rollout aimed at long-term market presences began in the mid-2020s. With the United Kingdom and Singapore as initial target countries, expansion was expected to build gradually across Europe and Asia. The company's deliberate, step-by-step approach appears to be ingrained in its culture. For example, applicants for franchises are rigorously screened and, if successful, rigorously trained. It's worth noting that Chick-fil-A is privately held, so there is no concern about stock-market pressure for rapid growth. Further, the deliberate approach has paid off in consistent revenue growth and profits, with the company's sales per location regularly topping the US fast-food industry.

Of course, the digital world moves faster, and it is possible to do low-cost market testing both rapidly and remotely. A common method is placing online ads in a potential market area. The ads can either have "fake doors"—a click-through takes the visitor to a page saying, "Thank you for helping us test"—or they can offer a chance to pre-order a product. Both allow you to gauge demand and get a reasonable proxy for conversion rate.

Testing in this way makes the most sense for comparing potential markets. The test markets can be countries (e.g., should we expand first to Thailand or Malaysia?), or they can be regions within a country (e.g., the Milan-Rome-Napoli metro areas). Running test ads may not give you definitive go/no-go answers, but the method allows for a lot of experimental tinkering with multiple variables, and it can be a valuable part of preliminary market R&D.

> ### *Key Takeaways*
>
> - **Local is ideal but not always available.** The strongest
>   market entries usually start with a local leader, but in many
>   emerging markets, true local leadership depth is limited.
>
> - **Third-culture talent is a superpower.** People who have
>   lived between cultures adapt faster, decode signals better,
>   and build trust in ways no résumé bullet captures.
>
> - **No country is one country.** Within any market lie
>   multiple subcultures, and real traction comes from
>   segmenting carefully, not assuming national homogeneity.
>
> - **Test before you build.** Pilots, pop-ups, and low-cost
>   digital experiments reveal the truth of a market long before
>   you spend real money.
>
> - **Presence matters, but permanence can wait.** Being on
>   the ground accelerates learning, but committing to a full
>   operation should follow evidence, not enthusiasm.

Joint Venturing as a Strategy

A joint venture (JV) with a resident company is a promising way to
enter a new market. If the JV is well-conceived and managed
properly, you get the home company's local experience and clout in
exchange for adding something new and valuable to their business. In
the best JVs, the partners work together to leverage each other's
strengths.

Netflix took its streaming service into Japan in 2015 through a
joint venture with SoftBank, known primarily as a telecom and
Internet services firm. SoftBank had the Netflix app installed on
phones that it sold, and customers of its wireless service were offered

Netflix subscriptions; payment was made easy by including the charge in their monthly mobile bills. Active collaborations by the JV included working together on local content for Netflix to stream.

Good synergy was achieved, too, when Starbucks joint-ventured to enter the Hong Kong market. The JV partner was (and remains) Maxim's, active across Asia and based in Hong Kong. Maxim's had experience operating its own branded restaurants and food outlets, along with a fine feel for partnering with others. This allowed the company to tweak the Starbucks product in little, localized ways that made a difference. For example, in its home US market and elsewhere, Starbucks had long offered a basic coffee-house experience: customers could have coffee with pastries on the side, and that seemed to be all they wanted. Maxim's had the Hong Kong locations offer sandwiches and lunch dishes as well—an appeal to busy Hong Kong businesspeople and similar patrons who could use Starbucks as a go-to place for lunchtime. It worked. Starbucks later went on to incorporate lunch menus even in the United States.

The Starbucks-Maxim's JV has been an enduring one that's expanded and evolved over the years. After the Hong Kong entry— which occurred in 2000—the partners went on to work together in various ways throughout a range of Asian markets, frequently adjusting the terms of the JV as times changed or as results indicated that changes should be made.

But much can be learned from failure stories. And since everybody loves them, here is a classic of the genre. It's about two companies that had the right motives and assets for a JV but were not able to make it work.

How a Joint Venture Failed: Tata × Docomo

In the 2000s, Japanese telecom company NTT Docomo was facing major obstacles to growth and profit in its home country: stagnant population growth and fierce competition within an already-mature market. These factors were "pushing NTT DoCoMo toward emerging Asian economies including India," per a journal article by two Indian researchers who studied the case.[1] For a JV partner in India, they were attracted to Tata Teleservices Limited (TTSL), the telecom arm of Tata Group, a huge traditional (founded in 1868) multi-industry conglomerate. Tata was able to provide market presence and a strong brand reputation India-wide. Its main motivation for seeking a JV was to gain expertise in wireless areas like moving to the globally adopted GSM technology, which was overtaking the more regional CDMA standard.

Tata Docomo was formed as an equity joint venture in 2008 and quickly scored a stunning success. The JV disrupted the market with pricing structures that made mobile use more economical for customers: a pay-per-second billing model for voice calls (others billed per minute, even if the full minute wasn't used) and billing per character for SMS rather than billing per message. In a nation of many price-sensitive consumers, the idea was a hit, pulling in about 10 million subscribers within a few months and drawing most of them away from competitors. As a strategy, however, the move amounted to a dangerous risk. Pricing structures cannot be patented, but they can easily be copied.

Tata Docomo had won big early with a competitive advantage that was innovative but unsustainable. The result was a race-to-the-bottom price war. Nonetheless, Tata Docomo survived and even kept on outpacing competitors—for a while. Then quarter-after-quarter losses became the norm and grew into losses of staggering magnitude.

Analysts have pointed to fatal mixture of "what went wrong" factors:

- **Where's the edge?** Once Tata Docomo lost its price advantage, the JV had a hard time finding other sources of competitive edge. In the vast Indian market—across a sprawling region, with many subregions—one key part of the game, when mobile service was evolving and spreading, was to stake out coverage and/or performance advantages in particular markets. Tata Docomo didn't manage to achieve a winning combination, or sustain it for long.

- **Regulatory friction.** While the industry and technologies evolved rapidly, India's regulatory policies also evolved in areas such as licensing and spectrum allocation. But sometimes the policies fluctuated unpredictably, not always in helpful ways. To quote the researchers we mentioned: "Though firms seeking IJVs give due importance to the economic environment, the case highlights that a more careful approach is required by factoring in 'policy stability' in the host country."

- **Timing.** Perhaps most critically, the JV's timing was unfortunate. In 2008, when Tata Docomo was formed, most of India had 2G wireless service and conversion to 3G was just beginning. NTT Docomo had gone 3G in Japan years earlier. The partner knew how to do it. But the JV still had to burn time and resources making the switch, while the next generation was dawning on the horizon.

India's government held an auction of 4G spectrum in 2010. A well-funded start-up—Jio, based in India—bought country-wide licenses. Jio then spent several years building toward a strong 4G launch, finally entering the market in 2016. Some observers have called this the nail in Tata Docomo's coffin. Even before Jio actually entered, everybody could see it coming, and that was not a good omen for a struggling JV.

It is possible for a business to ride out losses over an extended time. But to do that you need three things: the resources, the will, and a light at the end of the tunnel (i.e., a plan or hope for a way to profitability). Tata and NTT Docomo had resources but not the other two ingredients. The Tata Group had many other revenue sources—including from fixed-line broadband in telecom—and thus little motivation to keep on scrapping in wireless. NTT Docomo had come to India to make money, not lose it. The JV fell apart piece by piece, finally dissolving in 2017, accompanied by a painful legal hassle over the terms of exit for the Japanese firm.

And let's close our JV examination with a look at the other side of the picture. Whereas some JVs do not work out, one should be careful not to *miss* out, by overlooking chances to leverage the advantages a JV can offer.

An Opportunity Missed

When an expanding Asian fintech was about to enter the Indonesian market, the executive who'd been sent there to build up operations got an interesting visit. The visitors were from an Indonesian company with a useful niche product. They had developed software to handle online billing and payments for the country's small businesses. SMEs throughout Indonesia were already using the software. The newly arriving fintech didn't yet have anything like it. Therefore, the on-the-ground executive saw an ideal setup for a joint venture.

Through a JV, the fintech could add the software to its product line and would also get access to a pre-qualified customer base: the Indonesian firm's existing customers. That firm would of course get a share of the revenues from software sold through its new partner, while expanding its reach via the fintech's marketing campaign. And, there were opportunities for creative synergy. The fintech exec quickly perceived that the two parties could work together to design a complementary product to the billing-and-payment software.

But when the exec proposed a JV to top management at headquarters, the answer was "No. Why partner?" The fintech had in-house developers who could build a simple small-business solution. So the company chose that path, only to discover it was anything but simple. Developing the needed software from scratch was harder than expected. The resulting product still didn't fit particular Indonesian requirements, which meant more tweaking and time lost, along with revenue lost—because the could-have-been JV partner, the established Indonesian company, was left free to dominate the market segment.

The "not invented here" syndrome can be costly. Many companies have missed many boats by rejecting chances to incorporate the ideas and technologies of others. Today, in an age when expertise is global and when knowledge of local markets is especially valuable, it makes more sense than ever to use what others can offer. That's what joint ventures are for.

To close on the subject, there are plenty of joint ventures that manage to bridge different cultures and thrive, and there is never a one-size-fits-all rule for success. The balancing factors that bring equilibrium and pace to a JV can come from creative, unexpected solutions. One of our interviewees saw this happen when he was seconded to a diamond mine in Angola. This was a JV between a local Angolan team that ran the operations and a team of mining experts from Russia who moved to Africa long-term for the project. Despite using metal detectors and X-rays to prevent theft of the rough diamonds being processed, the Russians didn't trust the Angolans not to steal, and vice versa. The solution—the balancing factor—came from a third team, brought in from Nepal to help make the JV work. The Nepalese were seen as incorruptible by both sides and were trusted to manage the crucial final task of distinguishing between rough diamonds and rubble. This unusual setup helped bridge the cultural divide and allowed the JV to operate effectively.

> ## *Key Takeaways*
>
> - **Local strength is a multiplier, not a bonus.** A well-chosen JV partner gives you instant credibility, distribution, and cultural fit that no foreign entrant can manufacture quickly on its own.
>
> - **Synergy must be real, not assumed.** The best JVs pair complementary capabilities—like SoftBank's distribution or Maxim's local insight—that neither party could replicate efficiently on its own.
>
> - **Policy stability matters as much as market size.** As Tata–Docomo showed, shifting regulations and timing risks can overwhelm even the most well-funded partnerships.
>
> - **Competitive edges decay fast.** Advantages built on pricing or novelty are easily copied. Sustainable JVs need defensible strengths, not tactics that trigger a race to the bottom.
>
> - **Don't let "not invented here" kill opportunities.** Turning down a capable local partner in favor of building everything in-house often leads to delays, poor product-market fit, and missed market share.

When M&A Is an Entry Strategy: Strategic Acquisition

For start-ups and their investors, being acquired means a great exit, provided the price is right. But for cross-border expansion, the formula works in reverse. Buying into the right existing company at the right price can be a great way to enter.

Hisham Halbouny explains why he's seen the strategy succeed across African countries. "Launching from scratch into this continent is not necessarily the easiest route, because in most cases it's a scale game," he says. To be a significant player, "You need to build a network. It's breadth that you need; it's integration; it's more than one city in terms of expansion." All this, he observes, "takes time and it takes deep local understanding."

To complicate matters, Africa's immense diversity can bog down efforts at scaling from scratch. There are dense clusters of neighboring countries, many of them diverse internally as well. And then Hisham adds the kicker: "Whether you're B2B or B2C, average ticket size or average contract value is usually much smaller than in the US or Europe. So then scale matters even more."

He says most of the success stories he's seen have come through M&A, which he calls a "shortcut" to achieving scale and on-the-ground know-how. Citing two examples in Nigeria, "Stripe came in and acquired Paystack. That automatically gave it access to a few markets from day one, with a phenomenal leadership team. Then on the AI side, BioNTech acquired InstaDeep for its IP and its engineers. And also, there is a big cost arbitrage"—for while AI solutions can be sold globally, hiring talent and doing R&D are much less expensive in Lagos than in high-rent tech hotbeds like Silicon Valley.

The major downside, Hisham concludes, is that "M&A obviously comes with some integration issues and other impeding issues. But the risks there are easier to deal with. The problems are more evident and there are so many ways around them."

Likewise, we've seen M&A pay off for online shopping companies entering Southeast Asia. Online retail is both extremely popular and extremely tough to do business in. Competition is fierce, and each country's market presents a distinct set of human demands. These range from the types of goods that people want to buy to the relationships that must be built with merchants. Not to mention items such as designing (and constantly tweaking) a market-friendly user interface, arranging supply chains and delivery systems, and blending in related services to augment the razor-thin profit margins of online retail.

During the early to mid-2010s, numerous companies tried to carve out a place in the fast-growing Indonesian market. One failure was the Japanese firm Rakuten. They sent a senior person to Indonesia to build and lead a local team, backing him with sizable investment. And it just didn't work out. Although the man sent in was a seasoned manager, he had very little knowledge of Indonesia's cultural and business norms. The local hires were supposed to provide those elements—but it seems that a Catch-22-style paradox arose. How can you do a top-notch job of finding, recruiting, organizing, and motivating the best local people if you don't *already* know the local game? Or at least have the multicultural flexibility to learn fast on the fly, before competitors squash you or resources run dry? At any rate, difficulties persisted, and Rakuten pulled out of Indonesia within two years.

Alibaba's entry went much better. The Chinese giant bought a minority stake and then a controlling stake in Lazada, an online shopping start-up born in Singapore. Lazada had expanded quickly and gained a foothold in several SEA countries, including Indonesia. Alibaba kept the company's management team intact, along with customer-facing elements from brand to local operations. What they added, besides capital, was Alibaba's back-end software for automation of warehousing and business analytics. Lazada's leaders welcomed this synergy, running with it to become Southeast Asia's largest e-commerce platform.

The story doesn't have an entirely happy ending either. In recent years, Lazada has ceded its number-one SEA ranking to Shopee, a culturally diversified e-commerce platform started only a few years later. Shopee's advantage began with its origin story. Unlike Lazada, which was founded by Rocket Internet in Germany and initially run with a more European-style operating model, Shopee emerged from Garena, a homegrown Southeast Asian company that grew into Sea Group as it expanded from gaming into e-commerce. Shopee's leadership was more deeply embedded in the region's consumer habits, digital behaviors, and cultural nuances. Its market-by-market decisions often felt faster, more localized, and more intuitive to Southeast Asian users. Over time, that "closer to the ground" advantage compounded.

The M&A strategy has been applied in highly developed markets as well as emerging markets. Carro is a Singapore-based company with a platform for buying and selling used cars, along with providing related services. After expanding to several Southeast Asian countries, the company executed an M&A entry into Hong Kong in 2024. Carro bought Beyond Cars—a similar firm that already had built a customer base, a good reputation, and a savvy management team in Hong Kong.

Caveats and Failures

Although the M&A entry model might not be appropriate in every case, it's definitely the fast-track route to achieving on-the-ground presence and cultural relatability. But there is a caveat. For an M&A to work well anywhere, you have to get the fundamentals right. It won't work if you acquire the wrong company. And it will flounder if you don't do a good job of implementing the merger.

Several years ago we watched a fintech entering the market in a country overseas. Part of the entry strategy was to acquire native companies that had assets they would need. A certain company had licenses and infrastructure related to payment processing, and it was available at a nice price, so the fintech swooped in to buy it. That was a wrong choice. The price was cheap because the company was in crisis. Its customer base—a key part of the package you get when you acquire—had been shrinking, not growing. And though it's tempting to think that new owners can turn things around, turnarounds are not easy. You have to diagnose and treat the problems that are causing a company to bleed customers instead of attracting them. This company's problems were deep and complicated. For the fintech's leaders, already facing a long to-do list for market entry, the acquisition added the task of dealing with the mess they had bought—not a good bargain at any price.

Meanwhile, in Vietnam, a company made a potentially great acquisition but fumbled the follow-through. The misadventure unfolded in Ho Chi Minh City, where the South Korean company Baemin had planted an on-the-ground staff. Baemin's product, a food-delivery app, was targeted mainly to the city's large Korean immigrant community and linked them with the many Korean restaurants in the area. But Baemin had eyes on a much bigger market. The dominant player overall in food delivery was VietnamMM, popular with Vietnamese and expats alike. It could be hard to find people who *didn't* have the VietnamMM app on their phones.

Baemin acquired VietnamMM in 2019. The deal appeared to be too good to fail. With ownership of two apps, Baemin could have simply kept both as they were. Or, it could've run them in parallel for a year or so while iterating and learning how to merge them into a single master app. Unfortunately the company did neither. The plan looked more like a buy-it-to-kill-it strategy: close down VietnamMM after pulling away the customers.

VietnamMM's onboarding screen was scrubbed bare. When customers opened the app, they saw a link redirecting them to a new app Baemin had designed. And what awaited them there was an unpleasant surprise. The screen layout was utterly different from VietnamMM's. The language was mostly Korean, and the

Korean-centric food selection was good if that was the range of cuisine you wanted, but VietnamMM fans couldn't find many of the foods they had loved. In short, the trap that was meant to catch these customers drove them off.

Baemin closed down VietnamMM at the start of 2021. By then, few visitors were coming anyway, and another competitor was starting to steamroll the market. Baemin exited Vietnam shortly after—cutting losses that might have been profits, if the acquisition had been implemented better.

Course corrections and "lucky" deals

One case that could have played out similarly to Baemin's, but didn't, involved the soft drink market in India. US beverage maker Coca-Cola exited India due to regulatory issues in the 1970s, then re-entered in the 1990s. During its absence a new made-in-India brand, Thums Up, had surged to the top of the cola market countrywide. Coca-Cola then engineered a buyout of Thums Up. To market observers, it seemed that the acquisition was meant to let the Indian brand die out, as Coca-Cola allotted only a small marketing budget to Thums Up.

But Thums Up refused to die. Its founder had come up with a unique, strong-tasting cola formula that appealed to many Indian consumers and went well with spicy local foods. So the US-based owner shifted gears. Coca-Cola committed to a new course, selling Thums Up along with its own globally known drink, and this has paid off well. Thums Up remains a top cola brand in India and second in the nation's overall soft-drink market.

Successful M&A deals often also rely on unexpected factors, with luck playing a significant role. At the GSM World Congress in 1998, Edgar Auslander—today head of strategic partnerships at Meta—casually struck up a conversation with an Ericsson engineer about eliminating the wire in headsets. This chance encounter led to a series of improbable events, including the acquisition of Butterfly, a cordless phone chipset company, by Texas Instruments in 1999. The sequence of events, from Edgar's question to the engineer, to his meeting with key figures like Tim Haynes and Gideon Barack, and, ultimately, to the acquisition, seemed like a stroke of luck. However, as the old principle goes, "Luck is when preparation meets opportunity." A fortuitous meeting would have not translated into a deal had the opportunity not been picked up by Edgar, and successfully moved forward and closed.

Key Takeaways

- **Acquisition is often the fastest path to scale.** Buying a strong local player gives you instant market presence, embedded trust, and operational depth that would take years to build from scratch.

- **Local leadership is an asset you should preserve.** The most successful M&A entries keep the acquired team, brand, and cultural know-how intact instead of imposing a foreign playbook.

- **Integration issues can break even the best deal.** Poor post-acquisition execution, especially around product fit and user experience, can erase the advantages of buying in.

- **Choose targets based on fundamentals, not price.** A cheap acquisition can be costly if the company's core problems, customers, or reputation are deteriorating.

- **Respect what customers already love.** When you acquire a beloved local product, avoid radical changes that alienate its user base, because trust is harder to rebuild than to inherit.

Using a Distribution or Channel Partner

Another partnering approach—the final strategy we'll examine here—is to work with a local company for distribution and sales. That partner can provide valuable expertise. Or, in some cases, be a disaster waiting to happen. First consider the benefits.

Haribo, the German parent company of everyone's favorite gummy bears, saw customer demand for its product in Southeast Asia in the early 2010s. To begin market entry, Haribo chose an official regional distribution partner, DKSH. The firm's Consumer Goods unit had strong distribution and market-expansion capabilities in Southeast Asia. DKSH selected two markets to start, Singapore and Myanmar.

This was a tiered-geography strategy. Singapore is a highly developed mature market; Myanmar is an emerging frontier market. By having DKSH address both, Haribo was able to mitigate regulatory, infrastructure, and distribution risks.

Colossal Failure

There are cases in which a good company has such stupendously bad luck that the name should be omitted. We'll do so here.

The economic growth in Vietnam during recent times has benefited people throughout the country. It also has produced one of the fastest-growing number of millionaires worldwide. To target this market segment, makers of luxury goods began moving in. One was a European maker of exclusive high-end sports cars and sedans. The European car company found a distribution partner headed by a man who knew the terrain and seemed reliable. He bought an initial shipment of the cars outright and then proceeded to order more on a consignment basis.

The automaker, however, made a fatal mistake. It did not establish any presence or representative on the ground and relied

100% on the local partner. Time went by, and the European maker didn't notice sales results. A representative was sent to the distribution partner's location. What the rep found was shocking. Dozens upon dozens of beautifully designed and crafted automobiles, with retail prices well upwards of US$100,000 each, were parked in a huge open-air lot—where they had been left to bake in the sun and soak in the rain. Paint was fading and peeling on the once-gleaming bodies of the cars. Other signs of exposure damage were obvious, too. The cars, which had to be sold in perfect condition to uphold the brand's reputation, were now completely unsellable.

Why had the distributor left these assets to rot? It turned out that the partner certainly had the incentive to sell them, but couldn't, having miscalculated market demand in light of the pricing and taxes involved. And instead of admitting a mistake, the partner simply went on acting as if all was well. His company was distributing a lot of other brands; the high-end luxury cars represented only a small slice of turnover, and their loss could easily be absorbed. What was important to the partner was being able to keep the elite European brand's logo in his portfolio and use it to close on much higher-volume deals.

Another story, same European luxury automaker, using a distribution partner in another Asian city: the plan included building a showroom for the cars. This time the automaker had apparently learned a lesson and relocated a foreign representative from headquarters to manage the relationship with the partner. But still another fatal mistake was made. The representative decided to live in a different region and to follow the showroom work with periodic trips, instead of being on the ground in the target city and building a solid relationship with the partner. As opening day for the showroom drew near, the automaker's rep started worrying. Construction was behind schedule. But that's not unusual; construction delays happen everywhere, because so many factors are involved in getting the job done right. This job was indeed being done nicely—a sharp-looking, fully outfitted showroom was taking shape, appropriate for the cars that would be placed there—and the rep was assured that everything would be ready on time.

Which it was. The day before the scheduled grand opening, the rep arrived at the location and could see from the outside that everything looked perfect, except for one detail. The luxury automaker's name and logo were not displayed on the facade. Instead, there was the name and logo of a competitor. Stunned, the rep inquired what was up. The distribution partner's reply: "Two days ago they offered us a better deal."

The point of these stories is to be aware of the kind of market you're entering.

In fast-growing emerging markets, multitudes of players from everywhere jump in to try to profit from the boom. The cross-section profile of these players may not resemble that of a mature market. It is likely to include a number who have limited experience, or perhaps questionable motives, rushing to get what they can. It's a gold-rush situation.

A lesson to be learned—from the automaker's stories and from the entire chapter—is: don't rush. Be neither a perpetrator nor a victim of the overheated-bubble mentality that often is present in international business. Rather, be diligent in choosing markets, strategies, and partners. Be aware of who's around you and how the gameboard is changing while you enter to play. Moving fast isn't a magic key to success. The better formula is moving fast *enough* in the right directions.

> *Key Takeaways*
>
> - **Distribution partners can accelerate entry**—but only if they have real capability. A strong partner brings reach, infrastructure, and regulatory familiarity that would take years to build alone.
>
> - **Incentives must be aligned from day one.** If a distributor can earn more promoting someone else's product, they will—even at your expense.
>
> - **Trust is earned, not assumed.** In fast-growing emerging markets, the pool of distributors includes both excellent operators and opportunists. Rigorous vetting is essential before handing them your brand.
>
> - **Once again—you have to be there.** Managing a distribution partner requires building an in-person relationship. No relationship, no business.

Carro's Cross-Border M&A: Why the Playbook Cannot Travel Unchanged

A fitting wrap-up to this chapter comes from a company we met earlier, the used car marketplace-maker Carro. Carro's expansion across Southeast Asia shows that transcreation doesn't apply only to products and user experiences. It applies to dealmaking itself.

When Carro grew beyond Singapore, the team did not rely on a single playbook. Instead, they decided whether to build or buy based on the character of each market. In financial services, they found that organic growth worked better because it avoided legacy risk. In marketplaces, where trust and dealer relationships matter more than marketing budgets, acquisition delivered far faster results.

CEO Aaron Tan explained that acquiring a 20-year-old auction house in Thailand saved eight to ten years of slow relationship building. Deep dealer trust could not be accelerated by capital alone. Buying history was faster than trying to create it.

The company also learned that every country hides different risks. In Indonesia, the biggest threat was not competition or pricing. It was tax compliance. Carro once missed a filing deadline by two days and received a fine of roughly $500,000. This taught the team that in Indonesia, the regulator is effectively the counterparty, and even small administrative errors carry heavy costs.

Other risks were cultural. In Thailand, Carro tried to hire local leaders who fit the company's high-velocity style. They found capable people but few who were comfortable with aggressive scaling or direct confrontation. Consensus often took priority over speed. Carro eventually placed an internal leader as CEO to push the market forward.

Japan revealed yet another internal logic. Carro evaluated dozens of potential acquisitions, came close to several, and watched sellers walk away each time. Valuation was rarely the issue. Many Japanese founders struggled with the idea of selling a domestic asset to a foreign company. Even well-structured deals with clean logic failed at the final step. Aaron summarized it simply: Japan will talk to you at length, but closing is rare.

The combined lesson is clear. No matter how experienced the leadership team, the playbook must bend to the place. Markets are not blank canvases waiting for a strategy. They come with invisible rules, legacy expectations, cultural biases, and trust dynamics shaped by decades of local behavior. Leaders who recognize this early will avoid years of frustration and avoidable cost.

11 Hiring Teams Across Countries

Talent Eats Strategy for Breakfast

Behind every successful international expansion are the people who actually make it happen: the leaders who shape the market entry and the teams who implement it in the local context.

This chapter explores the quiet engine of global expansion—people—by showing how organizations identify, hire, onboard, and retain the right talent across borders.

Identifying the Right Talent in Different Countries

Who is best suited to lead an expansion into a new country? Conventional wisdom might say it's wise to have the top person (or at least, significant members of the leadership team) be native to the target country. These people know the culture instinctively, and they're likely to have strong local networks. Hisham Halbouny agrees that, in many cases, that has proved to be a good choice for his portfolio companies across Africa. But he's also seen exceptions, like a Turkish CEO who does a great job leading a company in Tanzania. This is because, when it comes to leadership, other factors than local knowledge become important. It's often best to choose someone who knows how to lead and is culturally adaptable.

Hiring Leaders to Drive International Expansion: Hire for "Distance Traveled," Not Just Gold Stars on the Résumé

Alexandre Lazarow takes this into account by looking for "distance traveled" in the background of the person being recruited: "What I want are team members who are humble enough to understand the market and curious enough to really try to figure it out locally. And I think that comes from some experience of having a multicultural background or experiences in traveling to many countries or even demonstrating the ability to adapt within a country through prior university exchange programs." In his book *Out-Innovate*, Alexandre also cites the example of Unshackled Ventures, a US-based VC firm purpose-built to support immigrant founders—handling visa sponsorship and employment so entrepreneurs could focus on building. Their thesis is based on the finding that outsiders, like immigrants who already had to live and adapt across different countries, have a strong competitive advantage when it comes to building something new.

Hiring for distance traveled, not job titles, is also one of Halbouny's main takeaways. The best cross-border leaders for building an expansion from scratch are often those who have demonstrated they can adapt, listen, and grow beyond their comfort zones while growing the business. Good sources for finding these people include the alumni networks of international study and exchange programs. One obvious example is the US-based Fulbright Program, which offers grants to support US academics and professionals for periods of work in other countries, and vice versa. Competition for the grants is intense, so those who qualify tend to be high achievers with a strong interest in gaining or expanding international experience. After their time abroad, Fulbright alumni—like those who've done similar programs—typically have enhanced abilities to adapt and operate in new cultures.

The deeper lesson is one repeated throughout this book: global ideas win only when they learn to speak local. And the leaders best suited to drive cross-border expansion are those who can combine local knowledge with international experience. "Africa rewards those who show up, listen, and build with partners who understand the terrain." As Halbouny put it, "Being on the ground turns assumptions into insight."

In practice, structure is what sustains trust at a distance. One useful approach—inspired by Adeo Ressi of the Founder Institute—is to avoid putting full control of a new market into the hands of a single individual. Instead, appoint two partners or co-leaders on the ground. This dual structure provides built-in governance, creates peer accountability, and ensures no single perspective dominates early decisions. It also signals that collaboration, not hierarchy, is the default operating mode.

Even beyond formal structure, trust grows through rhythm. Keeping recurring calls on the calendar, using WhatsApp groups to share small moments—from travel updates to lighthearted memes— and ensuring that every cross-border visit is treated as a cause for connection all help replace the spontaneity that distance takes away. Over time, these rituals become the invisible scaffolding that holds a distributed organization together.

Hiring Other Team Members: Scouting for Strong Talent Cross-Border

When hiring, you are focused on finding "the one"—the candidate that perfectly fits both the specific role and your business: the perfect head of sales, the strongest head of operations, etc. But an important detail to note when expanding internationally is that "the one(s)" may look different depending on the culture you're in. They will talk differently, be dressed differently, and be educated differently, for example. What is important is to acknowledge the differences in how they present themselves and instead be very clear in your head about the universal traits any strong candidate needs to have.

With respect to early start-up hires, the core traits to look for can be distilled quite simply. Integrity comes first. Beyond that, one executive with experience across four continents offered a useful shorthand. He suggested that strong candidates should have a "PhD": Professional, Hungry, and Driven. The challenge is that a PhD in Indonesia will look very different from a PhD in Sweden or Hong Kong. Recognizing real talent requires going beyond surface-level differences and resisting easy cultural assumptions.

How do you recognize a PhD? Time and physical presence. Spending time with the right people, testing them, and understanding if the traits you are looking for are consistently present in them. For example, some of the most talented team members Stefano worked with in Indonesia were faith-centered Muslims. At first, their colleagues from other countries didn't expect them to show the same "PhD" traits—professionalism, hunger, and drive—simply because their communication style, dress, and worldview were different. But once those initial assumptions faded, it became clear that their values and discipline strengthened the entire team. Their presence brought cultural depth and balance, showing that true talent often looks different from what people expect. The key point being that you need to recognize those specific PhD traits under the apparent cultural differences.

There is a key pitfall to avoid when hiring in new markets: the tendency to hire candidates with the same background as yourself. For instance, by focusing solely on candidates from prestigious Western schools, you risk limiting your talent pool and missing out on individuals who may not have had the same opportunities but possess great potential.

In Brazil, the executive noticed that many top candidates were from wealthy families who had studied abroad. This pattern also applies in Southeast Asia, where sons and daughters of successful industrial families tend to follow elite educational paths and eventually return to manage their family businesses. While these individuals are highly capable, sometimes they may lack the long-term drive needed for entrepreneurial ventures. Instead, the executive found a group of talented engineers from public universities who, though they hadn't had the same opportunities, displayed a stronger sense of motivation and resilience. This "PhD profile" emerged as an untapped source of raw talent that proved to be incredibly valuable in the long term.

A similar trend surfaced in more rural parts of Brazil, where engineers from less conventional backgrounds, demonstrated exceptional technical skills. These engineers were less polished, but they exhibited raw intellectual capability often overlooked by those focused on traditional urban talent pools.

When identifying talent, our PhD-seeking executive emphasized that it's not just about academic credentials but about personal drive. Candidates who've faced challenges—such as being the first in their family to attend university or overcoming significant personal struggles—often show a level of motivation that others may lack. These individuals are not only capable but also driven to prove themselves.

The executive recalled an interview with a candidate who, at first, seemed quiet and introverted but stood out by providing thoughtful, genuine answers. This candidate's ability to pause, think, and give a sincere response rather than the typical rehearsed answer demonstrated intellectual independence and authenticity.

One practical way to test for these traits is to listen for self-awareness and the ability to grow. Vinnie often asks candidates, "Tell me the biggest misperception others have of you." The answers reveal how honestly a person can look at themselves and how comfortable they are acknowledging blind spots. These are qualities that travel well across borders, because cross-border work constantly challenges your assumptions. A second question is, "What is a piece of feedback you received that changed how you work?" Many candidates offer safe answers like "I work too hard." The strongest ones share specific stories of growth and self-correction, which shows they can adapt, learn, and reset their behavior in a new environment.

Hiring Cross-Border Across Different Countries

Once the right people are identified, you can move to the hiring process. But when hiring cross-border, there are always two sides to consider.

The first is *the legal framework of the country where you plan to hire*. Each jurisdiction has its own set of employment laws—from probation periods to minimum wage requirements and contract durations. These rules are usually written clearly, so understanding them is mostly a matter of studying the law or consulting with local employment lawyers. Whenever you open operations in a new country, involving legal experts early in the hiring process is essential to ensure compliance.

For example, in the United States, most employment contracts are very flexible, and people can be fired at will, often with short notice. On the contrary, in other countries labor law can be pervasive and stringent. In the Socialist Republic of Vietnam, for example, a temporary employment contract cannot be renewed more than twice (and for a maximum of three years), after which the employee must be offered a life-time contract with no expiry date. In many European countries labor law is also incredibly stringent, and there is some truth in the joke according to which it is much easier and faster to end a marriage than to fire an employee.

The second aspect is more subtle: the *cultural differences surrounding employment*. These vary widely and are not always written into law but are deeply embedded in local expectations. In some countries, employees are expected to begin working the day they sign the contract or even right after a successful interview. In others, it is customary to have a few weeks between the job offer and the actual start date to allow for preparation and transition.

The same applies to things like probation and bonuses. Some countries legally require a thirteenth-month salary (some even a fourteenth-month salary!), while in others, it's not mandated but widely expected—and failing to offer it could make a company less attractive to candidates. You also need to be aware of which holidays are recognized, what days or hours people typically work, and when they are expected to stop.

In short, hiring globally means understanding not only the *written rules* defined by law but also the *unwritten ones* shaped by culture. Both are equally important, and the latter can only be learned through experience and time spent on the ground.

Key Takeaways

- **Hire for "distance traveled," not just pedigree.** The best expansion leaders are humble, curious, and adaptable enough to navigate unfamiliar terrain.

- **Look past surface differences.** True talent can present differently across cultures, so focus on integrity, hunger, and drive rather than familiar signals.

- **Legal frameworks are the easy part.** The harder part is mastering the unwritten cultural expectations around contracts, bonuses, notice periods, and work norms.

Onboarding

By onboarding we mean getting up to speed with the company itself, its processes, its tools, its software, its method of working and getting things done. The onboarding process gives new hires their first impression of the company they are joining—and it is thus fundamental to get it right. But onboarding can be made even more complex when it needs to be carried out across different countries and cultures.

The "Onboarding Buddy"

A common way to make the onboarding process smooth is by matching the new hire with an "onboarding buddy": an existing employee who is already familiar with the company and its processes and that for the first few weeks can be the go-to person for any basic questions the new hire may have. When expanding internationally, the "onboarding buddy" plays an even more crucial role, because they need to be a person either very familiar with the cultural background of the new hire or at least fully aware that they will need to help the new hire bridge many cultural gaps. The ideal "onboarding buddy," however, should be a peer or even someone junior to the new hire, so as to never be intimidating and to allow the new hire to truly ask anything—there should be no question "too naïve to be asked." In cross-border or multicultural organizations, the "onboarding buddy" can often be someone with the same cultural background of the new hire, who has already completed the process of integrating with the company and its culture and who therefore helps the new hire going through the same process and overcoming the same challenges they had to face.

Official Language(s) Used Within the Firm

Having one official language across the organization—especially at the management level—is essential for clarity, consistency, and cohesion. It ensures that all decisions, strategies, and communications are understood uniformly, reducing the risk of misinterpretation and inefficiency. A shared language promotes inclusivity among teams across regions, strengthens alignment with corporate goals, and enables faster, more transparent collaboration between departments and leadership.

A notable example of this was Rakuten's decision to make English the official company language of a traditional Japanese company with global ambitions. In 2010 the CEO, Hiroshi "Mickey" Mikitani, announced Englishnization—an aggressive two-year English proficiency mandate for all 7,100 of Rakuten's Japanese employees. A decade later, Mikitani pointed to this as a success of his business: "We have to be one team. That is why I want everyone to be able to communicate in English. Of course, I'm not saying it has to be perfect English. I, for one, make many grammatical errors. But that's fine. I don't worry about it. As long as we can understand each other, we don't need 'native' English to do great things together."

When Stefano was a junior executive operating in a foreign country, he initially thought it was disrespectful to require his team members in that country to speak a language different from their own. He quickly realized, to his surprise, that driven individuals all preferred to speak in English at work rather than in their native language. Actually, one of their main drives for joining a cross-border company rather than a local one was precisely to improve their English skills and to become fully familiar with a professional culture (and a language) different from their own.

Some large companies have adopted a hybrid approach. At Samsung Electronics, Korean remains dominant at headquarters, but English is required for global divisions and senior executives. For SAP out of Germany, all global documentation, product interfaces, and corporate communication are in English; internal meetings in Germany can be bilingual.

The Company's Dictionary

Another useful tip for a smooth cross-border onboarding is creating a "company dictionary." Stefano learned this in Aspire. When he joined the company in the early days (Aspire had just recently graduated from Y-Combinator), he was surprised to realize that he was the oldest employee. On top of it, he was coming not from previous start-ups but from a law firm, one of the most conservative industries, where people still use words such as "whereas" and "hereto" and others. He found himself all of a sudden immersed in a bunch of tech-savvy 20-year-olds who were using acronyms for virtually everything: CPT, PIC, GCT, etc. That's when he came up with the idea of a company dictionary, where all new joiners who came after him were able to find a clear explanation of the dozens of company-specific and team-specific acronyms used in Aspire.

> ### Key Takeaways
>
> - **Onboarding is cultural, not just procedural.** New hires don't just need tools; they need context, norms, and behavioral cues.
>
> - **The right onboarding buddy accelerates integration.** Peer-level guides reduce friction and give new joiners a safe place to ask anything.
>
> - **Shared language creates shared alignment.** A common working language, used consistently across leadership, eliminates ambiguity and strengthens cohesion.

Training

Training is not just a matter of teaching new skills or tasks. That is a mere 20% of the training. It is often less than that when you hire experienced professionals. Actually, when hiring your first few team members overseas, your aim is to hire people who are more knowledgeable than you and more well versed in their local market than you are: you want to hire people who will teach what they already know and who have the capability to train and manage their own team members. You want to hire people you can learn from.

This is even more important in those organizations—such as technology companies and start-ups—that are at the frontline of innovation and build new products and tools. In these companies, people need to create new things, rather than learn how to repeat existing ones. This was very visible during the first stages of the AI boom that started in the early 2020s. At that time, many tech companies around the world realized how quickly young people from completely different backgrounds could rise to the challenge when given access to new tools and opportunities. In Stefano's company, many of their interns came from Fulbright University—a remarkable college that nurtures curiosity and critical thinking. Some of them had studied subjects as far removed from technology as history or literature. Yet, once immersed in the right environment, they became outstanding coders, software developers, and eventually product managers.

Their success proved that what matters most is not what someone has studied but how they think, how adaptable they are, and how motivated they feel to learn. This is why, in the same way that top investment banks often hire graduates from mathematics or even humanities rather than economics, tech companies can find extraordinary talent in unexpected places. Mathematicians bring a sharp analytical mindset, while language students—especially those who have studied complex grammars like Latin or Greek—have a natural ability to absorb new frameworks and rules, much like learning a new programming language.

During that period, everyone witnessed something remarkable: young professionals with no formal background in computer science rapidly became some of the most efficient developers in the team. By mastering the new generation of AI tools, they quickly surpassed more experienced software engineers—even those who, just a year earlier, would have been their trainers.

The Company Culture

By far the most important component of what we call training is cultural: understanding and learning how people in the organization work together, share resources, resolve conflicts, and empower each other. And note that this is a component of the training process that cannot be automated by AI.

Cultural training is essential for any organization that operates across borders. A company's shared values are the foundation of its success, and these values must be deeply ingrained in how people work and interact. Mutual respect is non-negotiable. There can be no place for remarks or behaviors that are discriminatory—whether based on nationality, gender, socio-economic background, or any other personal characteristic. Inclusion must be fully embraced, and even a single inappropriate comment can be damaging to the culture the organization strives to build.

Many talented individuals may enter the company and perform exceptionally well from a technical or output perspective. Yet, they may not be the right fit—not because of their skills but because they may be unable to truly align with and embrace the company's culture.

Stefano recalls a case during his time managing a large engineering team in one country. One of our top engineers—technically brilliant and highly productive—was dismissed overnight. The reason had nothing to do with his performance but with the way he treated his colleagues. Messages he sent on Slack revealed a lack of respect and empathy that directly contradicted the company's values. As painful as it was to lose such a skilled professional, the decision to fire him was necessary to preserve the culture of mutual respect and care that sustained the team. Interestingly, the head of engineering who identified and raised the issue later became a close friend—and eventually Stefano's co-founder in his next venture.

Cultural alignment extends beyond interpersonal respect. It also includes how people demonstrate commitment to shared practices and routines. For example, in teams where daily meetings are essential, consistently arriving late can send a signal of disregard for the group's time and priorities. Even small breaches of respect can undermine cohesion and trust. Sometimes, taking decisive action on these cultural misalignments is more important than retaining a highly skilled individual. Skills can be taught; cultural values must be lived.

Keeping and Nurturing Talent

We have tried to distill more than 30 years of combined experience in managing cross-border teams into a few key principles.

First Principle: Talent Retention Is Key

All the effort you spent identifying, hiring, onboarding, and training the right people has little value unless those same people stay in your company long enough to create lasting impact. Unless you are hiring for a specific short-term project, your goal should be to build a team that remains, grows, and contributes meaningfully over time. When a talented person leaves too soon, the return on the time and energy invested is almost always negative.

Each departure forces you to start again—identifying, hiring, onboarding, and training a new person from the beginning. Beyond the lost time, the rest of the team can be negatively affected by the additional workload and uncertainty. The transition affects not only performance but also morale. Retention, therefore, is not just an HR metric; it is the foundation that determines whether your earlier hiring efforts were an investment or a loss.

Second Principle: People Do Not Leave Companies, They Leave Bosses[1]

If one of your team members leaves, the fault is all yours. When a talented team member decides to move on, effective leaders should first look inward. Across all types of organizations, hiring and retaining the right talent are the most important responsibilities of leadership—often more critical than short-term performance or strategy. Companies can pivot, restructure, or even rebuild within months, but great teams take years to form. And once they break, they are far harder to reassemble.

The solution begins with perspective: keep your team at the center of the organization. To lead effectively, a manager must understand not only the work their team members do but also their focus, motivation, and personal circumstances. Without that understanding, guidance becomes mechanical and detached. True leadership starts with genuine awareness—of the person, not just the role.

This kind of care cannot be faked. If employees are not truly valued, they will know it. When people genuinely feel that they are at the heart of the organization, they respond with trust, dedication, and exceptional commitment. To build this connection, leaders need to create moments of authentic conversation—discussions that go beyond work outputs, strategies, KPIs, or performance metrics. These moments should explore where each person is in their life: what matters to them, what challenges they face at home, and how they envision their future. Understanding these dimensions helps leaders see whether an employee's personal ambitions overlap with the company's—and what can be done to expand that overlap.

Stefano learned this at Aspire, where every manager was encouraged to hold, at least once a month, a "nonbusiness one-to-one" meeting with each one of their direct reports. Regular one-on-one meetings are essential to this process. At least once a month, take time to focus entirely on the individual. Let them bring up any topic, including those unrelated to business. They might want to discuss career aspirations, salary adjustments, or even personal matters that affect their performance. Some may be seeking new responsibilities or a title change—not out of vanity but because it influences how they see themselves or how they are perceived by peers. These conversations not only improve motivation and productivity but also reinforce trust and transparency.

A healthy relationship between a leader and their team member is one where both can speak openly about future plans. If someone cannot be honest about how long they intend to stay with the company or what they hope to achieve, it signals a lack of trust. As a leader, your role is to understand their agenda—what they want for themselves—and to find ways for the company to support that journey. Do they aspire to become executives, specialists, or future entrepreneurs? If so, what skills can they learn while in your organization that will help them reach those personal goals?

When people feel that their personal growth and ambitions are supported, their engagement deepens. They may eventually move on, but if their time in the company helps them progress toward their own goals, they will leave as advocates, not as disengaged employees. Such openness serves both sides: it gives the company visibility to plan ahead and it ensures individuals stay motivated and connected throughout their professional journey.

Third Principle: People Will "Go Through Fire and Hell" to Follow a Leader They Believe In

Working across several organizations, Stefano has seen people (including himself) willing to make immense personal sacrifices, from taking major salary cuts to relocating their family across continents, or living on savings for months, simply to work for a leader they trust and admire. This is because they are convinced that the benefits of working for that person (in terms of learning, potential future upsides, etc.) largely outweigh the present sacrifices; and that boss genuinely cares about them and their career and will "go through fire and hell" rather than letting them down.

Fourth Principle: You Can't Bluff Leadership, You Either Have It or You Don't

People can tell immediately whether a manager truly cares about the team or is driven mainly by self-interest. When leaders put their people first and when they genuinely care about their growth, success, and well-being, team members will respond with their full energy and commitment. They will follow you across new projects, new countries, new strategies, pivots, and the roller-coaster journey of international expansion. Even if you change departments or even companies, sooner or later they will find a way to follow you again.

The opposite is equally true. When leaders put themselves first, people sense it right away. There is no bluffing. No amount of charisma or strategy can conceal selfish intent. Bosses who treat others as instruments for personal advancement are not "leaders"—they are just employers. And people don't "go through fire and hell" for an employer. Team members will simply "use" their employer until a better job opportunity comes up.

True leadership doesn't require abandoning personal ambition; it requires aligning it—ensuring that personal goals advance, rather than compete with, the goals of the team and the company. When that alignment exists, doing the right thing for your team member also advances the company's and your goals, and everyone moves forward together.

Incentives That Drive Expansion

When expanding into a new market, the right incentives can make the difference between a short-lived effort and lasting success. Incentives are not only about compensation; they are about alignment. The most effective leaders design reward systems that connect personal ambition to organizational progress—where taking ownership, delivering results, and growing personally all move in the same direction.

The idea of aligning risk and reward is not new. It can be traced back centuries. When Ferdinand Magellan embarked on his voyage to circumnavigate the globe, his contract with the "lead investor" (the King of Spain) specified that he would be rewarded in direct proportion to his discoveries—he was promised a share of the profits generated from any new lands he found. Such a powerful incentive was sufficient to motivate Magellan and its crew to risk their lives by undertaking an endeavor that had never been attempted in history. Although Magellan did not survive the journey, the structure of his agreement perfectly illustrates the power of aligned incentives: the greater the success, the greater the personal reward.

There is no single formula. Incentives vary across industries and company stages, but the principle remains the same: reward impact.

For executives or managers tasked with opening new markets, this might mean bonuses tied to measurable outcomes such as revenue targets, customer acquisition milestones, or local profitability. For others, it can take the form of accelerating a person's role or title at the firm with higher responsibility or expanded scope. In start-ups, equity programs such as Employee Stock Ownership Plans (ESOPs) play a similar role—linking long-term personal gain with the company's success. When people hold a tangible stake in what they are building, their motivation naturally aligns with the organization's future.

Stefano experienced this firsthand during his time at Aspire. When he joined the company, he was hired to open a new market in Vietnam—effectively becoming the founder of that country operation and responsible for building the local team from the ground up. He was offered three compensation options: one with a higher salary and fewer shares, one balanced between the two, and one with a lower salary but a larger equity package. He chose the latter, accepting more than a 50% pay cut compared to his previous role as a New York lawyer. That decision sent a clear message to the leadership team— that he was fully committed to the company's long-term vision and willing to invest in its future. The alignment created by that ownership not only strengthened his relationship with the company but also fueled his motivation to build Aspire in Vietnam as if it were his own.

Career advancement itself can be one of the strongest motivators. Many companies, from Hewlett Packard to Uber, have long used international assignments as fast tracks for leadership growth. In markets like Singapore, it's common to see executives relocate from the home market to lead expansion and then return to headquarters two or three years later in significantly more senior positions. These rotations serve both sides: the company gains seasoned leadership on the ground, and the executive gains visibility, autonomy, and a springboard for career progression.

Autonomy, in fact, can be one of the most powerful incentives for entrepreneurial talent. Expansion leaders often thrive when they are given the freedom to operate almost like founders—shaping local strategy, building their own teams, and making market-level decisions with accountability for results. The ownership mindset that comes from such autonomy fuels both motivation and innovation.

Effective incentives also recognize the personal realities behind professional decisions. Entering a new market often means moving families, adjusting to new environments, and taking on risk. When companies design packages that account for these realities—for example, offering relocation support, flexible benefits, or coverage for international school programs—they align company goals with what matters most to the individual. Supporting both the professional and personal sides of an employee's decision strengthens long-term alignment and retention.

When incentives align risk, effort, and reward, the results compound. People stay longer, perform better, and think like owners. Financial rewards may initiate motivation, but it is the sense of ownership—of being trusted to build something meaningful—that sustains it.

Firing an Employee

Even the decision to let an employee go can and should be made with the best interests of both the company and the individual in mind. While it is never an easy step, firing an employee may sometimes be necessary to preserve the overall health and integrity of the organization—and, in many cases, to allow the affected person to find an environment where they can better thrive.

It is important to understand that the meaning and impact of firing vary greatly across cultures. In some countries, termination is viewed as a dramatic and deeply personal event, often carrying heavy social stigma. In other countries, such as the United States, it is seen as a normal part of professional life—a routine adjustment made when roles or expectations no longer align. A good leader must always take this cultural context into account when approaching such decisions.

Firing can also go wrong for reasons that have little to do with leadership intent and everything to do with context. Legal frameworks, cultural expectations, and company policies can all shape how separations must be handled. In some countries, such as France or Vietnam, employment law makes dismissals highly regulated and often time-consuming, while in the United States the process can be comparatively fast and flexible. The key is preparation. Regular performance reviews, clear documentation, and formal performance improvement plans help ensure that feedback is understood across cultures and that any eventual separation complies with local labor requirements. Understanding these frameworks early allows leaders to act with both empathy and compliance when difficult decisions arise. But beyond compliance, the way a leader handles these moments defines how the rest of the team perceives fairness, trust, and accountability.

Beyond culture, firing is ultimately a matter of alignment of incentives. When an employee consistently underperforms, resists collaboration, or creates a negative dynamic, their continued presence harms not only the company but also their own personal growth. Keeping someone in a position where they are disengaged or ineffective serves no one. Removing them gives both the organization and the individual the opportunity to realign—the company regains focus, and the employee has the chance to find a role or environment better suited to their strengths.

The decision also sends a powerful signal to the rest of the team. Allowing an unproductive or misaligned employee to stay communicates, implicitly, that performance and cultural fit do not matter—that mediocrity is tolerated. Taking decisive action, on the other hand, reinforces shared values and reminds everyone that alignment, contribution, and respect for the company's mission are non-negotiable.

Firing should therefore be handled with fairness, clarity, and empathy. If the misalignment lies in the person's role rather than their attitude or values, reassignment should always be considered first. But when no suitable position exists within the organization, it is kinder—and more responsible—to let the person go. In many cases, this opens the door for them to pursue a path where their skills and energy can be better utilized, whether in another company or in starting their own venture.

Naturally, things get even more complex when the decision to fire a person has to be implemented in a cross-cultural working environment. Oluchi Ikechi, who has been leading M&A teams across three continents, reflects on the ways that difficult personnel decisions—letting someone go, moving someone to another team, or navigating internal conflicts—played out very differently depending on the cultural environment she was operating in.

In New York, where she spent several years working with both American and British banks, Oluchi witnessed how direct and uncompromising the American style can be. For example, during a major divestment project, she watched a boardroom literally divided between key employees who would remain with the company and those who would be transferred to the divested entity. One team member, widely regarded as the most experienced in the room, became the focal point of tension as he made it clear that he did not want to move to the divested entity. The CEO, a British leader who had internalized New York's corporate culture, handled the situation with striking bluntness: "You're moving. Period." No diplomacy, no softening. That moment showed her how in the United States, tough decisions are delivered quickly, openly, and often with little emotional cushioning.

Her experiences with similar situations in the United Kingdom contrasted sharply with this. Decisions in London were still firm, but the communication was far more diplomatic and cautious. She recalled needing to remove a team member who was loud, confident, and pushy in group settings but lacked real substance and depth when pressed. The client had noticed this and had demanded that the person be removed from the team. Yet in the United Kingdom, the process required time, sensitivity, and careful handling. At the end, however, letting this person go sent a strong and positive signal across her cross-border team in India, the United States, and the United Kingdom: being the loudest voice does not equate to delivering value.

When Oluchi moved to Asia, she encountered yet another dynamic. Work meetings were mostly quiet. No one asked questions publicly. Even when team members admired her contributions during meetings and were excited to work with her, they still waited until after meetings to share their thoughts privately, never in front of the group. And cultural norms around deference and hierarchy made open challenges difficult. She also observed how Singapore's internal social hierarchy could influence who was let go. In some cases, the individual who ended up being removed was not the one who performed worst but the one who was socially perceived as an outsider; decisions could be shaped by this unspoken social order. Even though she was not the final decision-maker, witnessing these patterns was eye-opening.

From these three cases, Oluchi described a spectrum: the United States at the direct and blunt end of the scale; Europe and the United Kingdom as occupying a more diplomatic and measured middle ground; and Asia at the highly indirect end, where hierarchy and social norms guide both communication and decision-making.

Regardless of geographies, making difficult people-related decisions is part of maintaining the right environment and dynamics within the team. Leaders must stay attuned to the emotional and motivational well-being of their employees, especially in remote or cross-border settings, and act decisively when misalignment threatens to spread. Compassionate firmness is the key: protect the team, respect the individual, and always act in alignment with the company's long-term purpose.

Aligning interests across teams, individuals, and company is of course easier said than done. It's more of an art than a science and more of a constant strive than something that can be achieved once and for all. It is a never-ending task, and it always requires a lot of emotional intelligence and a lot of work. It becomes, however, even more complicated when your teams are spread across multiple countries, and your individual team members have different cultural backgrounds, values, and perspectives. That is what we will explore in depth in the following chapter.

Key Takeaways

- **Retention multiplies every earlier effort.** Identifying, hiring, and training pay off only when people stay long enough to have impact.

- **People follow leaders, not companies.** When they trust a manager who cares about them, they will endure difficulty and commit deeply.

(continued)

- **Incentives must align risk, effort, and reward.** Ownership, autonomy, and growth opportunities drive motivation more than salary alone.

- **When misalignment persists, decisive action protects the culture.** Letting one destructive person stay sends a stronger negative signal than letting them go.

12 Managing Teams Across Countries

Talent Eats Strategy for Lunch

Once Stefano was asked by the CEO of Aspire to share in front of the entire global leadership team what his secret was for managing his teams, as the drive and output of his team members had been noticed across the entire organization. He thanked the CEO for the opportunity, shared his screen during the leadership meeting, and simply played a four-minute YouTube video. Everything truly important about team management and "leadership"—he explained—is condensed in this video of Jack Welch, who was the CEO of General Electric between 1981 and 2001: https://mindthegap.to/welch. The following are the key takeaways from Welch's speech:

What makes you a leader?

1. *Be the chief meaning officer—Let everyone in the place know where you are going, why you are going there, and what's in it for them to get there with you.*

2. *Be the chief broomer officer—Get rid of the clutter, breaking down silos and bureaucracy so that people can act and do things.*

3. *Generosity needs to be part of your DNA—You've got to enjoy people's success and work toward their benefits: promotion, bonuses.*

4. *Be the chief fun officer—Make the job fun and celebrate even the small victories.*

5. *Recognize your privilege—Leadership lets you positively impact people's lives. It's both a responsibility and a privilege. Embrace it.*

This video is a must-watch for anyone who has a team to manage, no matter how big, diverse, or dispersed. In this chapter, we'll expand on the truths shared by Jack Welch, in the context of managing cross-cultural teams across borders.

How to Keep the Same Pace and Focus Across Different Countries

Keeping a team aligned across countries requires more than communication—it demands presence. One of the most effective ways to maintain unity is through regular in-person visits.

To Maintain Pace and Focus in a Country, Go There

Stefano learned this from the CEO of Aspire, who in the early days was managing four countries—Indonesia, Thailand, Vietnam, and Singapore. Despite having a young family, he spent each week in a different country, rotating through all four every month. It was exhausting, but it showed the level of commitment required to keep a regional team connected and moving at the same pace.

When Stefano later found himself in a similar role, he finally fully understood the value of that approach. Being physically present allows you to take the real temperature of the team—to sense the energy, challenges, and momentum that no report or video call can fully convey. It also allows you the deep on-the-ground understanding you need to push each local team to its full potential, without ever breaking it. It's demanding, but that's what leadership means: setting the pace by showing up.

Vinnie has witnessed the same truth across his firm, Golden Gate Ventures, spread over three continents. As a founding partner, he realized that absolutely nothing replaces genuine face-to-face time. Being physically present allows a leader to take the real temperature of the team, surface the harder or more uncomfortable issues in a setting of trust, and ensure everyone understands the unified mission. Presence also enables a leader to serve as what Jack Welch calls the "chief meaning officer"—reminding everyone where the company is going, why it matters, and, most importantly, what's in it for them. While town halls and partner-level calls across regions help, direct dialogue with individual team members cements alignment far more powerfully. Presence is not symbolic. It is operational.

As part of Golden Gate Ventures' company culture, the firm ensures that everyone has opportunities to connect in person through workshops, team-building events, and social gatherings, including a three-day annual general meeting (AGM) in Singapore during Formula 1 weekend. Team members fly in from three continents to be alongside the firm's key stakeholders, its investors, and portfolio CEOs, turning the event into both a business event and company alignment ritual.

Give Context and Direction: The Importance of Town Hall Meetings

In Silicon Valley's jargon, a "town hall meeting" is the gathering of all the employees in the company at once. There's something special about a town hall. It's not just another meeting on the calendar—it's the one moment when the entire team comes together, when you can pause the noise of daily tasks and remind everyone why we're doing what we're doing.

A good town hall sets the pace of the company. It gives clarity, energy, and direction. It's where you share the vision—not in abstract slides but in a way that connects every person to the bigger picture. The more context you share, the more empowered your people become. When they understand how their work fits into the broader journey, they can think, act, and prioritize autonomously and with purpose.

Context is not just information—it is trust. When leadership withholds context, teams work in silos, each focused on their narrow tasks until misalignment quietly grows. Opening the books and explaining the "why" behind decisions invites everyone to become a builder of the vision.

At Golden Gate Ventures, and across their portfolio, they apply the same principle while balancing global time zones. There is no perfect schedule that suits San Francisco, Singapore, Riyadh, and Amsterdam simultaneously. For internal all-hands, this sometimes means asking the New York team to join at awkward hours—and accepting that they start the next day later, a bit *jet-lagged*. With external stakeholders such as global investors, if live Q&A is crucial, they host two separate calls to accommodate different regions. Inclusion is intentional, not incidental.

Stefano saw at Aspire that when management began sharing more openly, morale and motivation surged. Employees stopped merely executing and started contributing. Town halls became moments of alignment—of truth and trust—where people lifted their heads to ensure they were still running in the same direction.

Constantly Ensure Alignment: The Daily Stand-Up

When teams are distributed across different countries and time zones, it becomes essential to create daily moments of connection. Bringing the team briefly together at least once a day—whether to discuss priorities, share progress, or raise challenges—helps maintain alignment and a sense of unity despite the distance.

In Stefano's company, these daily meetings do more than synchronize work; they also reinforce the company's culture. The way people communicate, support one another, and solve problems together during these sessions naturally shapes how the culture is lived day to day.

Over time, they evolved from one monolithic daily meeting to smaller working-group sessions. Each manager ensures that essential information flows across teams without requiring everyone to join every call. As organizations expand beyond 20–30 people, daily stand-ups become team-specific—for example, product separate from commercial—to keep meetings meaningful.

They rely heavily on asynchronous tools, such as Slack, concise emails, and AI-generated call summaries, to keep information current without adding meeting fatigue. The objective is not more meetings but smarter rhythm: enough connection to stay aligned, with room for deep work.

Reinforcing with Examples (Always Reinforce the Positive: It Sticks Better!)

To cultivate company culture, leaders must make it explicit and consistent. Culture unites people not through rules but through daily reinforcement of what works. It allows an organization to self-correct even when leaders are momentarily absent.

A 1,000-year-old management maxim captures the idea: "See everything; overlook a great deal; correct a little."[1] Trying to correct every deviation exhausts both leaders and teams. Instead, spotlight what excellence looks like.

Vinnie emphasizes this across his global teams. He tells every new hire that *failure* is not a bad word—it is the only way to learn.

A toddler cannot learn to walk without falling, and no one learns to sail without capsizing once or twice. He encourages people to move fast and take risks, expecting that mistakes will happen, but insists that they must learn and not repeat them. "If you keep making the same mistake, we have a problem," he explains, "but if you learn from it, you grow stronger.

As a manager, instead of focusing your attention on correcting every mistake, highlight examples of excellence. For instance, when a team member sends an email that reflects genuine customer care and professionalism, don't just acknowledge it privately; forwarding that email to the entire team and celebrating it as a model of communication can be far more effective than pointing out multiple errors made by other less effective team members in their customer emails. Positive reinforcement has a much greater and more lasting impact than negative feedback.

By consistently showcasing and celebrating positive examples, team members learn what behaviors and values are appreciated. They want to become the ones writing the next email that will deserve to be praised and forwarded internally. Over time, this repeated reinforcement helps everyone naturally align their "internal compass" toward those shared standards. In this way, culture becomes a driving force that overcomes challenges, ambiguity, and lack of structure—because people act with shared understanding and purpose.

This directly reflects the principle of "always reinforce the positive." Instead of focusing on what went wrong, leaders should continuously spotlight what went right, creating a self-sustaining culture built on trust, pride, and collective excellence.

Giving Feedback Across Cultures

A strong feedback culture is one of the clearest markers of a high-performing team. When done well, feedback becomes a form of respect. It signals care, trust, and a shared commitment to improvement. Drawing from Kim Scott's *Radical Candor*, the principle is simple: teams must both care personally and challenge directly. Neither is enough on its own.

The best teams make feedback normal, frequent, and safe. It is not reserved for annual reviews or moments of crisis. It happens in real time, between peers, across functions, across borders, and even across hierarchies. A great manager does not wait until something is broken to speak up. And a great team member does not hesitate to question a decision, raise a concern, or suggest a better way. Ideally, feedback is given in person. For international teams, that is not always possible, so many conversations will happen online. When that happens, we strongly recommend a short video call instead of a brief chat message, as tone and body language carry much of the message. Vanessa Van Edwards, author of *Captivate: The Science of Succeeding with People*, notes that much of what we communicate comes through nonverbal cues. Leaders should pay attention to facial expression, pacing, and posture to ensure that feedback feels supportive rather than confrontational.

In some countries, direct feedback is the norm; in others, it is softened, delayed, or avoided entirely to preserve harmony. Misunderstandings grow quickly when these styles collide. Once a company crosses borders, it becomes an international organization by default, and its team must reflect some shared norms, especially a growth mindset and openness to learning. Leaders must therefore set the tone: honest feedback is welcome, appreciated, and expected. Respect does not mean silence. Candor, when delivered with care, strengthens trust rather than weakening authority.

Practical habits help. Some leaders ask for feedback before giving it, which models humility and makes the conversation two-sided. Others use simple questions to open a dialogue, such as "What is one thing I could do better?" or "What did not work about how we handled this?" The goal is to make feedback something people look forward to, not something they brace for.

Across companies that get this right, candor is not an event. It is a rhythm. People ask questions openly in meetings. They point out risks early. They highlight blind spots without waiting to be invited. And leaders grow alongside their teams, not above them. When honesty becomes a shared language, teams operate with more confidence, clarity, and speed across borders.

In some cultures, on the other hand, honest feedback still always happens sideways rather than head-on, or sometimes doesn't happen at all. A person in our network recalled that during a business training with top executives on the topic of giving feedback to your superiors, an Asian executive shared her unique approach to giving difficult feedback. She would invite her boss out for dinner, get both of them drunk, deliver the full negative feedback, and then tell the boss the next morning "I don't know what I said yesterday; I was drunk, so don't worry about it." This method, she explained, softened the blow by delivering the difficult message, while still allowing both parties to save face by reassuring the boss that the feedback should not be taken seriously. While this is of course not an advisable way to ever handle feedback and tough conversations, when working cross-border it's important to keep in mind that this may be the default context that some of your team members are coming from.

Regional Autonomy and Performance Calibrations

Designing fair and motivating reward systems across countries requires sensitivity to both timing and calibration. In the Northern Hemisphere, bonuses are often distributed in December, while in Australia or New Zealand they usually come in July. In many Asian countries, however, the Lunar New Year marks the true midpoint of the year and serves as the key moment for bonuses. This period carries deep cultural and financial significance, as employees typically travel back to their hometowns and face additional expenses during the festivities. Recognizing such local traditions ensures that rewards are both timely and meaningful.

Equally crucial is the calibration of rewards across markets. A uniform approach—such as granting a flat 30% raise—can create stark disparities, especially if there are countries in which employees are paid less than in another country. For instance, a flat 30% raise may mean that a top performer in Indonesia with a low base salary might receive an extra $1,000 per month, while a lower-performing colleague at the Hong Kong headquarters gains $2,000 simply because of a higher base salary. Such inequities can erode trust and weaken the company's merit-based culture. Even when Stefano was working for one of the top global law firms worldwide, it was no mystery that associates in Italy were paid a fraction of their same-level colleagues in the United Kingdom, who in turn were paid peanuts compared to their peers in the United States.

Some start-ups illustrate this challenge vividly. Early employees often accept lower pay and heavier workloads in exchange for equity. When the company grows and begins hiring senior professionals at higher salaries, failing to recalibrate pay for long-serving staff creates frustration and disengagement. One notable fintech company, after raising a successful Series B round, lost several key early members because management did not proactively conduct a proper salary review—and when it finally did so, aggravated the situation by sloppily handling the recalibration internally rather than engaging an external professional expert.

Performance calibration is not about inflation adjustments (which is discussed in more detail later in this chapter); it is about ensuring fairness in how effort and impact are recognized across regions. It can be a great opportunity to fairly reward the team and consolidate its morale. Without it, even top global firms risk losing talent, as professionals "vote with their feet" and leave for environments that value them properly.

> ## *Key Takeaways*
>
> - **Presence is not symbolic; it is operational.** In-person time gives leaders the only accurate read on morale, alignment, and momentum across countries.
>
> - **Context creates autonomy.** Town halls and transparent communication empower teams to act independently while staying aligned.
>
> - **Rhythm beats control.** Daily stand-ups and smart async communication keep distributed teams moving together without adding long-meeting fatigue.
>
> - **Reinforce the positive.** Spotlighting great behavior shapes culture faster and more effectively than correcting every mistake.
>
> - **Fairness must be localized.** Reward systems require sensitivity to cultural timing and regional calibration, or they unintentionally damage trust.

Promoting the Company's Culture Across Different Countries

When we talk about a company's culture, we are talking about everything that brings people together to think and act in alignment with the company's goals and values. This includes norms, practices, and standards—some of which may be formally put in writing, and some just widely understood and mutually reinforced. And it includes the *spirit* of the company—the prevailing vibe and the shared attitudes that animate people (or in negative cases, drag them down) as they go about their work.

In a company where the people themselves come from different national or ethnic cultures, each with its own characteristics, the leader's task is to honor those while also bringing everyone around to living in accord with the company's culture. That is not always easy, but it's doable.

There Is No Single Right Way

One of the greatest challenges in leading across cultures is recognizing that there is no single "right" way of doing things. Most of us grow up believing that the norms of our own country—how they speak, express opinions, or make decisions—are the natural way to live and work. These beliefs shape how they interpret others and how they judge behavior.

It took Vinnie years of living and working abroad to unlearn that mindset. Over time, he came to understand that what feels natural to one person may feel foreign to another, and neither is wrong. There isn't a universal standard for how business should be done—only different approaches shaped by history, values, and environment. Success across borders begins with curiosity: the willingness to observe, learn, and adapt. It means paying attention to how people express disagreement, how they give feedback, or how they build trust. What works in one culture may backfire in another.

Vinnie often reflects that being unique is valuable, but leadership across borders means recognizing that—when it comes to culture—there are no absolute truths. His way is not "right" and another's "wrong." There are many ways to achieve a goal, and understanding that early helps leaders resonate more deeply across cultures.

"Culture Eats Process for Breakfast"

Every individual brings their own distinct traits and perspectives to a team, and this can sometimes create friction. Yet, when people with diverse backgrounds and personalities work closely together, these differences gradually smooth out. Over time, collaboration helps refine each person's approach and fosters mutual understanding.

At the heart of this process is genuine care. When leaders truly care about their team members—not only as professionals but as individuals—they build trust and loyalty. True care means asking questions that go beyond tasks: how someone is coping with a move, what their family needs, or what motivates them. These small acts of curiosity create psychological safety, especially in cross-cultural teams. When an employee decides to leave, taking the time to explore the reasons—and even supporting that decision when it's right for them—reinforces trust among those who stay. The organization signals that integrity matters more than convenience.

Vinnie and Stefano have both seen this dynamic repeatedly. In one case, a team member's open discussion about leaving prompted a conversation that revealed deeper misalignment among management versus the person. Instead of a quiet resignation, the process became a mutual realignment.

This mindset naturally encourages empathy across all levels. When senior members model care and attentiveness, junior members mirror the same behavior. Respect and kindness become embedded in daily interactions, forming a cycle of positive reinforcement that spreads throughout the organization, all the way to the last intern.

However, cross-cultural teams often face misunderstandings— especially where direct feedback or disagreement is culturally avoided. To counter this, leaders must actively create space for open conversation. They should invite different viewpoints, ask for opposing perspectives, and remind everyone that raising issues early prevents bigger problems later. A culture of respectful candor reduces the gap between intention and perception.

Ultimately, effective leadership goes beyond enforcing processes.

Processes bring structure, but culture sustains trust. When culture is rooted in empathy, respect, and accountability, it becomes a stronger unifier than any rule, system, or manual. As the saying goes, "Culture eats process for breakfast." By hiring people who embody shared values and by modeling care through daily actions, leaders build organizations that thrive across borders despite distance or differences.

Culture Starts with the Leaders

A company's culture doesn't emerge by accident—it starts with its leaders. Whether they are founders or executives, their behavior, values, and ways of treating people set the tone for everything that follows. If leaders are open, transparent, listen actively rather than simply instruct, and take time to coach and develop their teams, they will naturally attract and hire people who reflect those same traits. Over time, that pattern shapes the DNA of the organization.

For start-ups, this influence is especially powerful. Vinnie has seen companies that went public, such as Yelp, whose culture at listing still reflected the habits and energy of their founders nearly a decade earlier, when they were just two people working from a shared office. The tone those early leaders set—how they handled disagreement, celebrated wins, and built out a team—often becomes the unwritten code that endures through scale, funding rounds, and global expansion.

The leader's energy—whether collaborative or competitive—becomes the invisible code that everyone else follows. People pay more attention to what leaders tolerate than to what they say.

Over the years, Vinnie has learned how to identify and invest into companies that have the potential to go international. When assessing companies for investment, Vinnie has asked questions such as: Where have you traveled? What have you learned about other places, and about yourself? How would you build a team in a new country? What models from other regions do you admire, and why? These questions reveal whether someone can think beyond their home market and lead with openness.

Vinnie will also ask questions about how people build their own teams. A founder or executive who hires only those who look and think like them often struggles to scale internationally. By contrast, those who value diverse perspectives tend to naturally create global organizations—because inclusion starts in the first few hires, not after expansion begins.

Vinnie once spoke with a former intern who had just started her first job after college. She told him how much she missed the collaborative culture she had experienced at his firm. Her new company, still led by its founders, had a far more competitive atmosphere, particularly within the investment team. Curious and a little frustrated, she asked what she could do to make it more collaborative.

Vinnie's answer was simple: she probably couldn't, because culture comes from the top. If the leadership values competition over collaboration, the company will be built around that energy. Founders hire people who remind them of themselves—people they click with, people who reinforce their worldview. Even when teams are diverse, there's usually some shared quality that connects everyone to the founders' way of thinking.

That doesn't mean one approach is better than another. Some of the world's most successful companies, such as Apple and Uber, have thrived in highly competitive, high-performance cultures, while others succeed by fostering deep collaboration and openness. The key is alignment—knowing the kind of environment you want to be part of and ensuring it matches your own values and energy.

The Importance of the Company's Values

A key pillar for cultivating and sustaining a shared company culture across borders lies in clearly defining the organization's values. These values act as a universal compass—guiding principles that every employee, regardless of country or background, must follow. They set the tone for how people think, act, and make decisions within the company.

Values are especially critical when teams are distributed. In a global organization, leaders cannot be present everywhere at once. Values become the "operating system" that ensures consistency when no one is watching; they guide how people respond under pressure, how they treat one another, and how they make trade-offs when priorities compete.

The challenge is to make sure values are not just printed on posters but practiced every day. One way is to weave them into hiring during interviews. This helps identify alignment before someone joins the team. Another way is to bring values into performance reviews— asking employees to rate themselves against key behaviors that reflect the company's values. When done consistently, these touchpoints remind everyone that values are not abstract ideals but measurable expectations.

Here is an example of company values from Microsoft[2]:

Our corporate values

Our values align to our mission, support our culture, and serve as a declaration of how we treat each other, our customers, and our partners.

Respect

We recognize that the thoughts, feelings, and backgrounds of others are as important as our own.

Integrity

> *We are honest, ethical, and trustworthy.*

Accountability

> *We accept full responsibility for our decisions, actions, and results.*

It is essential that these values are not only written down but also consistently reinforced. Everyone, starting from the leaders, must abide by them. Leadership by example is crucial, even the highest-ranking executives should be open to being called out if they fail to live up to the company's principles. This sense of equality builds trust and accountability.

Vinnie recalls several instances where junior team members openly challenged leadership during meetings, not out of defiance but out of shared ownership in protecting the culture. These moments, while uncomfortable, are exactly what make values credible rather than performative.

A powerful example of this came during a company town hall. A team from the Gulf region shared candid feedback about a regional workshop they had attended in Asia—what hadn't worked for them and where they saw gaps. For a team member from the Gulf to voice such frank feedback publicly was itself counterintuitive, given how communication in that region often emphasizes respect and diplomacy. Speaking up so directly, and doing so live in front of the entire company, would typically be unthinkable across these two cultures. Yet instead of defensiveness, the Asia team welcomed the critique, and leadership praised the honesty. The exchange became a shared moment of growth and respect, reinforcing that honest feedback is not a risk but an expectation.

When values are lived in this way—when openness and respect coexist—they move from being words on a wall to becoming the company's true operating system.

To ensure these values truly permeate daily operations, they must be brought to life through concrete examples. Leaders should regularly highlight employees who embody them, illustrating what "aiming for excellence," "delivering results," or "defaulting to action" looked like in practice this past week or this past month. As highlighted earlier in this chapter, positive reinforcement is far more powerful than criticism. Praising one employee for acting according to company values leaves a lasting impression that motivates others to follow suit.

It is equally important to provide clarity and context for these values, especially in a multicultural environment where interpretations may differ. For instance, "aim for excellence" might, in some highly competitive cultures, be misconstrued as stepping over colleagues to get ahead. The leadership must therefore show, through consistent examples and discussions, that excellence means lifting the whole team, not competing internally. Similarly, values such as "speak your mind" may clash with cultural norms in regions where saying "no" is considered impolite. In these cases, leaders must explicitly encourage open dialogue and show appreciation when employees voice differing opinions—even when those opinions challenge authority.

Marek Kiisa, cofounder and managing partner at NordicNinja VC, shared a great example of this. He had envisioned a company value of "brutal honesty" among the partners in his fund. Then the day came when one of his junior Japanese partners challenged Marek explicitly and publicly about having missed a deadline. The moment tested the company culture: for a Japanese partner, openly correcting a senior is almost taboo. But Marek stayed true to the company's culture, took responsibility, and apologized. Instead of breaking trust, the moment cemented it. Both sides proved that directness could coexist with respect, and the company's values were truly upheld and not just there merely for show. They all learned that "Honesty feels rude until it builds trust."

Over time, this practice builds confidence across cultures. When team members see that speaking up is respected and rewarded, they begin to internalize these values as part of how the organization operates. Reinforcing such behavior in daily meetings, town halls, and one-on-one interactions ensures that values are not abstract slogans, but living, breathing principles that shape the company's collective identity.

Identify Champions: Reinforcing Culture with Examples

Another effective way to promote company culture is by consistently identifying and recognizing champions within the team—those who embody the organization's values in their daily actions. A leader's role is not to draw attention to themselves but to highlight others who demonstrate excellence.

When a team member closes an important deal or successfully solves a customer problem, showcasing a specific company's value, celebrate their accomplishment publicly. Share it with the rest of the team and explain why it stands out—because it shows empathy, grit, or commitment to service. This form of recognition leaves a stronger impression than any bonus or quiet compliment. Others will naturally aspire to earn similar acknowledgment, creating a cycle of positive reinforcement.

Vinnie has seen this dynamic across his own teams at Golden Gate Ventures. Whether it's a partner leading a start-up ecosystem event, an associate delivering a diligence report under time pressure, or a team member taking initiative to improve a process with measurable results, those moments are celebrated in company-wide town halls joined across all countries. The celebrations are diverse—from recognizing financial performance and competitive deal wins to applauding teammates who cover extra work when a colleague is on extended leave, or those who model work-life balance while hitting tough deadlines. Even personal milestones are acknowledged, reinforcing that success in the firm goes beyond numbers.

Each town hall features the person's photo and a short story of what they did and why it mattered. When possible, the recognition ties back explicitly to the firm's values. The same stories are shared again in a monthly internal newsletter, keeping a rhythm of positive reinforcement alive between meetings. Across borders, the tone stays consistent: public praise is universally appreciated, and team members are encouraged to say "thank you" rather than deflect recognition. Over time, these shared celebrations have become part of the firm's collective memory—a living reminder of what the culture looks like in action.

As a leader, avoid positioning yourself as the sole example to follow. People are perceptive; they will notice both your strengths and your flaws. Instead, point to the "superpowers" of different team members—the customer focus of one team member, the professionalism of another, the reliability of someone else. By doing this, you promote a culture built on shared excellence rather than hierarchy.

Your responsibility as leader is to keep your eyes open, recognize these champions, and celebrate them at every occasion. This approach strengthens the team far more than self-praise ever could. Leadership is not about being the best at everything—it's about empowering others to excel. The ultimate goal of a good leader is to make themselves unnecessary, to build a team that continues to thrive independently.

This principle becomes even more important in cross-border teams, where recognition often gets lost across time zones and cultural styles. In some markets, people hesitate to self-promote or publicly highlight success. In others, public acknowledgment carries enormous motivational weight. Good leaders adapt the format—sometimes a company-wide shout-out, sometimes a private thank-you—but the intent remains the same: to make people feel seen.

Great leaders don't stand in front and say, "Follow me." They say, "I've got your back." They build teams so capable that the direction becomes obvious. If you can't see people outpacing you in nearly every domain, you're building followers, not leaders.

Key Takeaways

- **There is no single "right way" to work.** Effective cross-cultural leadership begins with curiosity, the humility to unlearn your own defaults, and the willingness to adapt to others' norms.

- **Culture beats process every time.** Empathy, trust, and genuine care create alignment far more powerfully than manuals or rigid systems.

- **Leaders set the cultural temperature.** A company becomes a reflection of its founders and executives, so their habits and energy shape the organization across borders.

- **Values must be lived, not laminated.** Shared principles matter only when modeled daily, reinforced through examples, and applied consistently even when uncomfortable.

- **Recognition is your strongest cultural tool.** Highlighting champions across countries builds unity, teaches values through example, and creates a self-reinforcing cycle of excellence.

Local Brand, Global Identity

As companies expand across borders, their brand becomes more than a logo or tagline—it's the living expression of their culture, values, and vision in every market they enter. A brand should adapt its expression, but not its essence: *same values, different accent.*

For Golden Gate Ventures, maintaining a global identity while resonating locally is a constant balancing act. The firm's brand reflects the same values everywhere—founder-friendly, ecosystem-driven, willing to take bold risks, and guided by trust and conviction rather than imitation—but the *accent* changes by market.

In the Gulf, that accent emphasizes legacy, trust, and nation-building—themes that deeply resonate across the region's investor and founder communities. Relationships there develop through time and shared vision, not just data or performance metrics. Investors in Riyadh, for instance, often value one-on-one relationship-building and discretion over public visibility. The presentation style is more relational and vision-oriented, focusing on how a partnership contributes to long-term growth and national transformation. Even the visual language adapts: the GCC team might highlight regional partnerships, use Arabic-language materials, or reference family-business ties that signal respect for local tradition and identity.

In San Francisco, by contrast, the same brand voice takes on a sharper, more data-driven tone. There, credibility is built through insight, results, and clear articulation of competitive advantage of the firm's global network. The presentation style is analytical and fast-paced, but the underlying message remains the same: empower founders, take smart risks, and help ecosystems grow.

The goal is not to localize for the sake of difference, but to earn local understanding. That means being physically present, hiring local expertise early, and showing humility—even in small gestures, like

Vinnie being seen on his motorbike to do the kids' school run in Ho Chi Minh City. These actions demonstrate belonging. They communicate that global doesn't mean distant.

Across markets, Golden Gate Ventures keeps its brand consistent in look and tone, while allowing local teams to express it through stories and relationships that resonate with their audiences. Whether in Singapore, Riyadh, or San Francisco, the identity is the same—a global ambition rooted in local trust. The brand becomes the bridge between those two worlds.

Christian Jølck—founder and managing partner of Denmark-based ClimateTech Venture Fund 2150—emphasized that one of the most overlooked factors in global expansion is bringing to the target country people who carry the company's culture. Start-ups often rely on hiring a strong local leader when entering a new market, but culture and trust, not just local expertise, are what allow a team to scale quickly. The companies that succeed typically pair local hires with someone from the core organization who relocates for the first one to two years, to bridge expectations and transmit how the company works. This person does not need to be senior, Christian noted, but must deeply understand the culture. He illustrated this with an energy and construction-technology company originally based in Asia. After scaling in Hong Kong and Singapore, the company's largest opportunities were actually in Europe and the United States, which led the COO to relocate first to Europe, spending a couple of years in the region to lay the right foundation for expansion.

This model becomes even more crucial for hard-tech companies, where execution cannot be done remotely. Jølck described another case: a US biotechnology company with American IP but a first-of-its-kind factory built in Europe, where demand was stronger. The distance between where the team sat and where the work happened nearly exhausted the organization, and the company scaled only after redistributing people across continents and replacing those who could not manage the time-zone strain. As Christian noted, unlike software companies—for which global growth can often happen from a single location—hardware technology companies absolutely require people on the ground. Hardware born in one region may commercialize first in another, creating operational challenges that only a strong and portable company culture can support.

Direct Reporting Across Different Countries

When your direct reports live abroad—or when your boss does—some considerations come up that otherwise might not. Let's look at how to handle them.

Managing Direct Reports Living Abroad: Constantly Take the "Temperature" of Your Team, Especially If They Are Working Remotely

There's an Italian saying that goes, "Lontano dagli occhi, lontano dal cuore"/"What is away from your eyes is away from your heart." It captures perfectly the challenge of leading remote teams. When people are far from sight, how do you keep them top of mind?

The answer is simple but not easy: constant engagement and presence. Structured check-ins, weekly calls, and monthly town halls help, but real connection also comes from the unstructured moments—a quick message after a tough meeting, a personal note when someone does something well, or a small gesture that shows you noticed. Vinnie often sends short Slack notes or memes to team members when he sees something worth celebrating or when he senses someone's energy has shifted. While two different companies, both Vinnie's and Stefano's have separately evolved a wall of printed memes—a lighthearted reminder that connection doesn't always have to be formal to be meaningful.

Still, nothing replaces physical presence. When Stefano launched a new team in Indonesia during the COVID pandemic, travel restrictions kept him apart from his team for more than a year. The distance began to erode cohesion. When the borders finally reopened, Stefano was the first person in the company to fly in, spending weeks on the ground meeting everyone face-to-face. The difference was immediate—energy returned, alignment grew, and soon the team began expanding on its own. They started referring talented friends, mentoring newcomers, and naturally filtering those who didn't fit. Connection, once reestablished, became contagious.

When physical presence isn't possible, emotional presence becomes even more important. Both leaders emphasize the value of "human thermometers"—team members naturally attuned to mood and morale in group dynamics. As Vinnie describes it, "Without them, it's like driving a car with no speedometer." These people can sense when tension is rising or motivation is fading. For example, one legal manager Stefano worked with could sense when a team member was about to quit months in advance. She could understand the deep reasons behind that future move, give a heads-up to the management, and help address its causes. Her insights gave them time to act—to listen, support, or prepare—long before any resignation email arrived. Great leaders recognize this as a skill, not a coincidence, and ask the team member to lean into it—asking for their read on the group's morale and empowering them to speak up early.

In another team in East Asia, a member of the HR team had become the unofficial emotional anchor for the entire local team. She had a unique cultural touch—as a hobby, she enjoyed reading tarot cards to her colleagues during lunch breaks. The country manager never believed in tarots but realized this wasn't about the cards; it was about connection. Through those moments, the tarot reader was able to understand her colleagues deeply—their struggles, hopes, and distractions. She never betrayed their confidence, but she could give a very useful heads-up to the country manager, "Keep an eye on this person—he needs support right now."

Vinnie also makes a point to connect with team members he doesn't directly manage whenever he visits another city. A quick one-on-one coffee, casual questions about how things are going, or either a cab-ride or short walk after a meeting often reveal more than a dozen emails could. These moments are trust accelerators—ways to realign, listen, and understand what's truly happening on the ground.

Leadership isn't just about performance reviews or KPIs. It's about proximity—emotional and physical. Whether through structured check-ins or spontaneous human gestures, the closer they stay to their people, the stronger and more resilient their teams become.

Navigating a Boss Who Lives in a Different Country

When a manager is based in another country, it naturally provides team members with a greater degree of autonomy. Without constant supervision, individuals have more freedom to organize their work and make decisions. However, this independence also comes with increased responsibility.

Working with a remote manager requires deliberate effort to remain visible and engaged. Regular communication is essential—through daily updates, weekly check-ins, and even occasional informal conversations. These interactions should not only cover progress but also convey a complete picture of the situation on the ground, including challenges, achievements, and emerging opportunities.

Structure is what sustains trust at a distance. Recurring calls on the calendar, group chats for informal moments, and deliberate in-person visits replace the spontaneity that proximity once provided. Consistent rhythms matter more than frequency—they create reliability, predictability, and a sense of shared momentum even across continents.

Because opportunities to communicate are limited, preparation becomes essential. Each discussion should be well planned, with clear objectives, defined topics, and supporting data ready in advance. The goal is to make every exchange count—to bring clarity, direction, and confidence. Being able to explain and stand behind each decision demonstrates professionalism and builds trust.

Trust is not given by default—it must be earned over time. It develops through consistent reliability, transparency, and integrity. Once established, this trust reduces the need for constant justification, allowing smoother collaboration and faster decision-making, regardless of your physical proximity.

Clarity is the foundation of trust. Ambiguity is the enemy of remote collaboration—when expectations are vague, assumptions multiply, and alignment erodes. Clear written goals, visible priorities, and shared accountability allow people to operate independently while still feeling fully supported.

Communication styles, of course, vary across regions. In San Francisco, directness to a superior is expected; in Singapore, feedback tends to be measured; in Tokyo or Riyadh, employees rarely challenge their managers openly. When working with a boss across borders, it is essential to make sure communication is crystal clear by documenting key decisions in writing and using AI meeting summaries to keep everyone aligned regardless of time zone or language.

If reporting to a remote boss, don't wait to be asked—overcommunicate. Share updates instead of questions. Provide context about progress, including mistakes with lessons learned,

and what's happening locally, from market shifts to team morale.
Ask about objectives, how success is measured, and what projects you
can contribute to or learn from. Volunteer for new challenges and
signal curiosity. Consistent communication and initiative build
visibility—and, over time, trust.

Some Practical Tips

Here is some guidance on a few issues that are well worth
attending to.

Salary Calibrations Across Different Countries

Salary calibration across countries is never as simple as it looks. There
are written rules—the ones you'll find in policy books and labor
codes—and then there are the unwritten ones, shaped by culture,
reality, and empathy.

We learned this the hard way, managing cross-border teams
spread across multiple countries. Stefano once saw this go wrong
when an HR team tried to benchmark the average cost of living
between two countries: Singapore, which is a 5 million people
modern city-state, and Vietnam, which is a 100 million people
country, with a large rural population. The HR team forgot to
consider that our talented Vietnamese software developers did not live
in the rural countryside of Vietnam but in Ho Chi Minh City—a
13 million people city with a high cost of living, where we were
competing for talent with Google or Apple. The result was
disengagement and attrition—all because the formula missed the
lived reality.

A similar thing happened on a different occasion, when
headquarters tried to adjust all salaries for inflation. The HR team
initially took as reference the inflation rate publicly declared by each

country where our employees were based and adjusted salaries accordingly country by country. They did not consider, however, that certain emerging countries tend to heavily under-declare the inflation rates affecting their countries so that the real inflation rate affecting our teams on the ground was up to 3× higher than the "official" one. It was necessary for the leadership team on the ground to jump in and address the issue properly and fairly.

The Importance of Team Off-Sites

In-person off-sites aren't a luxury—they're essential for keeping global teams connected. While shared values and communication tools help maintain cohesion, it's real-world interactions that forge genuine trust. When people who have only seen each other through screens finally meet, misunderstandings fade, collaboration deepens, and energy returns to the team. The best off-sites strike the right balance between bonding and business. Focus only on fun, and you lose momentum; focus only on work, and you miss the magic of connection. When laughter, shared stress, and strategic discussion happen in the same space, alignment becomes effortless.

One of the most powerful team builders is a shared challenge. It's the same reason friendships from freshman year of university often last a lifetime—the bond that forms when people go through pressure together. A team climbing ropes in a forest canopy, racing high-speed go-karts, or simply navigating a packed three-day off-site will leave with the same feeling: we've been through something together. That sense of shared experience can't be replicated on Zoom.

At Golden Gate Ventures, annual off-sites have become an anchor for the firm's culture. Whether it's a team dinner, a collaborative workshop, or the flagship three-day gathering around the Singapore

Grand Prix, these events remind everyone that culture isn't built through slogans or slides—it's built through experiences that people remember and retell.

Managing Time Zones Fairly

In a world where teams are spread across continents, technology gives the illusion of togetherness. Zoom and Slack make it possible for everyone to appear in the same virtual room—yet real connection requires more than just logging in.

One of the biggest challenges in global teams is the invisible hierarchy created by time zones. Too often, one office—usually far from headquarters—becomes the one staying up late or waking up before dawn for every meeting. Over time, this erodes morale and sends an unspoken message about who matters most.

The solution doesn't have to be complex. The most effective leaders make small, thoughtful adjustments: rotating meeting times so no team consistently bears the burden. One week, the US team stays late; the following week, the Asian team starts early. This small act of balance reinforces that every member of the company, regardless of geography, stands on equal ground.

Inclusion also grows through moments of shared humanity. During global town halls, leaders highlight local holidays, birthdays, or small cultural traditions from different offices. Even symbolic gestures—like wearing the same color, sharing regional updates, or spotlighting a local win—transform a virtual meeting into a space of connection and pride.

At the individual level, discipline matters just as much as structure. Managing time zones successfully requires clear personal boundaries and communication habits. Vinnie, for instance, turns off all mobile notifications—both at work and at home—and uses apps that mute visual alerts during evenings and weekends when spending time with family. He tries to model a healthy work-life balance for others to follow.

Respecting "business time" also means understanding that weekends and workweeks differ across regions. In the Gulf, for example, the weekend falls on Friday and Saturday, while in much of the rest of the world it's Saturday and Sunday. Recognizing these differences—and avoiding meetings or deadlines that overlap with someone else's weekend—demonstrates both cultural awareness and respect.

Ultimately, maintaining culture across time zones isn't about perfect scheduling or polished presentations. It's about showing, through consistent actions, that every person—no matter where they are—is part of one unified team.

How to Handle Holidays Across Different Countries

Managing holidays across countries goes far beyond logistics—it's about understanding rhythm, respect, and humanity.

Every country has its own cadence. In Western cultures, work slows around Christmas; in Asia, it's during the Lunar New Year. In Muslim-majority countries, Ramadan brings a different kind of slowdown—not because people stop working, but because they're fasting, reflecting, and re-centering. Productivity may dip, but the spirit of the team strengthens. A company that understands this doesn't just tolerate differences—it grows through them.

In China and in Vietnam, the Lunar New Year can bring business to a near standstill for two or three weeks. Even before the official break, teams are preparing client gifts and tokens of appreciation—Christmas cards, Lunar New Year cakes, or Ramadan care packages that reinforce relationships and respect. At the same time, people are planning their journeys home, traveling to see family, and fulfilling long-standing traditions. During that time, revenue might drop significantly, and that's normal. Planning around it—rather than resisting it—shows respect for local culture and foresight in business.

There are also more subtle observances. In some countries, entire months are dedicated to honoring the dead. Superstitions may halt local players from entering into new contracts or partnerships during this period. No spreadsheet can change that—but awareness can help you plan around it.

Fairness matters too. Sometimes one office must lean in while another steps back. When a team in one region takes extended time off, another may step in to cover critical work. These moments should be exceptions, not the rule—and the effort should always be recognized. Publicly appreciating those who help during peak holiday periods reinforces that teamwork goes both ways.

Respecting rest must come from the top. Leaders who encourage their teams to unplug—and model it themselves—create stronger, more resilient organizations. At Golden Gate Ventures, Vinnie regularly reminds direct reports to go fully offline during breaks so they can return sharper and more energized. Failing to rest isn't just bad for the individual; it also signals poor delegation, depriving others of the chance to grow by taking on new responsibilities.

Communication is the simplest tool for preventing friction. When deadlines or major projects are shared early, everyone has the chance to flag conflicts with holidays or other priorities. Clear planning avoids unnecessary stress and helps local teams take ownership of their own rhythm.

Ultimately, it's not about enforcing uniformity—it's about building a culture where people understand, respect, and support each other through their differences. That empathy is what truly keeps a global team together.

Key Takeaways

- **Same values, different accent.** A global brand must stay consistent at its core while adapting its expression to earn local trust, respect, and relevance.

- **Presence creates connection.** Whether managing abroad or leading remote teams, physical or emotional presence matters more than process for building cohesion and loyalty.

- **Clarity and communication sustain remote leadership.** Overcommunicating context, documenting decisions, and keeping predictable rhythms maintain trust and alignment across borders.

- **Fairness must match lived reality.** Calibration of salaries, workloads, time zones, and holiday rhythms requires cultural awareness and on-the-ground empathy, not formulas.

- **Shared experiences build culture.** Off-sites, in-person gatherings, and even small gestures of recognition strengthen global teams more than any policy or handbook.

13 The Convergence of Business and Society

Explore and Work Where the Realms Meet

The lines between business and society have blurred. Companies are no longer seen as operating in a separate commercial sphere, bound only by commercial rules. Their decisions influence the well-being of communities, governments, and global systems, and those systems influence business in return. Whether you intend it or not, entering international markets puts you in the middle of this overlap.

That is why cultural awareness, social awareness, and an understanding of local needs matter. You are not selling into an abstract "market." You are selling to, and working with, people who live within specific social, cultural, and environmental realities. When companies pay attention to those realities, they not only create more value, they unlock new forms of impact that society now expects from global businesses.

Currently the realms of business and society are intersecting more than ever. For example, societies everywhere now see climate change and pollution as major concerns. Businesses are part of the problem; they're expected to be part of the solution, and some businesses are very actively providing solutions. They've created the renewable energy and cleantech industries—and are profiting from them—which societies are happy to see and support, because those industries are starting to make a big dent in the problem.

What we're seeing in this one area of concern, our natural environment, is a great convergence. It is a win-win converge of the interests and activities of business and society, on a global scale. And it's far from the only area of concern in which convergences are either in progress or sorely needed.

The key areas, the most widespread and pressing areas of concern, can be identified by turning to the United Nations. The UN has published and promoted a list of Sustainable Development Goals (SDGs) that ought to be met worldwide, if we want to have the kind of world in the future that human beings—indeed, all beings—deserve. The goals start with "No Poverty," "Zero Hunger," and proceed from there. Blue-sky as they may sound, the SDGs identify great needs and set the solution bar high. Member nations of the UN have signed on to the SDGs. We suggest that businesses pick goals that are relevant to them and go after them in international markets of their choice.

Why, from a business perspective, is it useful to look at the SDGs as a framework? Because they represent a broad consensus, among smart observers from many countries, that these are the world's equivalent of "grand challenges" in science and tech. They are problem definitions. And for a business, a problem is an opportunity. If you can find a solution and provide it at a price that people will pay, which also returns a profit, you will gain. And the bigger the problem, the bigger the opportunity. By focusing on the SDGs, you may stand to gain a lot.

Let's explore a few goals. For each we will frame the state of the problem as it currently exists, while seeing what businesses are doing and *could* be doing in this area.

Quality Education

SDG 4: "Ensure inclusive and equitable quality education and promote lifelong learning opportunities for all."

In nearly all countries, formal education is managed mainly by governments and nonprofits. But business has played a larger role than most people realize, for a long time. That role is now growing, while at the same time, the concept of education is expanding well beyond the traditional systems of elementary through high schools, universities, and other certificate-granting schools. (When you browse the Internet, are you being "educated"? Sometimes but not always? Or maybe sometimes in a "quality" way and sometimes not?)

There are plenty of hard challenges in education, too. Colleges and universities in the United States are generally of good quality, but they're outlandishly expensive for students.[1] Meanwhile, in the world's poorest countries, schools from the elementary grades on up are barely adequate, and many children are lucky if they can attend for even a few years. (Often the kids are pulled out to help support the family, which limits how long they can stay in school.)

This makes "quality education" a very complex goal. So, ratchet back and let's review what businesses already do. In many countries they create the textbooks and learning materials used in government-run schools. Private businesses also *operate* for-profit schools, including for-profit universities in a number of countries. Business relations with universities run deep: companies help to fund research at universities, in return for certain designated rights to use research results; they endow faculty chairs; they recruit graduating students as talent for their teams, and more. Businesses also provide alternative forms of learning—which range from edtech (education technology) programs online to test-prep services for students and more. Now to continue the deeper dive.

> Emerging economies often experience a growing middle class, and one area that ties directly into this trend is education. As more families have two working parents living in urban areas, away from extended family, there is increased demand for early childhood education services, such as learning-enhanced daycare and other foundational support. The shift is evident in countries like Indonesia and Vietnam, where investments in these areas are already being made.

An investor in an Indonesian edtech (education technology) start-up told us how the company is addressing the challenges faced by busy working parents with young children. The start-up introduced a tech-enabled educational daycare program, transcreated for local needs. In cities like Jakarta, where heavy daily traffic shapes people's routines, the company located care centers on the ground floors of large office buildings, making them convenient for parents with white-collar jobs. The edtech start-up also structured its scheduling and pricing to fit the needs of parents in Indonesia. Unlike in the United States, where people typically work 9-to-5 schedules five days per week, many Indonesian families may not need full-time childcare. Grandparents may often help, or one parent may not have a full-time job, so the start-up implemented a flexible pricing model. Whether a child attended for three days a week or five, the cost was adjusted accordingly. This locally tailored approach made the daycare both practical and economically viable.

Emerging markets tend to bring out another form of demand: rising aspirations. As a country moves up the development ladder, parents want their children to move up the socioeconomic ladder, ideally getting into a university and going on to a professional career.

The kids themselves pick up this desire as they grow. And in many cases, the country's public schools aren't yet geared to provide top-notch, university-prep education. A number of edtech start-ups in emerging markets have moved to fill the gap by offering mobile-learning apps that supplement classroom teaching. Young people across the region could use these apps to learn Singapore math, improve their English-language skills, or learn more about nearly anything.

One challenge is that mobile learning may not be commercially profitable on its own. However, it can serve as an entry point for other services. Mobile learning platforms frequently offer additional services like offline tutoring or upskilling programs targeted at college prep. This expands their commercial potential while helping customers meet their education goals.

When shifting focus to more mature markets, the landscape changes. For example, offline tutoring centers, which are often owned by private equity firms, have been successful in more developed economies. Also, international test-prep services and programs aimed at helping students and parents navigate the application process for international universities are significant business opportunities globally. These services align with the goal of providing quality education while also serving as commercially viable models.

As for adult education, Vinnie's VC firm has invested in a company in Indonesia that offers affordable upskilling services, supported by both government initiatives and large corporations like Indosat, a major telecom provider that funds these services for its workforce. This trend reflects a broader need for accessible education and skills training in emerging markets, benefiting both nations and companies providing such services.

When it comes to balancing the pursuit of profits with the need for measurable impact on education outcomes and skills development, the leadership's drive plays a significant role. The key question is whether the leadership is purely financially motivated or driven by purpose. In the education sector, we've seen both types. Some private equity firms view owning education centers similarly to owning other businesses, like restaurants, focusing primarily on financial returns. However, we've also met leaders who are deeply impact-driven, and that purpose shapes the company culture and the team they build around them.

In summary, quality education may often be perceived as a government need, but when viewed through a business lens, there are numerous emerging opportunities around the world that support this goal and are commercially lucrative.

Gender Equality

SDG 5: "Achieve gender equality and empower all women and girls."

What can businesses do to promote gender equality? We believe the best move, and one that pays real dividends, is to practice diversity within your company.

In our experience, gender diversity drives innovation and improves market understanding. Women and men bring different life perspectives to the table. Recruiting both for key teams, and having women in leadership roles, can lead to multiple benefits. Gender-diverse teams are able to generate a richer range of approaches to problem-solving and conflict resolution. Out in the market, women wield buying power, and women in companies can best understand their needs and preferences. Gender-diverse teams mirror the real world outside the company, where the genders coexist and co-decide. This should help avoid the risks of a business operating in a self-enclosed bubble. Last but not least, diverse companies lead by example, which can be an advantage in markets where inclusion is valued by customers, partners, or regulators.

The mindset of inclusivity becomes even more critical when expanding into new markets. One Golden Gate Ventures portfolio company sought a female director while expanding into Japan. Recognizing the lack of female representation in executive leadership compared to some other Asian countries, the company saw it as an opportunity to build out a more innovatively diverse team and ultimately tap into new growth avenues.

A similar approach can be seen with a consumer services start-up Vinnie sat on the board of, which initially focused much of its marketing on male consumers. Recognizing that women were also significant buyers, Vinnie pushed the management to hire a female chief marketing officer (CMO). With the previous male-dominated leadership, the company's messaging and promotional efforts had unintentionally missed a large portion of the market. By diversifying leadership, the company's marketing became more inclusive, speaking to a broader consumer base. This shift wasn't about prioritizing one audience over another but aligning the brand with inclusivity, helping the company connect with customers who had been overlooked. The result was significant business growth, as embracing gender diversity unlocked new opportunities and expanded the company's reach.

The concept of inclusivity goes beyond gender and extends to other forms of diversity. Many founders and leaders fall into the pattern of hiring people similar to themselves, often recruiting from familiar pipelines, whether that means their alma mater, former employers, or tight-knit professional networks. While this may lead to gender diversity, it can produce teams with a narrow cultural, social, and economic outlook. Such practices, though comfortable, limit the diversity of thought and experience. To build an international team that is truly inclusive, companies need to ensure representation across gender, ethnicity, culture, socioeconomic background, and other dimensions of diversity. This broader approach is essential for a company's international growth, as it enables teams to better understand and navigate global markets.

Building a diverse, inclusive culture starts from the top. At Golden Gate Ventures, promotions reflect performance. When Angela Toy became a partner and joined the firm's core global executive leadership team, it signaled that strong leadership and diverse perspectives belong at the center of decision making. GGV also reinforces this mindset with a fast-track program that helps gender-diverse teams reach the investment committee more quickly.

For company leaders aiming to promote inclusivity, it's important to build a culture where a broad range of backgrounds and experiences are recognized and valued. Stefano reinforces this mindset daily by highlighting contributions from team members who bring perspectives that are not yet well represented in the company. By recognizing contributions publicly, leadership sets the tone for how to embrace diversity. When employees see that contributions are acknowledged across a range of backgrounds and viewpoints, it reduces biases and reinforces the company culture.

Leaders must also actively maintain the company's culture, especially when addressing inappropriate behavior. If a colleague disrespects another team member, especially across gender lines, the leader must step in and address it immediately. Whether the issue is handled privately or publicly, this ensures that a culture of respect and inclusivity is upheld. And a decisive step-in shows that inclusivity is just as important as the company's financial goals.

By fostering an inclusive culture from the top down, integrating diversity into leadership decisions, and addressing issues as they arise, companies can create an environment where diversity is woven into the way the company operates. This not only strengthens the company's internal culture but also drives innovation, growth, and success across new markets.

Climate Action

SDG 13: "Take urgent action to combat climate change and its impacts by regulating emissions and promoting developments in renewable energy."

(Also related, SDG 7, Affordable and Clean Energy: "Ensure access to affordable, reliable, sustainable and modern energy for all.")

We briefly mentioned what's happening on this front earlier. Now let's dive deeper. Climate action has created new profit centers in sectors including renewable energy, electric mobility, battery storage, recycling, and waste management. These industries provide social benefits along with openings for profitable, self-sustaining businesses. In the past, such businesses were considered unprofitable without subsidies or philanthropic support. But they're now evolving into independent models that can thrive on their own.

To grasp one reason for this transformation, think of Sherlock Holmes, the famous English detective. Holmes had an extraordinary ability to identify things others couldn't see, simply because he *looked for them.* His focus on specific details mirrors how human ingenuity works. When we direct focus toward a specific problem, solutions emerge. The same principle applies to the climate crisis. As awareness of environmental challenges grows, brilliant minds are addressing the problems, and finding innovative solutions through deliberate focus and effort. This is not by chance, but a result of targeted action.

Technology has played a pivotal role in these efforts, too, making once-impossible solutions a reality. A historical example of this comes from thirteenth-century Florence. The city, already a powerhouse in banking and trade, set out to build a grand cathedral with the largest dome ever constructed. The project was so ambitious that the initial architects lacked the expertise to design a dome capable of holding up. But they trusted that future generations would develop a way to solve the problem. This faith in future innovation allowed them to proceed, even expanding other parts of the project. And their faith was rewarded when the final architect designed an ingenious self-supporting dome that still crowns the Florence Cathedral today. In modern times, industries like solar energy and battery storage have followed a similar trajectory. Early solar panels in the 1970s were inefficient and prohibitively expensive, but researchers kept working. Dozens of innovations since then have combined to cut the initial cost per watt by more than 99%. Rooftop solar and solar farms are now mainstream, with costs still decreasing while efficiency improves.

The rapid pace of technological progress in many industries in recent decades is closely linked to globalization. The advances of the past 25 years have been unparalleled, largely driven by global collaboration. Big multinational companies attract talent from all over the world, pooling expertise and ideas to fuel innovation. University research labs do the same, and start-up teams are increasingly international—and talent flows between all these places as people move around. This interconnectedness accelerates technological progress, enabling solutions to complex problems that were once out of reach. Today, industries such as solar energy are benefiting from this global exchange of ideas, transforming from expensive niche technologies into scalable solutions that are reshaping our world.

Barriers, while often viewed as obstacles, can also present major opportunities. Challenges such as dealing with complex regulations, or facing large competitors, are often mountains waiting to be climbed. Stefano emphasizes that problems, like barriers, are what bring people together to find solutions. That dynamic is evident in the way certain companies in the climate sector have thrived despite lacking capital at first. These companies began working without external financial support and, once progress was made, recognized the additional resources—such as capital—that could accelerate their efforts. Their willingness to start without knowing the solution mirrors the approach taken by the builders of the Florence Cathedral, who began constructing a massive dome, trusting that future generations would find a way to complete it.

Aside from all the progress that's being made, there are still market distortions caused by companies that create negative externalities such as pollution, without paying for the damage they cause. The vastness of the planet allows these companies to evade accountability, as environmental harm created in one region may go unnoticed by the affected parties. This highlights the need for accountability mechanisms to ensure that those responsible for environmental damage bear the costs. Just as a parent teaches a child to clean up their mess, companies must be held accountable for the mess they create.

The carbon market and other mechanisms, such as the European Carbon Border Adjustment Mechanism (CBAM), are steps in the right direction. These measures ensure that companies causing environmental harm are held accountable, making it clear that the costs of pollution should not be externalized onto vulnerable communities. Steps like these are vital for creating a fair and sustainable global economy.

Good Health and Well-Being

SDG 3—"Ensure healthy lives and promote well-being for all ages."

Health needs and resources to meet the needs vary immensely from highly developed nations to the least developed. We'll focus on emerging markets, where the opportunities for business to make a difference might be less widely known.

Access to healthcare in emerging markets is often limited by time, cost, and information barriers. The cost of living in these markets makes time a precious resource, and navigating the healthcare systems—especially public ones, which often rely on large government-funded hospitals—can be difficult. The hospitals tend to be located in city centers, far from where many people live, and visiting them can turn into an all-day event, a luxury that many can't afford. For those living paycheck to paycheck, taking a day off to seek medical care can be prohibitively expensive.

Telemedicine, in combination with pharmacies, holds potential for improving healthcare access. For instance, remote consultations could be paired with in-person verification from a pharmacist to prescribe meds. This approach ensures that patients receive proper care while avoiding unnecessary hospital trips.

And more advanced versions of the idea have already emerged. For example, in Indonesia, GGV invested in a company called Alodokter, which operates similarly to WebMD but with a richer, more interactive approach. Alodokter provides a platform where users can access reliable health information about various conditions. In addition, the platform links to full-time doctors who answer questions for free, allowing users to engage in conversations with medical professionals without the cost. If users have deeper questions, they can schedule consultations or telemedicine sessions with doctors. This service fills a critical gap by providing accessible healthcare information and consultation in a market where traditional healthcare might be difficult to access.

Another solution is on-the-spot clinical care. One example is a platform that has set up mini-clinics at work sites specifically for blue-collar workers. These clinics aren't just for emergencies; they cater to common ailments like colds or flu. Workers can get tested and rest without having to leave their workplace. This model of healthcare, similar to a family GP clinic, has worked well in Indonesia. GGV also invested in a similar model in Vietnam with FD Care, which operates family clinics catering to the emerging middle class. FD Care locates its clinics in dense residential communities, with the aim of making them close and convenient for large numbers of people. Also the care is focused on specific demographic groups, such as expectant mothers, parents with young children, and those caring for elderly family members. The company provides services such as transportation for elderly patients to and from clinics, which is included in the pricing for those within a certain region. The company's attention to the specific needs of these groups sets FD Care apart from typical local clinics in Vietnam. (For example, at one clinic site, a doctor's office was transformed into a large play area for young children, making the experience more comfortable for families.)

To ensure cohesive treatment and follow-up for patients, FD Care has strategic partnerships with leading hospitals, which include integrating and coordinating services. That's a key benefit in a country where the overall healthcare system is still fragmented across different layers of care. The whole picture adds up to a well-targeted approach.

There's a "hidden benefit" to working in emerging-market countries. While regulations can sometimes limit access to healthcare in many places, emerging markets often have a more flexible approach. For instance, during the COVID-19 pandemic, telemedicine was heavily regulated in more developed markets like the United States, where it was restricted to limited conditions. However, in Indonesia, the government embraced telemedicine as a way to address the country's healthcare needs, particularly in rural areas. The government even promoted services like Alodokter, encouraging citizens to use telemedicine for remote consultations. This more progressive stance in emerging markets allows for innovative healthcare solutions to emerge more quickly, addressing critical needs when traditional infrastructure is lacking.

There are also unique barriers to healthcare access that are related to the cultural and emotional challenges of certain medical conditions. For example, infertility treatments can be emotionally charged, and many individuals may feel uncomfortable going into a clinic. To address this, GGV invested in a company, Two Plus, which offers at-home self-insemination. The cost is much more affordable than a clinic—an important factor itself, for the majority of the world's population—and it allows couples to privately take charge of fertility without the public embarrassment that some may feel. This solution highlights how innovation can both help to broaden access and overcome the social stigma attached to certain conditions.

Altogether, these examples show that emerging markets, despite their challenges, provide fertile ground for innovative healthcare solutions, which often can be implemented and adopted faster than in more highly regulated, developed markets.

Key Takeaways

- **SDGs turn global problems into business blueprints.** They frame humanity's biggest challenges as clearly defined opportunities where solving real needs can unlock large, durable markets.

- **Purpose and profit reinforce each other.** Companies that genuinely tackle education, health, climate, or equality do not just "do good," they build stronger brands, deeper customer loyalty, and more resilient economics over time.

- **Emerging markets are fertile ground for SDG innovation.** Gaps in access to schooling, healthcare, finance, and inclusion are widest there, which means the upside for locally tuned, scalable solutions is often the greatest.

- **Diversity is a growth strategy, not a checkbox.** Teams and leadership that reflect gender and cultural diversity

> gain real advantages. They can see more angles, reach more customers, and avoid blind spots that leave markets and value on the table.
>
> - **Mission-driven companies attract outsize talent and energy.** When people believe their work moves the needle on climate, health, or opportunity, they work harder, stay longer, and bring in others who share that drive.
>
> - **Accountability mechanisms create new markets.** Tools like carbon pricing, progressive regulation, and impact data do not just punish bad actors, they reward innovators who design cleaner, fairer, more efficient business models.

The goals highlighted are the ones that resonated most in our work. The following is the complete list to help you reflect on which may be relevant to your business.

The UN Sustainable Development Goals

Goal 1: No poverty: "End poverty in all its forms everywhere."

Goal 2: Zero hunger: "End hunger, achieve food security, improved nutrition and promote sustainable agriculture."

Goal 3: Good health and well-being: "Ensure healthy lives and promote well-being for all ages."

Goal 4: Quality education: "Ensure inclusive and equitable quality education and promote lifelong learning opportunities for all."

Goal 5: Gender equality: "Achieve gender equality and empower all women and girls."

Goal 6: Clean water and sanitation: "Ensure availability and sustainable management of water and sanitation for all."

Goal 7: Affordable and clean energy: "Ensure access to affordable, reliable, sustainable and modern energy for all."

Goal 8: Decent work and economic growth: "Promote sustained, inclusive and sustainable economic growth, full and productive employment and decent work for all."

Goal 9: Industry, Innovation, Technology and Infrastructure: "Build resilient infrastructure, promote inclusive and sustainable industrialization, and foster innovation."

Goal 10: Reduced inequality: "Reduce inequality within and among countries."

Goal 11: Sustainable cities and communities: "Make cities and human settlements inclusive, safe, resilient, and sustainable."

Goal 12: Responsible consumption and production: "Ensure sustainable consumption and production patterns."

Goal 13: Climate action: "Take urgent action to combat climate change and its impacts by regulating emissions and promoting developments in renewable energy."

Goal 14: Life below water: "Conserve and sustainably use the oceans, seas and marine resources for sustainable development."

Goal 15: Life on land: "Protect, restore and promote sustainable use of terrestrial ecosystems, sustainably manage forests, combat desertification, and halt and reverse land degradation and halt biodiversity loss."

Goal 16: Peace, justice and strong institutions: "Promote peaceful and inclusive societies for sustainable development, provide access to justice for all and build effective, accountable and inclusive institutions at all levels."

Goal 17: Partnerships for the goals: "Strengthen the means of implementation and revitalize the global partnership for sustainable development."

14 Stories from the Frontlines

How the Playbook Works in the Real World

The lessons that matter most rarely appear in strategy decks. They surface in conversations with founders who navigated chaos, investors who watched patterns repeat across continents, and operators who built trust one misunderstanding at a time. This chapter distills those hidden truths.

Vision Beyond Borders Sets the Path Beyond Borders

Global success begins long before a company sets foot abroad—it begins with vision. Mario Scuderi of CPD Venture Capital emphasizes that the founders he's seen in Italy who broke through internationally were not only the most technically accomplished; they were the ones who paired deep expertise with an unapologetically global vision. He points to founders like Luca Rossettini of D-Orbit, who set out to build a *space logistics company* long before the category existed. (The company's tech systems deploy constellations of small satellites from a single rocket launch, making access to orbit faster and cheaper for clients who buy slots in a deployment.) D-Orbit has drawn funding from both global VCs and strategic corporates who saw its long-term potential in in-orbit services. Similarly, Claudio Padoacini of Energy Dome built a long-duration energy storage technology using CO_2 phase changes—an idea so contrarian and ambitious that it is now positioned at the center of global grid transition and AI-driven power demand. And with Cubbit, another Italian start-up, the founders reimagined cloud storage altogether, creating a distributed system that fragments and replicates data across centers as a more secure and energy-efficient alternative to hyperscalers.

None of these founders waited for Italy's ecosystem to mature. They operated from Italy while fundraising abroad, relying on vision, narrative, and technical clarity to convince international investors. As Mario puts it, "Global money follows global ambition."

This pattern is mirrored in Latin America, though the starting conditions could not have been more different. As Santiago Zavala of 500 Global explains, early LatAm founders weren't thinking globally because they couldn't. A decade ago, the region lacked nearly everything: venture capital, experienced operators, and even basic digital infrastructure. Founders tackled the most fundamental problems first—building payment rails, logistics networks, and the initial talent base. These companies were not just solving market needs; they were laying the foundation for an ecosystem.

That groundwork, Santiago notes, is what unlocked the shift happening today. The first wave of large-scale success stories, now with 1,000+ employees, has effectively become a training engine—producing operators who have managed country expansions, built cross-border teams, and learned to think bigger than their predecessors ever could. For the next generation, global ambition is no longer aspirational; it is expected. Or as Santiago frames it: "The first generation built the roads; the next one drives beyond them."

Across both ecosystems, the pattern is the same: global outcomes start with global intent. Ecosystems mature when founders lead with global vision, and infrastructure eventually follows that vision—not the other way around.

Where Limits Create Opportunities: The Geography of Global Ambition

In many ecosystems, going global is a strategy. In others, it's the only option. Across Central and Eastern Europe, the Baltics, and Israel, one pattern consistently emerges: when local limits close in, global horizons open up.

In Central and Eastern Europe, fragmentation itself becomes a teacher. As investor Maciej Małysz of Inovo.vc explains, founders grow up navigating a patchwork of 20+ small countries—each with its own language, currency, customer expectations, and regulatory quirks. The region may be compact, but culturally it feels like 20 different worlds stitched together.

In the Baltics, this creates clarity from day one. Markets like Lithuania or Estonia are simply too small to sustain a venture-scale company, so founders don't waste time building for a local niche. "No one is going to build a tech company for Lithuania," Małysz says. "If you want to build something global, you can't start by building for Lithuanians." With no domestic comfort zone available, global thinking isn't a stretch goal—it's survival.

Poland illustrates the opposite dynamic. Its midsize market is large enough to feel comfortable and safe, but small enough to limit a founder's vision. Founders can grow quickly by selling to local enterprises or relying on their own networks, but those customers rarely resemble global buyers. A Polish bank is not a proxy for a US enterprise. Choosing a "friend of a friend" as a first design partner often results in products built around local assumptions— habits that quietly anchor the company to a sizable but limited national market.

Meanwhile, the Baltics show how constraints accelerate ambition. With no domestic buffer, founders choose global customer profiles and global product standards from day one. They also benefit from a powerful social catalyst: visible outliers. A Lithuanian founder is often just "two WhatsApps away" from someone who built unicorns like Vinted or Wolt. As Małysz puts it, "The smaller the pond, the easier it is to see the big fish." In these ecosystems, strong ideas can build momentum quickly—they attract talent and support; employees take equity because they've seen peers become wealthy through stock options, and success becomes a lived reality rather than an abstract hope.

A similar pattern defines Israel. As Liron Azrielant of Meron Capital explains, the domestic market is so small that "no one is going to even pretend like it's big enough for a start-up," so Israeli founders are forced to build globally from day one. They excel at product and deep tech, but face a distinctive challenge: with no real home market to practice on, they must learn sales and go-to-market directly in the United States and other major markets. Yet this constraint has produced one of the world's most prolific start-up export ecosystems. In Israel, global ambition isn't a strategic choice—it's the baseline.

This shift has not been limited to emerging ecosystems. Even Silicon Valley had to evolve. Phil Wickham of Sozo Ventures saw that before almost anyone else. When he stepped into leadership of the Kauffman Fellows Program in the early 2000s, venture capital was still US-centric, relying on the same circles and the same ideas. Yet the founders Phil met were already building globally. "They were not American start-ups anymore," he recalled. "They were founders trying to take over the world." Phil responded by globalizing the Kauffman Fellowships well before the rest of the Valley realized how quickly entrepreneurship was moving beyond its borders, transforming accidental globalization into something intentional and structured.

Phil's insight revealed a deeper truth. Global strategy fails without global people. His work at Kauffman showed how powerful it is to identify globally minded leaders early and support them from every corner of the world. But for company leaders expanding into new markets, the next challenge was far more practical. They had to build cross-border teams with accuracy. The wrong hires slowed companies down. The right ones unlocked entire markets.

Hiring Across Borders: Beyond Language, Titles, and Optics

Once a company decides to enter a new market, its success often hinges on the first people it hires. Many leaders assume that finding a polished, English-speaking candidate will bridge the gap with headquarters and smooth the early operational hurdles. Shin Iwata of Miraise saw the opposite happen repeatedly. Foreign teams entering Japan often prioritized language fluency or impressive titles over the qualities that actually determine local traction. They would hire someone who communicated well with headquarters but lacked the cultural intuition, networks, and market awareness needed to navigate Japan's complex business landscape. The result, Shin noted, was leadership that "optimizes for comfort over growth," costing companies valuable time and traction.

True cross-border hiring requires more than linguistic or résumé credentials—it demands bicultural fluency. As Kieran Donovan of K-ID explains, the most successful hires are those who can bridge two worlds: individuals who deeply understand local norms but can also interpret and align with global expectations. At K-ID, a Japanese liaison with international experience became invaluable in navigating client relationships, etiquette, and hierarchy—turning potential cultural friction into trust. "The best hires," Kieran says, "live on both sides of the cultural equator."

This same pattern shows up in Western markets as well. As a senior public-capital investor in Europe told us, European founders expanding into the United States often hire a senior, well-connected American VP of sales who "fits" the market profile, hoping to compensate for cultural differences or accent insecurity—but these comfort hires rarely deliver. Lacking the founder's conviction, product understanding, and urgency, they may burn cash for months without closing deals. The investor's firm conclusion: "Do not leave your first million in sales to somebody else."

Shin Iwata and Kieran Donovan emphasize that early hires must match the reality of the market, not the assumptions of headquarters. Time and again, breakthroughs come only when company leaders step in directly when needed and realize that long-term success depends on hiring people who understand local needs and will move vigorously to meet them—rather than relying on polished résumés or familiar signals. It is a reminder that judgment cannot be outsourced. In a new market, context is everything.

The importance of context and culture came into sharp focus for Dr. Mark Thaller of Jebel Associates, whose work often takes him into conflict zones. In 2010, while traveling through Southern Sudan, he took the Yei Road near the border with the Democratic Republic of Congo, a route so damaged that abandoned trucks were half buried in enormous potholes. He was accompanied by a dozen soldiers from the Sudan People's Liberation Army (SPLA), who were guiding him to an old alluvial gold mine in the region. Even though a ceasefire was in place, fighting was still common. That night, they stopped in the town of Yei. One of the soldiers, who was from Yei, offered Mark his own bed in his family's small mud brick hut and slept outside himself. Only later did Mark fully understand this act of hospitality, which was deeply rooted in South Sudanese culture.

The next day, during a roadside stop, all of the soldiers took a bathroom break in a ditch while standing on the side of the road. Mark later said he was not shy, but for reasons that felt "proper" to him at the time, he stepped off the road and behind some bushes to find privacy. When he returned, the dozen soldiers were standing together, staring at him in silence. Mark asked what was wrong. They suddenly burst into shouting and laughter, pointing at him. When he asked his friend to translate, the answer was unforgettable. "They are saying, 'That mzungu is crazy. He just wandered off into a minefield and did not get blown up.'"

Mark later reflected that this became one of his most vivid lessons in cultural awareness. Actions that felt appropriate through a Western lens had produced radically different outcomes. One act of cultural misunderstanding led to unexpected generosity. Another nearly cost him his life. The lesson was simple: in a new environment, trust local knowledge and follow local norms. Or as he put it, "Don't step off the road into the bushes just to take a piss." Sometimes fitting in is not only respectful. It is survival.

How Communication Shapes Success Across Cultures

Shin Iwata explains that entering Japan requires an entirely different communication rhythm. Decisions move slowly, commitments are rarely explicit, and meeting feedback is often indirect or intentionally vague. Trust accumulates through repeated, respectful engagements rather than aggressive follow-through. Foreign founders often misread this silence, assuming disinterest when it may simply signal internal deliberation. Shin stresses the importance of having a local supporter who can observe subtle cues, identify the true decision-makers, and follow up privately to gather candid feedback. In Japan, progress is measured not by quarterly KPIs but by the steady construction of trust.

Phil Wickham adds that this dynamic is not unique to Japan—it reflects a broader truth about Asia. While Silicon Valley's hierarchy is visible and public, Asia's hierarchy is opaque. Titles may hide real influence, and decisions may hinge on relationships invisible to outsiders. Many Western founders pitch the wrong person simply because the org chart misled them. As Phil notes, in transparent systems, credibility is public; in opaque systems, it must be earned quietly and relationally.

For Nicolas Sauvage, President of TDK Ventures, operating across Europe, Asia, and the United States revealed something deeper: communication is not just about speaking clearly but about listening fully. He learned to slow down, absorb nuance, and treat cultural differences as signals rather than friction. "Diversity of thought is not a challenge to manage," he writes. "It is the lens that turns different perspectives into insight when we approach them with curiosity, patience, and genuine respect." Collaboration across borders begins when leaders stop assuming and start interpreting.

On the opposite end of the communication spectrum sits Israel, where boldness is a cultural norm rather than an exception. Liron Azrielant describes Israeli founders as unapologetically direct—so direct that "they'd cold call the Pope if it helped." This *chutzpah* (extreme self-confidence) is rooted in early responsibility: Israeli teenagers often handle real-life, high-stakes tasks during mandatory military service, giving them a sense of agency years before most peers worldwide. That early confidence shapes founders who push, ask, challenge, and insist until they get the answer they need.

One of Liron's defining anecdotes captures this perfectly. During her first week at MIT, she stopped a professor mid-lecture to question a logical step in an equation—an act that stunned the room. To her, it wasn't rebellion; it was the straightforward act of solving a problem she didn't understand. Only later did she realize why it became a campus story: in the US academic world, hierarchy often dictates when and how questions are asked. In Israeli culture, hierarchy is negotiable, but clarity is mandatory. As she puts it, "In Israel, hierarchy is optional; clarity isn't."

This contrast in communication styles points to a broader truth. Every market has its own logic, its own expectations, and its own interpretation of how things should work. That same variability shows up in both conventional and cutting-edge business expansions.

Yes, AI Has to Be Localized

One investor with plenty of on-the-ground, face-to-face experience across borders is Dany Farha, cofounder and managing partner of Dubai-based BECO Capital. He reminds us that "the real friction" for an expanding business, "whether it is structure, culture, dynamics, readiness, or even proximity, always hides beneath the surface"—and "the extent of that friction only becomes obvious once you are actually inside the market." Dany's advice: "Before you enter a new market, stress-test your thesis from all sides."

He also speaks firmly of the need for adapting uses of AI to local markets. "In an AI-driven world, local nuance becomes even more important," Dany told us. "Having a data advantage now means having more context, knowing how to apply it, and building feedback loops that continuously enrich the dataset." His firm invested in a company called ClearGrid, a digital debt-collection platform that uses AI and machine learning to generate "hyper-personalized" collection messages. Dany said that in some segments, the technology has boosted collection rates from a traditional 25% to over 45%. He attributes this to "Deep personalization, from tone to channel selection—WhatsApp, email, calls—and applying local understanding of personas to reach customers at the right time, through the right channel. For example, people in some cultures do not want to be called first thing in the morning about paying off a loan."

If you're integrating or expanding AI in your business, which you probably are, don't be late to the party. Heed Dany Farha's advice. See that cultural and personal awareness are built in.

When Regulations Collide Across Markets

Kieran Donovan sits at the center of one of global expansion's toughest problems: what to do when regulations directly conflict or, as in many emerging markets, aren't clear at all. For global consumer platforms—social media, gaming, AI—he explains that the first step is choosing a *baseline* regulatory environment that defines the minimum standard for product controls, maturity filters, and data rules. But once a company enters multiple markets, that baseline inevitably collides with local realities.

Some conflicts are structural. Gambling mechanics or randomized rewards may be legal in one country and banned in another. "If your game relies on randomized rewards," Donovan notes, "you cannot monetize in markets where they're prohibited." Other conflicts are ethical. Many jurisdictions forbid profiling minors; others have no restrictions. Companies must decide whether to apply one global rule or enable targeted features only where allowed.

To navigate this, Donovan applies a principle he calls "baseline plus elevation." Choose one jurisdiction as your global floor; then elevate selectively where regulation—or ethics—requires more. "You can't comply everywhere," he says, "but you can be consistent everywhere."

Yet conflict is only half the challenge. In many emerging markets, the issue isn't contradiction but ambiguity: vague laws, inconsistent enforcement, or multiple authorities with different interpretations. Donovan's answer (treated in detail in Chapter 5 under "Unclear Local Regulations") is a five-category framework that classifies every regulatory requirement into:

1. Enforced law

2. Codified law

3. Inferred law

4. Regulatory guidance

5. Best practice

This lets teams benchmark jurisdictions, understand what's required versus suggested, and decide their "risk peg" with intention rather than guesswork. Across both conflict and uncertainty, Donovan's message is simple: global compliance isn't about reacting to every rule. It's about building a structured, principled approach that can flex across markets without losing coherence.

A similar pattern appears in competition. Even when companies understand the rules, the competitive landscape can shift dramatically from one market to another. Being early is not always an advantage, and being correct is not always enough.

When Being First Isn't Enough: Competing in Markets Where Speed Doesn't Guarantee Success

In many emerging and hypercompetitive markets, business leaders have learned through hard experience that being early does not guarantee success. Fast followers are often better positioned than the original innovators, whether through easier access to capital, faster consumer adoption, or fewer regulatory hurdles. The first mover often absorbs the learning curve for everyone else. China is the clearest illustration of this dynamic. As Wee Liang Chua of LUN Partners Group explains, "Competition there is not only intense. It is *relentless, fearless, and unconstrained.*"

In the United States, a frontier sector like humanoid robotics might have a handful of serious players. In China, Chua has seen 500 companies rush in at once. Saturation doesn't deter entrants—it *attracts* them. The prevailing mindset: copy fast, adapt faster, and overwhelm the market with speed and iteration.

In such an environment, the Western ideal of "first-mover advantage" loses much of its power. The fast follower—the player who refines, repackages, and scales more aggressively—often ends up ahead. Chinese local and provincial governments fuel this pattern too, each backing its own robotics base, EV cluster, or climate-tech hub. Dozens of near-identical companies emerge overnight, margins collapse, and soon even successful founders look outward for better profits, a trend the Chinese describe as "chu hai"—"going overseas."

This creates a different kind of competitive reality. Winning isn't about entering first or raising the most capital. It's about agility: knowing when to align with stronger partners, when to step aside, and when to let the market's momentum carry you instead of fighting against it.

In environments like China, influence isn't secured through contracts or early entry; it's earned continuously in motion. The strongest players are the ones who adapt fastest, iterate relentlessly, and understand how to navigate shifting power structures.

Being first opens the door—but adaptability is what keeps you in the room.

Local Pricing Strategy? It All Depends

Spotify, the Swedish-based streaming content provider, localizes its pricing worldwide. In relatively affluent countries where Spotify has a strong market presence, monthly subscriptions have been priced up to 10 times higher than in the lowest-cost countries. This strategy has allowed the company to penetrate new markets while profiting from business in its more mature markets. And it has been made possible by a transcreative approach to Spotify's supply chain. Spotify doesn't own the music and other content that it streams. The owners of the rights are music production and distribution companies and individual creative artists or groups. They've all had to agree to change their licensing arrangements, accepting lower returns in some markets along with higher returns elsewhere. The case shows that transcreation applies to more than the front-end aspects of a business. It can be applied to any aspect, including to negotiations with suppliers and partners on the terms of their participation.

Meanwhile, a US-based global company practices an approach that is just the opposite of Spotify's. FedEx uses essentially the same pricing structure everywhere for overnight package delivery. The thinking here is that guaranteed overnight delivery is a premium service, targeted to customers who need it and are willing to pay for it. Charging equivalent rates per package size and distance may lose the company some potential customers in less affluent markets, but the strategy helps FedEx uphold its brand reputation while paying for implementation of the service. (This is costly, requiring sizable investments in aircraft and other equipment in addition to operating expenses.)

These contrasting cases show once again that there is no single formula for success across borders. You will do best by localizing to the extent and, in the ways, that best fit your business and the market(s) you're entering.

In a Cross-Border Negotiation, an Interpreter Can Be Your Greatest Ally—or Your Worst Enemy

When meeting with a counterparty who doesn't speak your language, always make sure to find out whether you will be assigned an interpreter. If the answer is yes, bring a printed copy of the key points and concepts you need to convey. If possible, try to meet briefly with the interpreter before the meeting and hand them the copy—or at least the highlights—of what you need to discuss. They will be grateful, as you're making their work easier, and at the same time you will ensure they can perform at their best for you, having had a chance to see the main concepts or jargon you are going to use. (Sometimes they are not expert in the matter, and they may need a moment to think about how to express certain concepts in their language.) Exchange a few words; get a sense of how this person speaks, the pitch of the voice, and the accent; and give them the chance to hear you before the negotiation starts.

An interpreter can be your greatest ally or your worst enemy in a negotiation. You want them to like you, to want to help you, and you should give them all the tools to do so. When you're the guest, you can never predict whether you'll get an excellent interpreter or not, but you certainly want to find out beforehand who you're dealing with.

Stefano learned these tips from his sister Annalisa, who worked for the United Nations across five continents for more than 10 years. A gambit she often uses to start a conversation with the interpreter is to joke about how fast she speaks, adding that the interpreter can just give her a sign if she needs to slow down. Why is this so important? Because there's nothing more awkward than listening to a decision-maker on the other side deliver a passionate speech in a language you don't understand, looking straight into your eyes, followed by silence as everyone in the room stares at you waiting for your brilliant answers to their complex concerns—until the interpreter finally mutters a short, bored, and unspecific "We disagree."

Women in Cross-Border Negotiations

Annalisa, drawing on her experience across several continents, shared that for many women, their role in negotiations, their legitimacy as trusted partners, and even their professionalism are still things they must prove repeatedly. Annalisa's point is not about victimhood, but awareness—recognizing bias allows women to navigate it deliberately and shape their professional image with intention.

She hopes this will change, but in many countries, walking into a meeting with a male colleague often still triggers the assumption that he has more authority. Taking offense only weakens your position, she says; it is far more effective to remain calm, confident, and composed. Most people act on subconscious biases, not malice, and confronting them emotionally usually backfires.

One early experience crystallized this for Annalisa, she recalls being 27 and sent abroad by the UN as their lead expert to speak with a foreign government in Africa. The event organizer approached her to ask when "the expert" would arrive, assuming she was just an assistant. When he realized she was indeed the expert, his surprise bordered on offense—not because he misidentified her role but because someone had dared to send a young woman as the lead expert. She stayed composed, delivered her work professionally, and the meeting was a success. The same organizer later became one of her strongest supporters—not because she argued but because she did her job well.

Oluchi Ikechi shared similar stories from her own career, which led to her becoming a partner at one of the "big five" business consulting firms. After doing business as a woman in different parts of the world, she explains that bias appears in two forms: the quiet, unspoken assumptions people carry, and the overt moments when your gender, age, or background enter the room before you do. She has experienced both—across the United Kingdom, Singapore, and the broader Asian region—and those encounters shaped the confident, intentional way she now enters high-pressure environments.

For the subtle bias, she learned to build a mindset strong enough to carry her through any room. She describes developing the ability to walk in as the only woman, or the only person who looked like her, and not only feel comfortable but actually thrive. Her mental script became simple: whatever you expect, I will outperform it by the time this meeting ends. That mindset protected her confidence in senior rooms where expectations were low or unspoken.

But she also talks about the more obvious moments. In London, she recalled preparing to present on a major topic to a prospective client when the partner she worked with told her, "This client prefers gray-haired people." It was a coded message: you're too young; you don't look like what he expects. Yet she was still the one carrying the content. She went into the meeting with heavy pressure to prove herself—and she did. Her company won the work. Later, she reflected that the bias may have been the client's, or it may have been her colleague's projection. Either way, the lesson for her was the same. You can't control other people's perceptions, but you can control how you show up.

Oluchi's experiences in Asia added another layer. The region's hierarchy meant that even with her seniority, she often had to navigate rooms where older male clients naturally gravitated toward other older men. She described one meeting with the CEO of a major Singaporean bank where, despite that she was the subject-matter expert, he spent the first half of the conversation engaging only with her older male colleague. To break that pattern, she used subtle tactics—holding eye contact with her colleague so the client would follow his gaze and delivering sharp, story-driven insights that made the client want to pay attention.

It wasn't about ego; it was about value. Over time Oluchi realized that in any country, in any culture, the only universal denominator is your ability to add value. If she could bring insight, connection, or clarity into the conversation, she could shift the room, one sentence at a time.

That understanding—combined with the resilience built from years of dealing with bias—made her unafraid of entering new markets or new rooms. As she put it, the real formula is simple: show up with confidence, speak with substance, and let the quality of your contribution carry you past whatever bias may exist.

Ernestine Fu Mak of Brave Capital has led negotiations in countries where it is often rare for women to have a primary seat at the table. She does not, however, view this as a formidable challenge. For one thing, she is present as a foreigner, which often brings recognition that she comes from a culture where gender roles differ.

Furthermore, she is often accompanied by, and leads, a team of men that is able to gain acceptance more easily.

Building on this, Annalisa also shared practical cultural insights for women traveling for work in unfamiliar environments. Her point was not about memorizing rules but about understanding how small actions can be interpreted very differently across cultures. Interrupting a speaker, for example, is widely considered rude, but in some societies interrupting a man can carry additional weight because of social hierarchies. The same applies to body language. Showing the sole of your shoe may be seen as disrespectful, and in certain cultures, men will not shake hands with women for religious reasons, making it important to wait for them to initiate. Even minimal physical contact can be misread. Annalisa once experienced a brief, accidental touch on someone's arm being interpreted as flirtation.

Etiquette varies as well. In some places men expect women to enter a room first, while elsewhere you should follow them. In certain cultures, women speaking directly about money is seen as improper, so it may be better to let a colleague introduce the topic before contributing. And while one's appearance should reflect confidence and professionalism, it should also remain culturally neutral. Business attire, with light adjustments to local norms, is safer than attempting to dress like locals, which can sometimes appear inappropriate or even disrespectful. In the end, cultural fluency is not a constraint. It is a strategic advantage.

15 The Global Expansion Checklist

A Summary of All Key Takeaways

There is no single magic bullet or secret sauce for expanding across borders successfully. That should be obvious by now. Every international market entry is a dive off the high board, into the waters of business uncertainty and cultural complexity.

But I hope we've been clear on the point that it is eminently possible to do it right and do well. There is just a lot to think about—many factors to address, many principles to keep in mind.

The following send-off should be useful. It's a compilation of the key takeaways from every chapter in the book, presented together as a master checklist. The list conveys our best thinking and best advice on everything of importance that you'll need to deal with.

Chapter 1—It's an Adventure

- **Surprise is the starting point.** In a new culture, the first thing you'll encounter isn't opportunity, but unfamiliar behaviors that challenge your assumptions.

- **Growth accelerates outside your comfort zone.** When you step into unfamiliar cultures and environments, your assumptions get tested, and your learning curve sharpens fast.

- **Small gaps cause big consequences.** Most cross-cultural failures begin with tiny misunderstandings that snowball when assumptions go untested.

- **Reserve judgment when things feel "wrong."** What looks irrational or unprofessional through your lens often makes perfect sense within the local context.

- **Learn the pattern behind the behavior.** A surprise tactic is only surprising once; after that, you gain an advantage by understanding why it happens and preparing for it.

- **Trust moves at different speeds in different places.** A handshake in one culture seals a deal, while in another it's only the beginning of proving you're trustworthy.

- **Connection is the real work.** Closing deals across borders is ultimately about reading people, earning trust, and adapting to how relationships are built locally.

Chapter 2—Prepare to Be Unprepared

- **Expect the unexpected.** No amount of reading prepares you for the cultural surprises that only show themselves on the ground.

- **Practice mindfulness.** Inner awareness keeps you steady in environments full of ambiguity, pressure, and social signals you may not yet understand.

- **Suspend judgment.** Different isn't wrong; every culture optimizes for what it values, and you must learn to see the logic beneath the surface.

- **Sharpen your intuition.** It's your early warning system in unfamiliar settings, helping you read cues correctly and recover faster from mistakes.

- **Stay humble.** Starting with "I know nothing" opens the door to genuine learning and protects you from dangerous assumptions.

- **Reality beats roadmaps.** Strategies that worked elsewhere must be revalidated in each new market, no matter how confident you feel.

- **Frequent reality-testing keeps you aligned with the market.** Does what you're thinking and doing correspond to what you actually see playing out day-to-day?

- **Lean on locals.** Surrounding yourself with people who know the culture accelerates your learning curve and prevents rookie errors.

- **There's no better education than a start-up.** Launching or joining one when you're young can be a great move. The risks you take will pay off later.

- **Go where other cultures actually live.** Time spent in a distant country rewires your intuition, giving you the mental fluency needed for real business interactions.

Chapter 3—Getting Ready to Expand

- **Preparation is everything.** "Be prepared" isn't just a motto—it's the foundation for cross-border expansion. Success abroad depends on readiness, not just ambition.

- **Success at home doesn't guarantee success abroad.** What works brilliantly in one market can fail fast in another. Each country has its own culture, economics, and competitive dynamics.

- **Focus is a finite resource.** The 1880 CEO's attention was divided between multiple launches, draining leadership bandwidth and weakening oversight—a common pitfall in global expansion.

- **Choose expansion for the right reasons.** Go international because it's strategic, not simply because "it's there." Expansion should serve growth objectives, competitive positioning, or market opportunity—not ego or impulse.

- **Study market fit and cultural alignment deeply.** Differences in consumer behavior and competition can easily blindside even experienced executives. Understanding local context is just as critical as getting the financial model right.

- **Be realistic about capital and capacity.** Even good ideas fail if the expansion burns cash faster than it builds value. Each new market should be approached with clear runway, ROI targets, and contingency plans.

- **Own your mistakes and learn from them.** Marc Nicholson's public accountability for 1880's failure is rare but admirable. Honest reflection turns a failure story into a learning story.

- **Timing is everything.** Entering a new market too early risks unmet readiness; too late, and competition closes the window. Base expansion timing on data and real market signals, not external pressure or hype.

- **Choose the market, don't let it choose you.** Picking the right country for expansion isn't simple or obvious. Evaluate it through business-specific metrics—customer readiness, operational feasibility, and local talent fit—rather than assumptions or narratives.

- **Resist supply-side pressure.** Investor or board expectations can distort priorities. Move when your company is operationally ready, not when others say you "should."

- **Avoid the Fear of Missing Out.** FOMO-fueled expansion often leads to half-built operations and costly retrenchment. Sustainable growth comes from strategic conviction, not fear.

- **Trust ground truth over spreadsheet theory.** Expansion decisions made from afar often miss the nuances that determine success. Spend time on the ground, test assumptions locally, and let firsthand understanding guide the plan.

- **Let pull guide your path.** The strongest signal for expansion is not a spreadsheet forecast but real, on-the-ground demand—customers asking, partners inviting, champions opening doors. Follow where the pull is genuine.

- **Time "in" market beats time "to" market.** Visiting repeatedly, listening, and observing reveal whether a market is truly calling you in. Don't launch until local traction and a hiring network start forming naturally.

- **Organic growth compounds trust.** Expanding through existing clients or referrals reduces uncertainty, lowers costs, and builds knowledge you can reuse in future markets.

- **Push carries power—and risk.** Blitz-scaling can capture short windows of opportunity, but capital and speed alone rarely create staying power. Without local foundations, early wins evaporate fast.

- **The best companies balance both.** A mature expansion strategy blends pull and push: pulled by authentic demand, but supported by the resources and urgency to seize it at the right moment.

Chapter 4—You Have to Be There

- **Mutual trust is the foundation for everything else.** To succeed across borders, you must signal credibility early and earn enough trust for people to engage with you—while also learning whom to trust in return. Relationships, not credentials, open doors.

- **Be your best self, with local awareness.** Honesty and authenticity build credibility, but so does respecting local customs. Cultural fluency strengthens relationships and prevents unnecessary friction.

- **Deep trust takes time.** First impressions help you get in the door, but meaningful trust develops gradually. Some cultures move quickly once reputation is proven; others need repeated interaction before business begins. Patience earns far more than pressure.

- **Use intuition—and don't gloss over red flags.** Instincts can reveal character where words fail, but they sharpen only with experience and reflection. Trust your read of a situation, especially when something feels slightly off, and follow up rather than dismissing the signal.

- **Trust removes complexity, which creates speed.** As Carl Fritjofsson, general partner at Creandum, explains, "The benefit of Nordic culture is that it's incredibly trust-heavy, which allows for speed and removes complexity. That can actually be an advantage compared to Silicon Valley–style aggressiveness."

- **Online research is a starting point, not a strategy.** AI-enhanced tools and data can help you map the terrain, but they can't show you how a market actually feels or functions day to day.

- **Learn through proximity.** You can't understand a market from a screen. Being on the ground reveals the signals, systems, and human nuances that remote work can't.

- **Expand step-by-step.** Start with industry events and regional forums to build familiarity, then follow up with repeated visits and local meetings. Gradual presence leads to deeper insight and stronger networks.

- **Local conversations uncover truths the web can't.** Talking with former employees, clients, or even competitors can surface hidden pitfalls and behind-the-scenes lessons that never appear in press releases or reports.

- **Groundwork reduces uncertainty.** Every visit replaces assumptions with verified knowledge. Over time, local presence transforms ambiguity into clarity and builds resilience for future challenges.

Chapter 5—How to Get the Deal Done

- **Contracts travel differently.** In some markets, a signature closes the deal. In others, it only starts the conversation. Learn to read which kind of field you're on before you play.

- **When the law can't protect you, alignment must.** If a country's legal mechanisms are less than fully effective, you cannot rely on a signed contract to preserve a business relationship. Keep it a commercial win-win instead.

- **Win-win cuts both ways.** This holds true when your partners, suppliers, or employees feel they're losing out—and it holds just as true when you're the aggrieved party. In either case, whether you need to help out the other side or apply leverage, keep coming back to balance.

- **Flexibility is the real protection.** Build optionality—secondary partners, backup licenses, alternative paths—so leverage never depends on one contract.

- **Anticipate the renegotiation.** Assume success will trigger new demands. Plan for it early, as Stefano did with Aspire, and you'll stay in control when terms start to shift.

- **Alignment beats enforcement.** When rules evolve mid-game, those who adapt with fairness and foresight keep both partners—and progress—intact.

- **Trust begins before proof.** In volatile environments, you often have to extend a small act of trust first to invite reciprocity.

As Dr. Mark Thaller puts it, you must "sail toward the horizon before proving the world is round."

- **Ethics travel, but the definitions shift.** What looks like corruption in one culture may be considered loyalty or survival in another. Learn the local frame without abandoning your own standards of legality and integrity.

- **Integrity is your strongest defense.** In places where the law can't protect you, your conduct often determines whether you're targeted or trusted. Never trade ethics for convenience.

- **Be wary where order breaks down.** If you must operate in highly unsettled or violent contexts, use extreme caution in vetting partners—and know when to walk away.

- **Expect friction at the other extreme.** In hyper-regulated, risk-averse systems, strict compliance can slow growth but also signal reliability. Adapt your pace and paperwork to match the local definition of readiness.

- **Government policies can make or break your expansion.** Incentives, restrictions, and regulations all shape how you can operate. Whether you're entering Singapore or São Paulo, staying aware of how government policy impacts your sector is critical.

- **Policies change—sometimes overnight.** Even stable governments rewrite rules that affect industries. A new administration, a new minister, or sudden public pressure can shift the playing field dramatically.

- **Use frameworks to clarify gray areas.** Operating in gray areas without certainty of how the rules will be interpreted is a gamble. Always aim for proper structure and reputable partners. As shared by Kieran Donovan of k-ID, his team developed a five-part framework that classifies each business requirement as either an enforced law, a formal rule, an inferred obligation, regulatory guidance, or best practice. This approach helps executives see which rules are absolute, which depend on interpretation, and where cautious behavior is the smarter move.

- **Local insight is your best defense.** Success depends largely on the people around you. Choose local partners who understand the landscape, maintain credibility, and have the influence to guide you through shifting regulations.

- **Blend local expertise with global guidance.** The strongest approach combines local advisors who know the terrain with international firms that ensure compliance and global alignment. Budget for both. It's not optional—it's insurance for your expansion.

Chapter 6—The Power of Transcreation

- **Transcreation outperforms translation.** Examples such as motorbike-based mobility, cash payments, and daily driver payouts illustrate how genuine transcreation outperformed global incumbents. And many products can't succeed at all across borders without fundamental adaptation to local habits, expectations, and cultural norms.

- **Technology adoption depends on cultural acceptance.** Trust, hierarchy, time orientation, and user behavior vary substantially across markets.

- **Culture is dynamic.** Effective market entry requires understanding current norms and anticipating the direction of cultural change.

- **The "now-future" is already visible.** Early prototypes of emerging technologies exist in the present. Thinking ahead to how you might use them is better than letting them make you obsolete.

- **Winning globally means thinking locally.** The companies that scale effectively are the ones that rebuild their models for each market rather than assuming a universal fit.

Chapter 7—Cultural Code-Switching

- **Credibility is cultural, not universal.** Behaviors that signal confidence and competence in one context can undermine trust entirely in another.

- **Hierarchy changes the rules of engagement.** In cultures that value seniority, publicly challenging someone above you is interpreted as disrespect rather than rigor.

- **Mirroring buys trust and time.** Active listening, reflection, and restraint can defuse tension and keep negotiations on track.

- **Assertiveness and deference are situational tools.** The skill is knowing when to push forward and when to step back.

- **Team presence sends a signal before words do.** In some cultures, showing up with colleagues signals seriousness and resources, while going solo suggests weakness.

- **Cultural code-switching is adaptation, not performance.** It is situational awareness that allows you to stay aligned with your goals while adjusting how you pursue them.

- **Signals don't always translate.** What looks like confidence in one culture can look like arrogance or disrespect in another.

- **Dress codes are cultural codes.** A hoodie may signal power in Silicon Valley but immaturity in Singapore or Tokyo.

- **Body language speaks volumes.** Mirroring posture and attentiveness shows respect and builds trust.

- **Team presence matters.** In East Asia, bringing colleagues signals seriousness and resources. In Silicon Valley, the same move can look like wasted resources.

- **First impressions are fast and sticky.** Small cues in the first minute can reinforce deep cultural perceptions and decide whether business moves forward.

- **Time is culture-bound.** A "few minutes late" may be acceptable in Southern Europe but deeply offensive in Northern Europe or Japan.

- **In some places, lateness signals status.** In parts of Southeast Asia, arriving late can imply importance, while punctuality may be read as desperation.

- **In others, punctuality signals respect.** In Northern Europe and Japan, being on time shows professionalism and courtesy.

- **Code-switching is ongoing.** Leaders often juggle different cultural expectations—relaxed at home, precise in global business.

Chapter 8—When "Yes" Means "No"

- **Extreme demands can be signals, not expectations.** In some cultures, asking for far more than is realistic is a way to probe limits, not a literal position.

- **Scarcity shapes strategy.** In societies with histories of insecurity, negotiators may push until they're stopped; knowing this helps you hold firm without overreacting.

- **Global founders must read intent, not just numbers.** Learn to ask: is this a test of limits, or a breach of trust? The answer determines whether you push back, concede slightly, or walk away.

- **Distinguish the stage of negotiation.** An aggressive counter bid (like 80/20) can be a tactic to test your walk-away point, whereas changing terms after an agreement risks breaking trust.

- **Remember the human baseline.** We share the same species and many universal traits—but culture, history, and external events often produce contrasting behaviors that are not easily made to converge.

- **Code-switching is your edge.** By being conscious of these cultural dynamics, you can play a pivotal role in bridging gaps and creating convergence where others cannot.

- **The speed of building trust looks different across cultures.** In some places it's granted quickly; in others, building trust can take years (time well spent).

- **Start with who you know.** The most powerful shortcut is doing business with entities you already trust. Beyond that, personal recommendations from your existing network are the most reliable path to new partners.

- **Trust is layered.** People may test your honesty, intentions, ability, discretion, resilience, fairness, values, and long-term alignment.

- **In open networks, speed cuts both ways.** In the United States, trust can be won quickly but lost instantly when broken.

- **Match your directness to the culture.** Trying to push the process forward too quickly, or being overly direct in a relationship-driven culture, can close doors instead of opening them.

- **In relationship-driven cultures, process matters.** Meals, social settings, and family connections are not side activities—they are where deals actually move forward.

- **Code-switch to fit the culture.** The way you build trust in Silicon Valley won't work in Jakarta or Riyadh; adapt to the process that fits.

- **Beware of death by politeness.** A "yes" is not always a yes. In many cultures, agreement may mask hesitation or a polite escape.

- **Context is your compass.** The setting, stakes, and relationships often reveal whether words mean what they say.

- **Match your pace to theirs.** Silence or delays rarely mean disinterest, they often mean your counterparty is navigating internal processes, politics, or hierarchy that are invisible to outsiders.

- **Spot the actual decider.** Influence often sits with the person others glance at for approval. Build trust with them. Sometimes the real decision-maker may not even be in the room, and that is perfectly normal in the early stages.

- **Lead with patience, not directness.** Trying to push the process too quickly, or being overly direct in a relationship-driven culture, can close doors instead of opening them.

- **Study the culture where it lives.** Restaurants, cafés, and local hangouts teach you more about norms than any briefing.

- **Look for everyday signals.** Watching sports events, entertainment, and even TV commercials show you what people find funny, respectful, or offensive—insight you can't get from meetings alone.

- **Always be honest.** Highlight your strengths, but never misrepresent. In a culture where you're already an outsider, dishonesty can be fatal.

- **Listen between the lines.** Tone, cadence, hesitation, and body language often carry more truth than the literal words.

- **Code-switch your ear.** Develop intuition for reading signals in your home country—then apply it abroad with humility and patience.

Chapter 9—Deals Are Human

- **Cultural fit beats product strength.** Even world-class products fail when they ignore the tastes, habits, and expectations of local users.

- **Clarity beats confidence.** Over-communicate early, define every term, and surface hidden expectations before they turn into conflict.

- **Create a culture where dissent is safe.** True cross-border collaboration requires environments where all partners can challenge, question, and push back without fear.

- **Assumptions kill deals.** What feels "standard" in one country may be unacceptable in another, so never assume shared definitions of fairness, ownership, or process.

- **Politeness is not agreement.** Silence, nodding, or soft language often signal deliberation or discomfort, not consent.

- **Equal partnership must be explicit.** Don't rely on goodwill or intuition—set shared rules for how decisions are made and how disagreements are handled.

- **Global business isn't borderless.** Even in advanced tech fields like quantum, legal, regulatory, and cultural norms diverge more than people assume.

- **Regional labels hide real complexity.** Treating Africa or LatAm as single markets leads companies to overgeneralize, overlook risk, and misread opportunity.

- **Honest debate builds real partnership.** Teams that challenge each other openly—regardless of age, title, or culture—create stronger, more resilient decisions.

- **Global clarity enables local flexibility.** Companies that decide what must stay global and what can be adapted locally move faster, scale cleaner, and avoid wasted effort.

- **Subcultures shape markets more than national labels.** Within any country, regional, urban–rural, and industry-specific cultures create wildly different behaviors and buying patterns.

- **The real segmentation is often invisible.** What looks like geography or income on paper may actually be lifestyle, identity, or worldview—like the pickup-truck versus sedan divide predicting US political and cultural values.

- **Generations can be different cultures entirely.** Young leaders across countries often share more values with each other than with older people in their own nation, reshaping sectors like climate tech and sustainability.

- **Shared mindset beats shared nationality.** Alignment of purpose, speed, and values—not borders—is often the strongest predictor of productive cross-border partnerships.

- **Values drive behavior, even more than rules.** What people protect, pursue, or fear reflects their cultural value system—and those values often override policy manuals or contracts.

- **"Collectivism" has two sides.** In some cultures, loyalty to the group means protecting shared assets; in others, it implies shared entitlement to those same assets. Knowing which version you're dealing with prevents costly misreads.

- **Consequences must match the local value scale.** Arguments that work in one culture (lost revenue, brand damage, lawsuits) may have little effect elsewhere. The persuasive lever might instead be social shame, legal exposure, or community consequence.

- **Never assume your logic is universal.** What looks like misconduct to you may feel justified or morally neutral to someone shaped by a different cultural framework. Diagnose the value system first, react second.

- **Transcreation beats copy-paste.** A model requires you to understand people's behaviors, not just market stats.

- **Trust has a price point.** Consumers may happily shop online for low-ticket items, but the moment the stakes rise, trust thresholds shift.

- **Adaptation compounds across markets.** Lessons earned in one country can be re-exported to others—but only when leaders resist the temptation to assume they've "found the formula."

Chapter 10—Strategy in a Strange Land

- **Remote looks easy, but it's costly.** What seems efficient from afar often leads to lost time, missed signals, and expensive course corrections once reality sets in.

- **You can't fix what you can't see.** Without firsthand experience in the market, the data tells only part of the story—and often the wrong part.

- **Proximity wins.** Teams that show up learn faster, adapt sooner, and earn trust before their competitors even know what's changing.

- **Local presence beats perfect plans.** The most valuable insights and opportunities emerge through personal interaction with potential partners and clients.

- **Test before you leap.** Small experiments reveal what slides unnoticed from afar, saving months of missteps.

- **Local is ideal, but not always available.** The strongest market entries usually start with a local leader, but in many emerging markets, true local leadership depth is limited.

- **Third-culture talent is a superpower.** People who have lived between cultures adapt faster, decode signals better, and build trust in ways no résumé bullet captures.

- **No country is one country.** Within any market lie multiple subcultures, and real traction comes from segmenting carefully, not assuming national homogeneity.

- **Test before you build.** Pilots, pop-ups, and low-cost digital experiments reveal the truth of a market long before you spend real money.

- **Presence matters, but permanence can wait.** Being on the ground accelerates learning, but committing to a full operation should follow evidence, not enthusiasm.

- **Local strength is a multiplier, not a bonus.** A well-chosen JV partner gives you instant credibility, distribution, and cultural fit that no foreign entrant can manufacture quickly on its own.

- **Synergy must be real, not assumed.** The best JVs pair complementary capabilities—like SoftBank's distribution or Maxim's local insight—that neither party could replicate efficiently on its own.

- **Policy stability matters as much as market size.** As Tata–Docomo showed, shifting regulations and timing risks can overwhelm even the most well-funded partnerships.

- **Competitive edges decay fast.** Advantages built on pricing or novelty are easily copied. Sustainable JVs need defensible strengths, not tactics that trigger a race to the bottom.

- **Don't let "not invented here" kill opportunities.** Turning down a capable local partner in favor of building everything in-house often leads to delays, poor product-market fit, and missed market share.

- **Acquisition is often the fastest path to scale.** Buying a strong local player gives you instant market presence, embedded trust, and operational depth that would take years to build from scratch.

- **Local leadership is an asset you should preserve.** The most successful M&A entries keep the acquired team, brand, and cultural know-how intact instead of imposing a foreign playbook.

- **Integration issues can break even the best deal.** Poor post-acquisition execution, especially around product fit and user experience, can erase the advantages of buying in.

- **Choose targets based on fundamentals, not price.** A cheap acquisition can be costly if the company's core problems, customers, or reputation are deteriorating.

- **Respect what customers already love.** When you acquire a beloved local product, avoid radical changes that alienate its user base, because trust is harder to rebuild than to inherit.

- **Distribution partners can accelerate entry—but only if they have real capability.** A strong partner brings reach, infrastructure, and regulatory familiarity that would take years to build alone.

- **Incentives must be aligned from day one.** If a distributor can earn more promoting someone else's product, they will—even at your expense.

- **Trust is earned, not assumed.** In fast-growing emerging markets, the pool of distributors includes both excellent operators and opportunists. Rigorous vetting is essential before handing them your brand.

- **Once again—you have to be there.** Managing a distribution partner requires building an in-person relationship. No relationship, no business.

Chapter 11—Hiring Teams Across Countries

- **Hire for "distance traveled," not just pedigree.** The best expansion leaders are humble, curious, and adaptable enough to navigate unfamiliar terrain.

- **Look past surface differences.** True talent can present differently across cultures, so focus on integrity, hunger, and drive rather than familiar signals.

- **Legal frameworks are the easy part.** The harder part is mastering the unwritten cultural expectations around contracts, bonuses, notice periods, and work norms.

- **Onboarding is cultural, not just procedural.** New hires don't just need tools, they need context, norms, and behavioral cues.

- **The right onboarding buddy accelerates integration.** Peer-level guides reduce friction and give new joiners a safe place to ask anything.

- **Shared language creates shared alignment.** A common working language, used consistently across leadership, eliminates ambiguity and strengthens cohesion.

- **Retention multiplies every earlier effort.** Identifying, hiring, and training pay off only when people stay long enough to have impact.

- **People follow leaders, not companies.** When they trust a manager who cares about them, they will endure difficulty and commit deeply.

- **Incentives must align risk, effort, and reward.** Ownership, autonomy, and growth opportunities drive motivation more than salary alone.

- **When misalignment persists, decisive action protects the culture.** Letting one destructive person stay sends a stronger negative signal than letting them go.

Chapter 12—Managing Teams Across Countries

- **Presence is not symbolic; it is operational.** In-person time gives leaders the only accurate read on morale, alignment, and momentum across countries.

- **Context creates autonomy.** Town halls and transparent communication empower teams to act independently while staying aligned.

- **Rhythm beats control.** Daily stand-ups and smart async communication keep distributed teams moving together without adding long-meetings fatigue.

- **Reinforce the positive.** Spotlighting great behavior shapes culture faster and more effectively than correcting every mistake.

- **Fairness must be localized.** Reward systems require sensitivity to cultural timing and regional calibration, or they unintentionally damage trust.

- **There is no single "right way" to work.** Effective cross-cultural leadership begins with curiosity, the humility to unlearn your own defaults, and the willingness to adapt to others' norms.

- **Culture beats process every time.** Empathy, trust, and genuine care create alignment far more powerfully than manuals or rigid systems.

- **Leaders set the cultural temperature.** A company becomes a reflection of its founders and executives, so their habits and energy shape the organization across borders.

- **Values must be lived, not laminated.** Shared principles only matter when modeled daily, reinforced through examples, and applied consistently even when uncomfortable.

- **Recognition is your strongest cultural tool.** Highlighting champions across countries builds unity, teaches values through example, and creates a self-reinforcing cycle of excellence.

- **Same values, different accent.** A global brand must stay consistent at its core while adapting its expression to earn local trust, respect, and relevance.

- **Presence creates connection.** Whether managing abroad or leading remote teams, physical or emotional presence matters more than process for building cohesion and loyalty.

- **Clarity and communication sustain remote leadership.**
  Overcommunicating context, documenting decisions, and
  keeping predictable rhythms maintain trust and alignment
  across borders.

- **Fairness must match lived reality.** Calibration of salaries,
  workloads, time zones, and holiday rhythms requires cultural
  awareness and on-the-ground empathy, not formulas.

- **Shared experiences build culture.** Off-sites, in-person
  gatherings, and even small gestures of recognition strengthen
  global teams more than any policy or handbook.

Chapter 13—The Convergence of Business and Society

- **SDGs turn global problems into business blueprints.** They
  frame humanity's biggest challenges as clearly defined
  opportunities where solving real needs can unlock large,
  durable markets.

- **Purpose and profit reinforce each other.** Companies that
  genuinely tackle education, health, climate, or equality do not
  just "do good," they build stronger brands, deeper customer
  loyalty, and more resilient economics over time.

- **Emerging markets are fertile ground for SDG innovation.**
  Gaps in access to schooling, healthcare, finance, and inclusion
  are widest there, which means the upside for locally tuned,
  scalable solutions is often the greatest.

- **Diversity is a growth strategy, not a checkbox.** Teams and
  leadership that reflect gender and cultural diversity gain real
  advantages. They can see more angles, reach more customers,
  and avoid blind spots that leave markets and value on the
  table.

- **Mission-driven companies attract outsize talent and energy.** When people believe their work moves the needle on climate, health, or opportunity, they work harder, stay longer, and bring in others who share that drive.

- **Accountability mechanisms create new markets.** Tools like carbon pricing, progressive regulation, and impact data do not just punish bad actors, they reward innovators who design cleaner, fairer, more efficient business models.

Chapter 14—Stories from the Frontlines

- **Small markets create big thinkers.** When the home market cannot sustain scale, founders learn to build for the world earlier and more deliberately.

- **Constraint is a catalyst.** Scarcity of talent, capital, or infrastructure forces teams to innovate, adapt, and globalize sooner than peers in mature markets.

- **Local comfort can mislead.** Early traction at home can anchor a company to assumptions that collapse when it enters real global markets.

- **Comfort hiring slows expansion.** Fluent English or a polished résumé does not equal local influence or cross-cultural intuition.

- **Bicultural talent is a force multiplier.** The best early hires understand the local context deeply and can translate those realities back to headquarters.

- **Early revenue cannot be delegated.** Leaders must engage directly with customers in a new market until they understand the rhythms, incentives, and signals.

- **Context determines survival.** Behaviors that feel respectful or logical in one culture can be dangerous, offensive, or counterproductive in another.

- **Localization is reinvention, not translation.** Products that look identical on the surface often require entirely different workflows, trust-building, and positioning in new markets.

- **Technology travels, trust does not.** The same device or feature can inspire curiosity in one country and suspicion in another, as we saw with a Square-style payments prototype in Mexico.

- **Communication norms shift across borders.** Silence, hierarchy, directness, and feedback all carry different meanings depending on the culture.

- **Hierarchy is not universal.** Titles may hide real power, and influence often sits behind the visible org chart.

- **Regulation has no single standard.** Markets interpret the same behaviors differently, often with conflicting or ambiguous rules.

- **First mover advantage can be misleading.** In hyper competitive markets, fast followers often win by learning from early entrants' mistakes—agility is a winning strategy.

- **Patterns repeat, outcomes don't.** The same idea can succeed in one market and fail in another when cultural norms, trust, or incentives differ.

- **Global playbooks work only when they evolve.** Expansion succeeds when leaders apply principles, not copy tactics.

If this book sparked an insight, changed how you operate, or helped you avoid a cultural misstep, we'd love to hear about it. Your feedback helps more people navigate the gaps.

https://mindthegap.to/review.

And may your playbook evolve spectacularly, with results to match.

The world needs great companies. Make yours one of them. Wherever you go.

NOTES

Chapter 10

1. "Instabilities in international joint ventures: a study of the Tata DoCoMo case," *International Journal of Entrepreneurship and Innovation Management*, January 2016. Authors: Utpal Chattopadhyay of the National Institute for Training in Industrial Engineering—now Indian Institute of Management (IIM) Mumbai—and Pragya Bhawsar of IIM Ahmedabad.

Chapter 11

1. The concept "People Leave Managers, Not Companies" is explored in more depth by Victor Lipman in his book *The Type B Manager*, in which he offers a unique lens through which to view the challenging problems of management.

Chapter 12

1. The author of this formula is Saint Bernard de Clervaux. He was born in France in the year 1090 and was a remarkable founder and "CEO." He launched and scaled in the span of a few years a community of monks (the Order of Cistercians) that covered tens of countries and that is still active today, from Switzerland to Vietnam. He definitely knew something about leadership and building a "company" culture that lasts.

2. From the Microsoft website at https://www.microsoft.com/en-us/about, accessed 21 November 2025.

Chapter 13

1. US President Barack Obama, didn't finish paying off his student loans until the age of 43, in 2004, just a few years before he moved into the White House—and costs have skyrocketed far above what they were in Obama's student days.

ACKNOWLEDGMENTS

This book grew out of decades of conversations, travel, and cross-cultural experiences, and we are grateful to everyone who helped turn those lessons into pages. Writing this book has been a journey across countries and time zones. It would not have been possible without the people who supported, encouraged, challenged, and believed in us along the way.

We begin by thanking our families, who carried the greatest load throughout this project. Vinnie extends his deepest thanks to his wife, Kristine, and to his children, Rocco, Beatrix, and Oscar. Stefano extends his heartfelt gratitude to his wife, Elizabeth, and to his children, George, Teresa, Camilla, and Rex. Thank you for your patience and understanding during the many weekends, soccer games, and family moments we stepped away to write or to travel for business. This book came together because you gave us the space to do the work and because you carried more than your share at home. Every chapter reflects your support.

Vinnie thanks his partners at Golden Gate Ventures, many of whom have worked together for over 15 years, for their support and belief in this project. He also thanks his three-time co-founder, Paul Bragiel, who has always challenged him to think bigger and push further. Stefano thanks his co-founder, Jarek and his entire team at Aquila, for their encouragement throughout the writing of this book.

We want to thank our writing partner, US-based freelancer Mike Vargo, for the care, patience, and clarity he brought to the manuscript. Thanks also to Nguyễn Nhật Lam of Aquila, who spent countless hours interviewing both of us and asking the difficult questions that pushed our thinking well beyond where it began, and to Minh Do of Golden Gate Ventures for his help in the final stages of the project.

Vinnie gives special thanks to Samuel Yates, the artist behind *The Color of Palo Alto*.

His remarkable art project was a source of early inspiration, revealing a layer of Silicon Valley's spirit, curiosity, and determination that shaped Vinnie's perspective long before this book was written. And it provided the colors behind this book's cover.

Stefano gives special thanks to Alessandro Necchi Villa della Silva and Prof. Carlo Granelli, who taught him how to write and supported him when he first moved to California. To his family, Sergio, Alessandra, Annalisa, Marcello, and Ludovico, who taught him a relentless work ethic and the importance of relationships, to Giorgio and Ruggero, who taught him how to dream big, and to Liz who showed him his potential and broadened his horizons.

We appreciate the support of Wiley for bringing this project to life, and we thank Syd Ganaden for reaching out and guiding us through the publishing process. We are also thankful for the modern tools that helped us stay organized and reflective throughout the writing process. New AI technologies assisted us in analyzing interviews, tracking themes, and refining ideas, although every story and perspective in this book remains entirely our own.

Cross-cultural work is complex, and we know we may not always get it perfectly right. We have tried to remove our own biases wherever possible, and if we have fallen short at any point, we apologize. Our goal has been to reflect on cultures as outsiders who care deeply about the places we have worked in and to bring together insights from people with different backgrounds and lived experiences.

We close by thanking the many founders, executives, operators, and investors who contributed interviews for this book. Their stories brought both nuance and honesty to the pages. Many of these individuals are Kauffman Fellows or Berkeley alumni, and we are grateful for their openness, their time, and their willingness to share experiences that will help others navigate cross-cultural work.

These are the interviewees and contributors who shared their time and insights:

- Hussain Abdulla, Golden Gate Ventures
- Edgar Auslander, Meta
- Liron Azrielant, Meron Capital VC
- Christopher Beselin, Endurance Capital
- Andrea Campagnoli, Bain & Company
- Meredith Carson, Growth Ensemble
- Wee Liang Chua, Cowin Capital
- Federico D'Amico, EQT Group
- Gianluca Dettori, Primo Capital
- Kieran Donovan, K-ID
- Fernando Fabre, Kauffman Fellows
- Nathanael Faibis, Alodokter
- Dany Farha, BECO Capital
- Carl Fritjofsson, Creandum
- Ernestine Fu Mak, Brave Capital
- Hisham Halbouny, P1 Ventures
- Justin Hall, Golden Gate Ventures
- Oluchi Ikechi, EY-Parthenon

- Shin Iwata, Miraise VC
- Christian Jølck, 2150 VC
- Kat Kennedy, Kickstart VC
- Marek Kiisa, NordicNinja VC
- Roman Kniazev, Nuravax
- Alexandre Lazarow, Fluent Ventures
- Michael Lints, Golden Gate Ventures
- Ashley Lundström, EQT Ventures
- Jonathan Lynch, Red Sea Global
- Maciej Małysz, Inovo VC
- Ricardo Melare, ASBZ Advogados
- Vinod Nair, MoneySmart
- Jeffrey Paine, Golden Gate Ventures
- Annalisa Pellegrino, United Nations
- Hoa Phan, FDCare
- Jose Romano, European Investment Bank
- Nicolas Sauvage, TDK Ventures
- Michelle Scarborough
- Mario Scuderi, CDP Venture Capital SGR
- Gustavo Rugani do Couto e Silva, Machado Meyer
- Aaron Tan, Carro
- Dr. Mark Thaller, Jebel Associates
- Olivier Tonneau, Quantonation
- Angela Toy, Golden Gate Ventures
- Phil Wickham, Sozo Ventures
- Santiago Zavala, 500 Global

INDEX

A

Abdulla, Hussain, 42

accountability, 175, 191, 212, 239, 243

active listening and mindfulness, 11–12

actual decision maker, detection of, 124

advisors, 80–81

affordable and clean energy (SDG 7), 237, 244

Africa, 132, 161

AI (artificial intelligence)
    humanoid commercialization
        trajectory, 92–93
    localization in new markets, 253
    meeting summary alignment, 222
    tool mastery generational shift, 184

Airbnb, 16

Alibaba, 162

alignment-beats-enforcement, 70

Alodokter, 240

annual general meeting (AGM) alignment
    ritual, 199

Apple, 210

Aquila green-finance incentive leverage, 76

Asia, 59, 88–90, 101, 118, 194, 212, 251, 260

Aspire, 37, 182, 187, 190, 198, 200

assertiveness, 98

Auslander, Edgar, 165

authenticity, 46

autonomy
    -driven growth momentum, 23
    incentive for entrepreneurial talent, 191

Azrielant, Liron, 248, 252

B

B2B2C model, 142

Baemin, 164

Baltics, 247

Barack, Gideon, 166

BECO Capital, 253

Beselin, Christopher, 61–62

Beyond Cars, 163

bias
    cultural, 14
    gender, 258
    in global consulting environments, 259

bicultural hires, 249

BioNTech, 161

blitz-scaling
    push model, 36–37
    strategy, 26

body language, 101–102, 261

Booksy, 51, 88

Brazil, 65, 66, 177

business and society
    convergence of, 229–244
    See also Sustainable Development
        Goals (SDGs)

business attire and cultural neutrality, 261

Butterfly, 166

C

Careem
    female-driver recruitment strategy, 91
    Saudi mobility adaptation, 87
    Uber regional acquisition strategy, 92

Carro, 141–144, 163, 170–171

CEO-led vs product-team-led M&A
    model, 120

Chick-fil-A cautious, 152–153

chief marketing officer (CMO), female
    appointment, 235

chief meaning officer, 197, 199

China
    Airbnb expansion failure in, 16
    hypercompetitive markets, 255
    informal trust-building, 63
    MOU nonbinding perception, 59
    weak enforcement in, 67

Chua, Wee Liang, 59, 63, 67, 69, 255

"chu hai" (going overseas), 255

circumstance-based "yes" decoding, 108–109

clarity
    and communication, 228
    radical, 129
    vs hierarchy, 252
cleantech government incentive programs
        (Australia), 75
ClearGrid, 253
climate action (SDG 13), 237–239, 244
climate change and sustainability, 229–230
climate hero targeting strategy, 137
ClimateTech Venture Fund 2150, 218
Clinton, Bill, 96
Clip fintech Mexico adaptation case, 86
code-switching, cultural. *See* cultural
        code-switching
collectivism dual-interpretation dilemma,
        140, 141
communication styles, 99–100, 251–252
company's culture, promoting, 206–216
company values, as universal compass, 211–214
compassionate firmness leadership balance, 195
competitive vs collaborative culture, 210
confusion-to-clarity transformation, 4
connection, as real work, 8
consequence matching persuasion principle, 141
contract
    -signed vs deal-completed distinction, 58
    as starting-point snapshot, 60
    -travel-differently principle, 70
copycat application threat, 68
creative balancing factor solution, 159
cross-border expansion preparation, 25
cross-border hiring
    beyond language, titles, and optics, 249–251
    legal framework, 178
cross-border negotiations
    interpreters in, 257–258
    women in, 258–261
cross-border onboarding, 180
cross-cultural mindset cultivation, xx
Cubbit, 246
cultural awareness, in product adaptation, 83
cultural bias, 14
cultural code-switching, xiv, xx, 16, 45,
        95–105, 125
    as adaptation, 99
    art of, 99–101
    definition, 96
    make-or-break (international) skill, 96–98
cultural fit
    adjustment analysis, 30
    dynamic evolution, 90
cultural fluency, as strategic advantage, 261

cultural mediator role, in negotiation, 113
cultural misalignment, as seed of failure, 4
cultural pace and value system, 6
cultural training primacy, over technical
        training, 184–185
culture-change leverage, 91–92
"culture eats process for breakfast" maxim, 207–209
culture gaps
    in international business, xi
    layered onto business uncertainty, 3
"culture starts with leaders" principle, 209–210
"cultures within cultures" targeting strategy, 7
cut-and-paste expansion risk, 17

D
daily stand-up alignment rhythm, 200–201
D'Amico, Federico, 18–19, 109–111
Darwin, Charles, 95
deal-closing definition variability, 57–60
deal-definition cultural contrast, 74
death by politeness, beware of, 124
December vs July bonus cycle contrast, 204
decision-making
    differences, across teams, xv
    and hierarchy, 100
direct-launch model, 147–153
    feature-heavy app performance failure, 148
    human-presence digital-dependency
        paradox, 150
    mobile-infrastructure misfit case, 148–149
    MoneySmart example, 149–150
    on-the-ground representative
        selection, 151–153
    remote-launch visibility gap, 148
    remote vs on-the-ground entry contrast, 147
directness balanced with courtesy, 46
direct reporting, across different countries, 219–221
"distance traveled" hiring criterion, 174–175
distribution partners, 167, 170
diversity
    as growth strategy, 242–243
    of thought, 235, 252
divide and manage negotiation strategy, 113
DKSH, 167
Donovan, Kieran, 78–79, 81, 249–250, 253–254
due diligence, 20, 58, 72

E
early deadline communication planning, 227
ecosystem event leadership, 214
edtech (education technology), 232
egalitarian vs top-down hierarchy models, 100

emergent business-practice risk, 57
emerging markets, 3, 18, 37, 53, 57, 66, 76, 79, 169, 232, 239, 241–242, 253–254, 283
emotion vs intuition distinction, 12
Employee Stock Ownership Plans (ESOPs), 190
employee termination, 191–195
employer-of-record contrast, 73
Englishnization corporate mandate, 181
Ericsson, 165
Europe, 57–58, 133, 178, 247
European Carbon Border Adjustment Mechanism (CBAM), 239
exclusivity-clause strategic error, 68
expect-the-unexpected principle, 23

F
Fabre, Fernando, 34
face-building, in negotiations, 3
failure
    as capability acquisition, 21
    as learning, 201
    small misunderstandings escalating to, 8
fairness, 227, 228
"fake-door" (low-cost digital) testing, 153
false consensus trap, 128
Farha, Dany, 253
FD Care, 240–241
Fear of Missing Out in expansion, 33
FedEx, 257
feedback, 204
50–50 joint-venture deadlock risk, 63–64
first-mover vs fast-follower advantage, 255
five-dimension cultural framework, 99–100
500 Global, 246
fixed-deadline vs approximate-target perception, 105
Florence Cathedral dome, innovation analogy, 238
foreign-ownership perception risk, 30
4G spectrum auction disruption, 157
France, 192
Fritjofsson, Carl, 49
Fulbright Program, 174
Fulbright University, 183
Fu Mak, Ernestine, 119–120, 260

G
Game Freak, 127
gender equality (SDG 5), 234–236, 243
General Electric, 197
generosity in leadership DNA, 198
global collaboration in innovation, 238
global compliance strategy, 255

"global ideas speak local" principle, 175
Gojek ride-hailing ban incident, 76
Golden Gate Ventures (GGV), xiv, 39–42, 76, 199, 200, 214, 217, 224, 227, 235–236
good health and well-being (SDG 3), 239–242, 243
"go through fire and hell" leadership loyalty effect, 188
governments
    roles of local, 75–77
    stability, in business terms, 30
gray-area legislation, 77–79
growth mindset, 203
GSM World Congress, 165
Gulf region, 41–42, 58–59, 212, 217, 226

H
Halbouny, Hisham, 131–133, 161, 173–175
Hall, Justin, 26
hare-and-tortoise growth dynamic, 37
Haribo, 167
Haynes, Tim, 166
healthcare
    access gaps, in emerging markets, 239
    system fragmentation, 241
Hewlett Packard, 190
hire-people-who-teach-you mindset, 183
Ho Chi Minh City
    cross-border contract finalization in, 1
    talent competition, 223
Hoffman, Reid, 6, 26
holiday
    planning across countries, 226–227
    and work hour alignment, 179
honesty, 116, 123
"honesty feels rude until it builds trust" insight, 213
Hong Kong
    financial infrastructure readiness, 53
    M&A entry (Carro), 163
    vs Singapore market misfit, 26
human thermometers, 220
humility, 16–17, 72, 174

I
identify-champions culture reinforcement, 214–216
Ikechi, Oluchi, 193–194, 259–260
"I know nothing" humility mantra, 16
incentives, 189–191
inclusive culture, top-down responsibility, 236
inclusive marketing strategy, 235

India, 109, 157
Indonesia, 32, 37, 103–104, 121, 142, 162, 171,
        198, 220, 232, 240
Indosat, 233
industry-conference networking entry point, 52
inferred legal obligation, 79
inflation, 223–224
innovation, and gender diversity, 234
innovative start-up, 77
in-person relationship, 170
InstaDeep, 161
integrity first hiring, 176
intercultural mindset development, 10
international advisory firm necessity, 80
interpreters, in cross-border
        negotiations, 257–258
intuition, 110
    as cross-cultural decoding tool, 14
    as early warning system, 23
    emotion vs, 12
    as mistake-correction mechanism, 15
    in partner evaluation, 47
Israel, 248, 252
Italy, 246
iterative execution, 19
Iwata, Shin, 127, 249–251

J
Japan, 97–98, 249
    acquisition closing reluctance, 171
    age-based deference risk, 130
    compliance conservatism, 73–74
    deliberative consensus culture, 13
    gaming industry, 127
    indirect communication style, 251
    market expansion, 235
    offline trust dominance, 144
    organic expansion vs acquisition
        strategy, 144
Jio, 157
joint venture (JV) entry model, 154–155
Jølck, Christian, 218–219

K
Kauffman Fellows Program, 248
Khan, Kublai, 9
Kiisa, Marek, 129–130, 213
Kniazev, Roman, 115
knowledge transfer, from startup to VC, 4
"know nothing" expansion mantra, 51
Korean multi-form "yes" refusal
        spectrum, 108–109

L
languages, used within the firm, 180–181
Latin America, 246
Lazada, 162
Lazarow, Alexandre, 87, 174
leadership
    accountability for inclusion, 236
    preference, culturally adaptable, 173–174
    as privilege mindset, 198
    proximity, 221
    remote team, 219–220
    responsibilities of, 186
    women in, 234
Lee, Admond, 26, 54
Li, Fei-Fei, 135
linguistic code-switching illustration, 96
Lints, Michael, 42
Lipman, Victor, 287
listen-between-the-lines principle, 125
livestreamed e-commerce adoption (Asia),
        88–90
local
    advisor strategic value, 80
    brand/global identity, 217–219
    conversation truth discovery, 56
    pricing strategy, 256–257
Luckin Coffee fabricated revenue case, 48
Lunar New Year
    bonus significance, 204
    operational slowdown, 226–227
Lundström, Ashley, 133–134
Lynch, Jonathan, 118–120

M
M&A as market entry strategy, 160–163
Magellan, Ferdinand, 189
Mak, Ernestine Fu, 43
Mallory, George, 27
Małysz, Maciej, 51, 247–248
market demand miscalculation, 168
market entry
    strategy typology, 147
    vs cultural entry, xi–xii
Melaré, Ricardo, 43
MENA (Middle East-North Africa)
    early scouting phase, 41, 42
    limitations of lumping diverse
        regions, 132
Meta, 165
Meyer, Erin, 99
Microsoft, 211
Mikitani, Hiroshi "Mickey," 181
Mindar humanoid example, 92

mindfulness
  in ambiguity, 23
  as internal-external awareness, 11–12
"mind the gap" principle, xviii
missed-JV opportunity syndrome, 158–159
mistake sharing, as trust accelerator, 46
mobile-banking initial resistance, in Thailand, 90
mobile learning platforms, 233
"move fast and break things" mindset, 13
mutual
  realignment, 208
  respect, non-negotiable, 184
  trust, xii, 44

N
Nair, Vinod, 150
"natural leverage" contract structuring, 61
negative externalities, environmental costs, 239
negotiations
  cultural mediator role in, 113
  face-building in, 3
  forewarning strategy in, 2
  silence during, 110–111
  stage of, 114
  See also cross-border negotiations
Netflix–SoftBank Japan JV, 154–155
never-reject-invitation rule, 119
Nicholson, Marc, 28, 29
Noah, Trevor, 138
no-bluff leadership authenticity, 188–189
nonexecutive director advisory role, 20
nonverbal
  cues, 14, 110, 203
  signal recalibration, 45
NordicNinja VC, 129, 213
Northvolt supplier consequence example, 62
"no single right way" leadership lesson,
    207, 216
"nothing beats selling in person" principle, 43
"not invented here" cost, 159, 160
now-future concept, 92–93

O
Obama, Barack, 288
"onboarding buddy" integration, 180
1880 Singapore private club, 25
online research, 50, 55
on-the-ground
  cultural immersion, 10
  presence before launch, 39, 50
organic expansion (pull approach), 35–36
organic trust compounding, 38

outsider advantage in foreign cultures, xv
overheated-bubble mentality, 169

P
P1 Ventures, 131
Padoacini, Claudio, 246
Paine, Jeffrey, 19
paper-based due diligence limitations, 20
paper money vs metal currency mental models, 9
parallel-track execution strategy, 19
patience as strategy, 111
pay-it-forward ethos, 6
Paystack, 161
peer accountability, 175
people-leave-bosses principle, 186–188
performance calibration, 205
"PhD" hiring, 176
Poland, 51, 247
polite-evasion signaling, 109
Polo, Marco, 9, 12
pop-up store pilot method, 153
portfolio of market-specific roadmaps, 18
positive reinforcement, 201–202
preparation-meets-opportunity principle, 166
"prepare to be unprepared" principle, xx, 9–24
presence
  creates connection principle, 228
  as operational, 199, 206
  as pace setting principle, 198
private equity–founder alignment conflict, 63
product and strategy localization, xii
product-market-fit timing misalignment, 32
professionalism, 202, 222, 258, 261
profit vs purpose alignment, 233–234, 242
proximity as leadership core, 221
proximity-based market learning, 55
psychological safety, 208
public praise universal appreciation norm, 215
public university untapped talent pool, 177
punctuality as respect norm, 104
purchasing-power proxy indicators, 34
push vs pull expansion framework, 33–38
put option, 143

Q
Qatar, 84, 89
quality education (SDG 4), 231–234, 243
Quantonation, 128

R
Radical Candor framework, 203
Rakuten, 162, 181

rapid exit vs slow cash bleed, 37
raw intellectual capability recognition, 177
reality vs strategic roadmap alignment, 17–19
reassignment-before-termination consideration, 193
recognition, 66, 214–216
regional autonomy and performance
    calibrations, 204–205
regulations across markets, conflicting, 253–255
regulatory guidance, 79
relationships, personal, 44–45
relationship-vs structure-driven trust, 116
remote manager autonomy and responsibility
    balance, 221–223
remote team leadership, 219–220
renegotiation, 60, 67
renegotiation-anticipation mindset, 70
renewable energy
    and cleantech industries, 232
    practice leadership, xiv
reputation, 20, 42
resilience
    through early mistakes, 21
    fairness assessment and, 116
    motivation and, 177
    reach vs, 36
respect vs weakness distinction, 71
respect-with-directness coexistence, 213
Ressi, Adeo, 52, 175
rest, as leadership modeling principle, 227
risk-averse vs entrepreneurial culture, 100
risk-management in unstable regions, 71
risk navigation trust framework, 115
risk–reward incentive alignment history, 189
risk-taking, 21
Rocket Internet, 36, 163
Rossettini, Luca, 245
rotating meeting times fairness model, 225
Rugani, Gustavo, 65–66
The Runway Ventures newsletters, 54
Russia, 115

S
salary calibration, across countries, 223–224
same values, different accent principle, 217, 228
Samsung Electronics, 181
San Francisco, 217
SAP, 181
Saudi Arabia, 87, 91, 120
"sauna culture" brutal-honesty norm, 130
Sauvage, Nicolas, 252
"scale of values" cultural contrast, 138–140
scarcity shaped negotiation strategy, 114
Scott, Kim, 203

Scuderi, Mario, 245
Sea Group, 163
"see everything; overlook a great deal; correct a
    little" maxim, 201
self-awareness, 177
serendipitous network building, 22
shared
    challenge bonding effect, 224
    experiences build culture insight, 228
    language alignment, 181
    routine commitment expectation, 185
Shopee, 162–163
silence during negotiation, 110–111
Silicon Valley
    dress-as-power signal, 101
    entrepreneurship, xiii
    network-building culture in, 6
    rapid execution ethos, 13
    shift to global venture model, 248
    trust dynamics, 5
Singapore, xvi, 198
    Grand Prix team gathering, 224–225
    social-hierarchy firing dynamic, 194
    trust-building processes, 5
    venture capital firm launch in, 4–5
Slack, 185, 201, 219
Soho House, 26
Southeast Asia
    as complex business ecosystem, xv–xvi
    ride-hailing market entry, 85
Southern Europe, 104
Southern Sudan, 250
South Korea, 119
Spotify, 256
Starbucks–Maxim's Hong Kong JV, 155
state-owned enterprise dominance, 69
stereotyping trap, 131–134
strategic acquisition shortcut, 160–163
strategic investor alignment, 63
strength-of-invitation metric, 34
Stripe, 161
"subculture as market segment" insight, 136
Sudan People's Liberation Army (SPLA), 250
"super-connectors," 20
supply-side pressure distortion, 33
surprise
    as element of cross-border business, 2
    as starting point in new cultures, 8
"survival of the most adaptive" principle, 95
suspend-judgment principle, 12–14
Sustainable Development Goals (SDGs), 230
    affordable and clean energy (SDG 7), 237, 244
    as business blueprints, 242
    clean water and sanitation (SDG 6), 243

climate action (SDG 13), 237–239, 244
decent work and economic growth
   (SDG 8), 244
gender equality (SDG 5), 234–236, 243
good health and well-being (SDG 3),
   239–242, 243
industry, innovation and infrastructure
   (SDG 9), 244
life below water (SDG 14), 244
life on land (SDG 15), 244
no poverty (SDG 1), 243
partnerships for the goals (SDG 17), 244
peace, justice and strong institutions
   (SDG 16), 244
quality education (SDG 4), 231–234, 243
reduced inequality (SDG 10), 244
responsible consumption and production
   (SDG 12), 244
sustainable cities and communities
   (SDG 11), 244
zero hunger (SDG 2), 243
Swedish credit-extension contrast, 62
symbolic inclusion gestures, 225

T
talent eats strategy principle, 173, 197
talent retention, 185–186
Tan, Aaron, 144, 171
target-country evaluation framework, 29–32
task-technology-culture fit framework, 84
task-technology fit, 84
task-vs relationship-based trust, 100
Tata–NTT Docomo JV formation, 155–158
tax loan seasonal product, 149
team-centered leadership mindset, 186
team composition, 102
team off-sites, importance of, 224–225
technical brilliance vs cultural misalignment
   dismissal, 185
technology
   adoption, depends on cultural dependency, 93
   role in climate solutions, 237
Texas Instruments, 166
Thailand, 90, 171, 198
Thaller, Mark, 71–72, 74, 250–251
third-culture professional concept, 151
thirteenth-month salary norm, 179
Thums Up, 165
time expectation cultural alignment, 104
time "in" market vs time "to" market, 38
time-orientation spectrum (flexible vs punctual), 100
time zone, managing, 225–226
Toca Boca, 134

Tonneau, Olivier, 128–129, 133
town hall meetings, importance of, 199–200
Toy, Angela, 236
Toyota Production System, 13
training, scope of, 183–184
transcreation, xvii, xx
   Carro cross-border dealmaking, 170
   from international team, 141–144
   localization as, 88
   as market-entry strategy, 83
   in supply chain negotiations, 256
   vs translation distinction, xvii, 85, 93
transcreators, Uber vs, 85–86
travel, as intercultural training ground, 22
"true decision maker" identification, 119
trust
   authentic conversation, 187
   breach, 2
   building, xii, xv, 8, 39, 44–48, 100,
      114, 122, 251
   clarity as foundation of, 222
   in digital payments, 86
   gesture, 7
   -granting culture, 5
   hierarchy and ritual process, 118
   after hours trust-building (East Asia), 118–119
   layered, 122
   meal-as-trust-building mechanism, 121
   multi-layer dimensions, 116–117
   price point sensitivity, 145
   slow granted, 118
   slow trust relationship dynamic, 120
   task-vs relationship-based, 100
   as two-way evaluation, 115
   velocity differences across cultures, 8
trust-speed-complexity trade-off, 49
Two Plus, 242

U
Uber, 78, 85–86, 91–92, 190, 210
uncertainty reduction, 55, 56
unit economics stress-testing, 27
United Kingdom, 51, 153, 194, 205
United Nations (UN), 230, 259
United States, 2, 51, 57, 72, 76, 85, 89, 115, 117,
      135, 152, 178, 192, 194, 205, 231, 255
Unshackled Ventures, 174

V
values
   as operating system principle, 211
   in performance reviews, 211

Van Edwards, Vanessa, 203
Vatanasakdakul, Savanid "Nui", xvi–xvii, 83–85,
    88–90, 92–93, 135
venture investing, in emerging tech
    ecosystems, 39–40
Vietnam, 3, 178, 198
    communist-market hybrid system, 40
    economic growth in, 167
    as emerging growth market, 7
    family clinic model, 240
    fintech bank-dependency, 68
    labor law, 192
    motorbike as necessity value frame, 139
    portfolio rebalancing toward, 41
VietnamMM, 164

W
Walmart, 16
Welch, Jack, 197, 198
Wickham, Phil, 248, 251

win-win continuity requirement, 60–64
Wirecard accounting scandal, 48
women
    in cross-border negotiations, 258–261
    cross-cultural etiquette for, 261
    in leadership roles, 234
work-life balance, 225–226

Y
Yelp, 209
"yes"
    as acknowledgment vs commitment, 111
    means "no" communication
        paradox, 107–125
    as "not yet" interpretation, 110–111

Z
Zavala, Santiago, 86, 246
zero-tolerance trust-breach culture, 117